Modern Initiatives for Sustainable Food Production

Modern Initiatives for Sustainable Food Production

Friedrich Huth and
Sara D. Garduno-Diaz

Delve PUBLISHING
www.delvepublishing.com

Modern Initiatives for Sustainable Food Production

Friedrich Huth and Sara D. Garduno-Diaz

Delve Publishing
224 Shoreacres Road
Burlington, ON L7L 2H2
Canada
www.delvepublishing.com

Email: orders@arclereducation.com

ISBN: 978-1-77469-022-2 (Hardcover)

ABOUT THE AUTHORS

Friedrich Huth has a background in Business Economics with a Master's Degree in Business Administration from the University of Brandenburg, Germany. He further specialized in Corporate Finance at the Institute of International Studies at the Ramkhamhaeng University in Bangkok. When a type 4 arthrosis diagnosis ended his career as a professional Athlete and Captain of the German U16/U18 Basketball National Team at an early age, he dedicated his life to helping a variety of small and medium sized companies grow their business as Operations, Marketing and Finance Manager while personally exploring measures to cure his joint-condition and regain his physical abilities. Thus, he started working on functional nutrition in 2017 when he became a first line member of Her1, an Ecommerce startup for Nutritional Supplements.

Currently he is responsible for a unit of consultants with focus on all German Companies in the Agriculture, Life Science, Pharmaceutical & Chemical Industries. Due to his professional environment he is exposed to first line insights on the practices and strategies of the main players in related fields to modern food production.

His approach to Food Production and Nutrition is based on his personal nutrition-induced full recovery from a condition with a prognosis to be irreversible, mixed with his professional interest in micro- & macroeconomic trends and correlations.

Sara D. Garduño-Diaz has a background in nutrition with a PhD in Nutrition and Food Science from the University of Leeds, United Kingdom; she has further specialized in Sports Nutrition with the International Olympics Committee, Switzerland. Dr Diaz has worked as Research Fellow for several EU-funded research projects and was awarded research grants from CONACYT (Mexico) and the BBSRC (UK). She currently works as Nutrition Consultant for companies in Germany, Kuwait, England and the United States. Dr Diaz has been working on functional nutrition and wellness since 2014 when she co-founded her first company. Since then she has joined various start-ups as part of the R&D department.

Dr Diaz sits on the editorial board of various international journals. She is the author of several peer-reviewed publications and books. Her research interests include the dietary patterns of migrant populations and their impact on health, as well as investigating the environmental factors that influence food selection.

Dr. Garduño-Diaz is a member of the Academy of Nutrition and Dietetics, the American Overseas Dietetics Association, Professionals in Nutrition for Exercise & Sport, and the World Public Health Nutrition Association, for whom she is a member of the executive committee.

With over 10 years of experience in the field of nutrition, and having lived and worked in various continents, Dr Diaz's approach to food is one of integrating strategies to design individual programs based on her client's wellness needs. Dr Sara advocates for real food and the art of sustainable eating.

TABLE OF CONTENTS

LIST OF FIGURES

LIST OF TABLES

LIST OF BOXES

SUMMARY

Discussions about sustainable practices in the global food system circle around the need to set up technologies and practices that minimize adverse impacts on the environment and are simultaneously accessible to and effective for farmers and other food producers. Regardless of significant progress in agricultural productivity over the past half-century, with crop and livestock production vastly driven by increased utilization of fertilizers, water for irrigation, agricultural machines, pesticides and land, the link between food production and said practices is likely to stay linear in the upcoming years.

Novel approaches are required for the integration of biological and ecological processes into global food production practices. Paramount will be the attention to minimizing the use of those non-renewable inputs which cause harm to the environment or to the health of farmers and commensals; ensuring productive use of the knowledge and skills of farmers, avoiding substituting human capital for costly external inputs, and making productive use of people's collective capacities.

As part of present and future food production systems, synergy will be required to solve common agricultural and natural resource problems, including: pests, watershed, irrigation, inadequate forest and credit management. Addressing these problems aids in the setup of important capital assets for agricultural systems: natural; social; human; physical; and financial capital.

Improving natural capital is a central aim for modern initiatives of sustainable food production. Its dividends will then derive from making the best use of the crop and animal genetics as well as from the ecological conditions under which they are grown or raised. The ecological management of agroecosystems that addresses energy flows, nutrient cycling, population-regulating mechanisms and system resilience can lead to the redesign of agriculture at a landscape scale.

The outcomes of modern initiatives of sustainable food production can be positive for food productivity, reduced pollution and overall improving the global living environment. Significant challenges, however, remain with the development of national and international policies to support the wider emergence of more sustainable forms of agricultural production across both industrialized and developing countries.

Key words: food sustainability, sustainable diets, dietary patterns, food economics, sustainable food systems

PREFACE

Food production is a key challenge in the politics of sustainability due to its effect on the environment, health of individuals and communities, social integration, and economics. Numerous important challenges high on current policy agendas all over the World can help exemplify how broad the problem is.

Consequential environmental problems linked with food production and consumption practices cover climate change, water pollution and scarcity, soil degradationand loss of biodiversity. Further, food consumption is connected to most of the international water usage and is the source of a large part of greenhouse-gas emissions. (Poore and Nemecec, 2018)

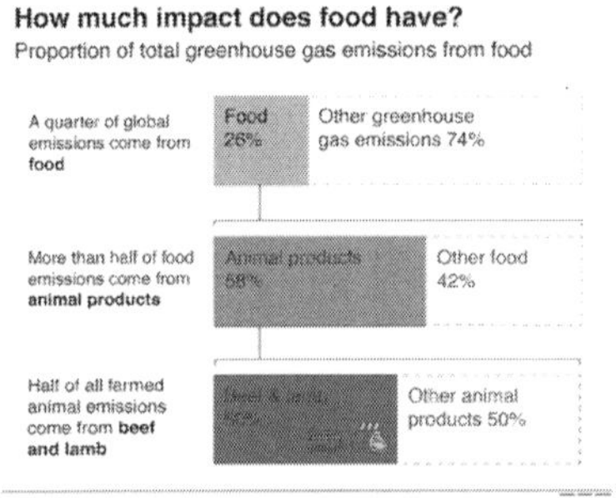

Figure 1. The impact of food production.

Demographic growth and fluctuating developments in the economy are likely to augment the requirement for energy, food, and water—what is referred to as the energy-food-water nexus (Bazilian et al. 2011)—which will endanger the sustainable utilization of natural resources and could further increase stress at a social and geopolitical level.

It is estimated that about 800 million people around the world experience on-going hunger and insufficient food intake. In addition, inaccessible and insufficient safe drinking water is still a worrying issue (Coff et al. 2008; Millstone & Lang, 2008). Simultaneously, 1 to 1.5 billion people are overweight with 300 to 500 million of them categorized as obese. This is now an ever-growing trend in the majority of countries around the World strongly linked to dietary modifications towards a higher intake of sugars, animal protein, and trans fatty acids.

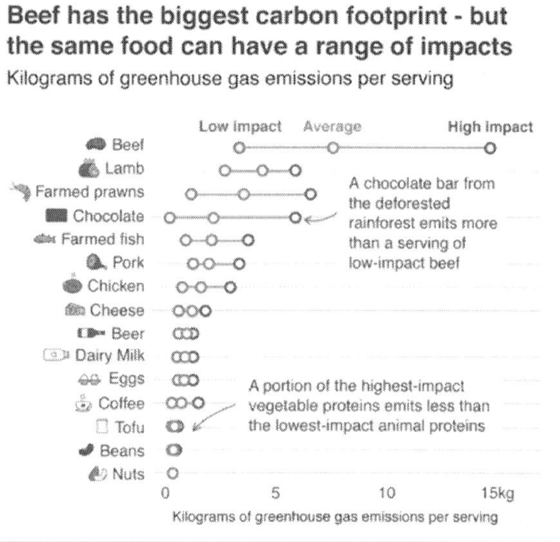

Figure 2. Carbon footprint of selected foods.

Health conditions linked to food selection and lifestyle, including cardiovascular diseases and diabetes, are becoming more prevalent among younger demographics (CEC, 2007). At the same time, this phenomenon strongly augments the costs for health care systems (BCO, 2007), while social cohesion is in constant threat since health is tightly linked to socioeconomic status.

New trends make transforming the food system more difficult. As people move out of poverty, they buy more meat, increasing the amount of land used to raise and feed animals, and further burdening overexploited fish stocks. Disruptions from climate change-related disasters and recently, from COVID-19, can lead to lower production and more food insecurity, demonstrating a need for more resilient supply chains. Simultaneously, humanity gets 75 percent of our food from just 17 species, decreasing resilience to diseases and other climate-related stresses and shocks. Finally, with 30 percent of food lost, a third of the food system's environmental impact happens without feeding anyone.

New data-rich technologies, combined with the revival of traditional practices such as intercropping or indigenous fisheries management, hold great promise. But new business models are required to bring these approaches to far more people, while further innovation is still needed to transform the food system at scale.

The concept of sustainable diets can be defined as the link between diet and sustainable food systems. This concept addresses the fields of agriculture, health, the environment and culture. Beginning from defining the basic unit of nutrition, usually understood as the nutrient, which derived from the agricultural model of nutrition. A diet has also been considered as the basic unit, more of a multi-sectoral model. Food systems are complex and can illustrate the many connecting areas related to sustainable diets. Recommendations include: availability of culturally acceptable food baskets, promotion of consumption of nutritional-rich local foods as well as their sustainable use, addressing the pandemic of overweight and obesity, and bringing together sectors such as agriculture and health to develop policies that will work together. A key area to address is the livestock sector. High intake of food of animal origin can increase the risk of diseases although they are nutrient-rich. At the same time, livestock is a synergic part of pasture lands, contributing to carbon balance. Additionally, animal ethics must also be taken into account in the discussion of dietary sustainability. While humans cannot eat pastures, these contribute to the biodiversity of systems which in turn help maintain sustainable food systems. The essence of sustainable diets is an ecosystem approach. To build a global narrative towards 2030, people must be empowered and be given agency to develop sustainable food systems. In addition, the Right to Food Volunteer Guidelines must be supported.

The World is off track on the nutrition and health targets set internationally and is also losing previously made gains. International nutrition and health targets like the policy briefs for 2025 set by the WHO address the needed changes due to malnutrition issues. Unfortunately, the World is off track on these targets and even losing previously made gains. Micronutrient deficiencies, in addition to problems of overnutrition, are some of the concerns. Another issue is that our diets globally are not healthy. Our food systems are failing us by not providing the foods that contribute to a healthy diet. The gaps to get back on track to the Sustainability Goals include making difficult decisions. Policymakers do not always have the tools needed to make decisions between trade-offs. The consumers will also be the agents of change in regards to sustainable healthy diets. While no one (single) diet fits all, sustainable diets can take different forms: they must contribute to all forms of development and health, including hunger and undernutrition as well as problems linked to malnutrition. The FAO and the WHO have put together 16 guiding principles for sustainable healthy diets including the following characteristics: diverse, balanced across all food groups, high in plants but also some animal-based products, to list a few. In addition, pollution, food losses and waste must be considered as part of the guidance for sustainable healthy diets.

The Sustainable Development Goals carry a common thread of gender equality. Gender equity is not about women, nor about women and men being the same, but rather about rights, responsibilities and opportunities being the same between women and men. Agriculture is strongly affected by gender inequality which does not allow for development and addressing issues such as hunger. Seaweed cultivation in Indonesia is an example of women participating in the food system. In this case, they have received support from their government to establish multi-sectoral partnerships in business and food system development. Covid-19 has shocked the food system further by giving place to risks including trade and investment restrictions, rising unemployment, movement limits and restrictions on accessing credits. The priorities for gender equity across sustainable food systems include gender equality, increase in women's voice and agency, a trans-disciplinary approach, investment in better data for assessment of what is and is not working, strong monitoring networks, capacity building at multiple levels for advocacy, and establishing policies to support nutrition sensitive agriculture inclusive of gender dynamics.

Box 1. Women in agriculture.

Largely around the world, the face of farming is female. Internationally, reports the United Nations' Food and Agriculture Organization (FAO), the majority of economically active women in the least-developed regions labor in agriculture. In addition, according to the 2012 Census of Agriculture, approximately 30% of farmers in the U.S. are female. The problem? Gender-specific obstacles—such as lack of access to land, financing, markets, agricultural training and education, suitable working conditions, and equal treatment—put female farmers at a significant disadvantage before they ever plow a field or sow a seed.

Arguably, the biggest roadblock is land rights. In developing countries, only 10 to 20 percent of landholders are women, and in some parts of the world, women still cannot legally own or control land. When a female farmer isn't empowered to make decisions about the land she works, it is impossible for her to enter contract farming agreements that could provide higher earnings and reliable sources of income.

In addition, entrenched gender roles in developing countries can prevent women from bringing their crops to market or even leaving their villages without their husband's permission. While female farmers in the U.S. don't face the same restrictions, Lorie Fleenor, 33, an eighth-generation Bristol, Tennessee, farmer, says persistent gender bias in agriculture makes it "easier" to have her husband, Ben, handle business transactions and phone calls for the family's Magna Vista Farm.

Yet, even with female farmers expending extra effort (worldwide, women work more hours per year than men), they substantially lag behind their male counterparts when it comes to crop yields and earnings. On average, women-run farms produce 20 to 30 percent less than farms run by men. The reasons for this "crop gap," according to the FAO, have nothing to do with an aptitude for farming and everything to do with the gender-specific obstacles.

To conclude, this book outlines five specific and implementable strategies. For each of these, there is a strong enough evidence base, and modeling and analysis demonstrates their effectiveness for achieving a Great Food Transformation:

Strategy one: establishing an international commitment towards more plant-friendly diets. The scientific targets set out by expert groups provide guidance about the necessary shift, which consists of high consumption of plant foods and substantially limiting animal source foods. Ample research has demonstrated that this will reduce environmental impacts and lead to better health outcomes. This concerted commitment can be demonstrated by investment in public health information and sustainability education, and better coordination between departments of health, environment and economy.

Strategy two: reorienting agricultural priorities away from producing 'more' food and towards producing 'better' food. This means focusing on producing a diverse range of nutritious foods from biodiversity-enhancing food production systems rather than aiming for an increased volume of a few crops, much of which is now used for animal production.

Strategy three: sustainably intensifying food production, generating more high-quality output. The current food system in the world is unsustainable, transgressing the scientific targets for sustainable food production within the boundaries defined. A new agricultural revolution is required, based on sustainable intensification, and driven by sustainability and system innovation. This would entail closing yield gaps on current cropland, radical improvements in fertilizer and water use efficiency, recycling of phosphorus, redistribution of global use of nitrogen and phosphorus, implementing climate mitigation options including changes in crop and feed management, and enhancing biodiversity within agricultural systems.

Strategy four: Tighter governance of land and ocean utilization. This implies implementing a zero-expansion policy of new agricultural land into natural ecosystems and species-rich forests, management policies aimed at restoring and reforesting degraded land, establishing international land use governance mechanisms, and adopting a "Half Earth" strategy for conservation of biodiversity in intact ecosystems. Moreover, there is a need to improve the management of the world's oceans, to ensure that fisheries do not negatively impact ecosystems, fish stocks are utilized responsibly, and global aquaculture production is expanded sustainably.

Strategy five: reducing food waste and losses by at least 50%, in line with global sustainable development goals. Substantially limiting the quantities of food lost and wasted at all levels of the food chain, production to intake wise, is paramount for the international food system to stay within its non-hazardousworking sphere. Both technological solutions applied across the food supply chain and the application of public policies will be required to achieve a 50% reduction in food waste.

Food will be a defining issue in the 21st century and unlocking its potential will catalyze pathways for the global implementation of better eating practices from sustainable food systems, which is fundamental to achieving the SDGs and Paris Agreement. An unprecedented opportunity exists to develop food systems as a common thread between many ambitious international, national, and business policy frameworks aiming for improved health of the global population and environmental sustainability goals. Establishing clear, scientific targets to guide food system transformation is an important step in realizing this opportunity.

Chapter 1 Introduction

When attempting to discuss sustainable food production, thought must be placed on context and consideration given to related aspects including population growth, urbanization, growing wealth, changing habits in consumption, and globalization, in addition to climate change and the total utilization of finite resources. This scratch to the surface illustrates the complexity of defining, implementing and evaluating initiatives for sustainable food production.

Modern initiatives in food production have produced numerous positive results. Among these are the development of off-farm job creation from developments in the food industry, as well as the increasing variety of food availability beyond local staples, hence modifying modern eating practices.

Nevertheless, the linked structural transformations rapidly taking place have also made way to other significant challenges, with high potential for effects on food security and nutrition at a global scale. These changes include the ever-increasing number of ultra processed food items replacing traditional foods, high-energy and low-nutrient food items becoming widely available and regularly eaten; reduced access of small-scale producers to competitive markets; huge levels of food loss and waste; compromised food safety with resulting negative impacts on animal and human health; and a strong and likely non-reversible ecological footprint resulting from current food supply chains.

For all of these reasons, a more well-rounded exploration into how a wide variety of food systems work is paramount to ensuring that said systems grow with minimal negative impacts and maximal positive contributions.

Modern practices of producing food are turning ever more ultra-processed at an international level, with food items increasingly trending towards higher standardization. Foods that were once subject to seasonal availability can now be accessed nearly continuously throughout the year, with food products moving internationally (Oosterveer& Sonnenfeld, 2012). In countries where agriculture is highly industrialized, food production practices are getting stronger and output per hectare has been steadily increasing in the past several years. This increasing productivity is an outcome partially linked to rationalization and specialization, in addition to developments in plant engineering and oin occasions the implementation of genetically modified (GM) seeds. These developments, likely to be carried on, also progress with various side effects.

As of current standing in which the market plays a paramount role, an emerging direction can be observed in which an attempt is made to link agricultural production to environmental protection. This process has been made central thanks to the factors comprising the modern food system, including intensive production techniques from farms to international markets via food processing, marketing and global distribution networks (Goodman et al, 2002). Farmers, once easily identified as food producers, have now become simply providers of raw materials to be reconstituted at a later stage into desirable consumable products to be traded multinationally (Schlosser, 2001).

Over the new years, an unprecedented level of pressure will be experienced by food systems world-wide. From a demand standpoint, world demographics will see a jump from nearly seven billion today to eight billion by 2030, and very likely to more than nine billion by 2050; a significant slice of the global population will probably manage to purchase more and more food, establishing a request for a more diverse, high-quality diet necessitating additional production resources. From the production standpoint, competition for goods including land, water and energy will strengthen, with the impact of environmental degradation becoming increasingly tangible. The need to reduce greenhouse gas emissions and adjust to a dynamic climate will become a given. Throughout all of these changes globalization will carry on, conducting the food system towards new economic and political stressors.

Regardless of the instability across markets in the prices of food in the recent past, the food system remains able to produce sufficient and relatively inexpensive food for most of the world's peoples. Nevertheless, the food system world-wide is failing in two main fronts:

- Hunger remains far-reaching. In 2018 it was estimated that approximately 820 million people experienced hunger: significant parts of the global population do not have access to sufficient macronutrients (carbohydrates, fats and protein) regularly.
- An additional section of the population is thought to experience "hidden hunger" (see Box 2). On the contrary, approximately one billion individuals are considered over-consumers, contributing to the public health epidemic involving chronic health conditions linked to food selection such as type 2 diabetes and cardiovascular disease. The global food system can be seen as highly responsible for a vast number of these three billion people having suboptimal diets.
- Numerous systems for food production are not sustainable. Left to its current standing, the food system world-wide will keep degrading the environment and put at risk the global ability to ensure future food production. In addition, it will keep adding to shifts in the environment and the elimination of biodiversity. Widespread problems exist with soil loss due to erosion, poor soils, salination and other forms of land degradation. In numerous locations, the degree of water utilization for irrigation are is higher than replenishment rates. Excessive fishing is a far-flung concern; and a heavy dependency on fossil fuel-derived energy for the production of intensely used fertilizers and pesticides remains a common practice. Additionally, food systems regularly emit significant quantities of greenhouse gases and other contaminants that accrue in the environment.

Box 2. Hidden hunger.

Hidden hunger is the term given to a lack of vitamins and minerals. Hidden hunger occurs when the quality of food eaten by an individual or population does not meet their daily nutrient requirements. This is usually due to food being deficient in micronutrients such as the vitamins and minerals that are required for adequate growth and development.

Its effects can be devastating, leading to mental impairment, poor health, low productivity, and even death. Its adverse effects on child health and survival are particularly acute, especially within the first 1,000 days of a child's life, from conception to the age of two, resulting in serious physical and cognitive consequences. Even mild to moderate deficiencies can affect a person's well-being and development. In addition to affecting human health, hidden hunger can curtail socio-economic development, particularly in low- and middle-income countries.

It is estimated that approximately 2 billion people suffer from vitamin and mineral deficiencies around the world. Factors that contribute to micronutrient deficiencies include a poor diet, increased micronutrient needs during certain life stages, such as pregnancy and lactation, and health problems such as diseases, infections, or parasites.

Women and children in families of low-income levels often do not receive sufficient vitamin a, iodine and iron, and sometimes other essential nutrients. Hidden hunger limits their growth, development, health and working capacity.

Ensuring people get vitamins, minerals and essential nutrients will help prevent malnutrition and its resulting effects on the development of entire communities.

When referring to a food system one must remember that it is not a single entity being referred to, but rather a somewhat self-organized umbrella of coworking factors. As a way to illustrate this point, the food systems of various countries are now connected at all levels, from raw material trade to the out coming processed edible items. Apart from on-farm production, capture fisheries and aquaculture are also paramount, in terms of both being a nutrient source and in providing livelihoods, particularly for the pauper.

Box 3. Which foods are unsustainable?

Following a vegan lifestyle has become ever trendier world-wide. Followers of such a lifestyle claim it as not just being environmental-friendly, but also one of the most beneficial lifestyles for human health. Nevertheless, a vegan lifestyle may seem a bit extreme for people who are still looking for a more suitable way to follow an eating plan with a lower environmental impact than the average western diet.

In that context, below we list five of the most unsustainable food items currently available and possible alternatives. By opting for an alternative it may be possible to lower your carbon food-print without needing to follow what may seem a more extreme eating plan such as veganism.

1. Factory beef

Most of the meat available for human intake is produced in factories referred to as concentrated animal feeding operations (or CAFOs), which the Environmental Protection Agency (EPA) considers one of the strongest contributors to the contamination of the environment. In addition to the energy used up by CAFOs, the animals themselves also produce significant quantities of methane, which is one of the most harmful greenhouse gases (GHGs) linked to the increase of the Earth's temperature. Hence, limiting meat consumption is an adequate and feasible way to move towards a more environmentally-sustainable way of eating.

2. Lamb

Even though lamb meat is less popular than beef, it produces approximately twice the carbon footprint, ranking it as a highly unsustainable dietary option. As a way to illustrate this point, it has been estimated that eatingmerely a single portion (200g) of lamb produces about the same amount of carbon emissions as driving a car for 24 kilometers. While the ideal situation would be to avoid red meat all together, is this is not an option a second-best is to opt for locally grown, corn-fed chicken or rabbit as possibly the most environmentally friendly options for foods of animal-origin.

3. Selected seafood

Shrimp and tuna are amongst the most unsustainable seafood options due to their on the rest of the food chain. The EPA has estimated that intake of shrimp may have a 200%-500% impact on additional species in similar living environments, leading to a ripple effect that can carryover whelming negative consequences for all forms of ocean life. Concerning tuna, their location at the top of the food chain translates into regular accumulation of significant quantities of mercury in their bodies, a detrimental characteristic in any source of food for humans. A recommended alternative is to opt for prawns rather than shrimp and trout or bass in lieu of tuna.

4. Corn

Because corn represents a the main food source for humans in addition to being a source of feed for animals, it has a gigantic production demand and thus is grown in huge quantities often with the aid of chemicals that are harmful for to the environment. Run-offs from agricultural practices cause said chemicals to infiltrate bodies of water and waterways. Even though high-resolution monitoring aids in river conservation, the contamination can strongly reduce the amount of oxygen and nutrients in watery environments and make it difficult for animal and plant life to survive. An alternative is to choose sweet corn, due to its less intensive farming methods when compared to standard corn. Another option is to source corn produce locally.

5. HFCS foods

A large part of the previously mentioned corn is grown to be transformed into high-fructose corn syrup (HFCS). HFCS is used as an artificial sweetener in food and drinks. In addition, the production methods used in the development of HFCS are much more fuel-consuming than other corn growing techniques. They further lead to soil degradation. Opting for natural sugars in the form of fruits and switching soft drinks for water in an alternative to avoid the consumption of HFCS and products that list it as an ingredient.

Numerous at-risk communities procure a large quantity of food from the wild ('wild foods', see Box 4), which augments resistance to possible food shortages. The majority of the added economic value of food, especially in developed countries, originates from processes out of the farm in the form of intense food processing and retail. These two stages of food production make up a significant part of economic activity world-wide.

Towards the final stages of the food chain, the commensal makes known her or his preferences which in turn have a strong impact on food production, while Big Food has a strong political and social impact, in addition to pushing for favorable policies shaping consumer preferences. These points translate into the obligation to consider the intricate consequences of possible future steps in policy modifications of the international food system.

In 2007–2008, an already weakened food system entered an additional crisis. The initial challenge revolves around the role of the farm. It is then paramount to consider whether a renewed policy is needed, one which emphasizes the role of the farm; or should policy deal with the food system as a whole and put farming into the full food chain production process? The majority of the general reports have centered on agricultural production, although in the recent past the debate has shifted thanks in part to social scientists, emphasizing the importance of a systems approach to farming and the entirety of the full food supply chain. Certain research has demonstrated how farming has been ever more turned into a commodity production. In this way, it has transformed into the initial link in a dynamically complex food chain. This food chain now straddles the globe and has turned into a labyrinthine system of contracts and specifications (Barrientos and Dolan, 2006). Researchers have traced the on-going development of the application of efficiencies set by stakeholders (mainly supermarkets) addressing perceived requirements of increasingly urban-based consumers (Burch and Lawrence, 2007; Barling et al,. 2009).

What has come to be known as 'farm against food' policy tension has escalated, having has now extended into the discussion of key aspects including fair trade, supermarkets and their influence, and which population groups gain the most from the various steps of the processed food chain. In the United States alone, the policy during the 19th and 20th centuries centered mainly around agriculture. In this fashion, most countries had Ministries of Agriculture, rather than Food. As society has become ever more urban, the connection from primary producers to consumers has become greater. Whole novel sectors have sprouted, for example, logistics. Regardless, during the

2007–2008 crisis, the focus of public policy returned to a focus on primary production and limited attention was given to adjusting governance.

This return to normal is unexpected in that attention to power dynamics is usual in the food universe. A point of view of food systems is required, ranging from food production to intake. The fact that "food system" as a term has entered daily discussions hints at an awareness of its various components (Ericksen et al. , 2010; Tansey and Worsley, 1995), yet policymakers remain in the grey zone when it comes to addressing the connected components of the food chain and the entire food cycle. The usually followed process of policymaking tends to focus more on single issue problems, rather than on the connections of, for example, the production cycle with its effects on environmental, natural resources and ecosystems. Another example could be the lack of attention given to the effect of consumption on waste production or public health. The dependence on 'market' mindsets to solve this complex practice translates into attention placed on the price setup and the dynamic participation of consumers. Nevertheless, as farmers living in developed as well as developing countries report, the force of consumers is dwarfing in comparison to the power of retailers, traders and trapping contracts.

Labor Efficiency in Agriculture

Farming and other forms of agriculture remain the prime source of employment around the world, yet the popular approach to financial development continues to observe a change in direction of labor from rural (agriculture) to urban (off--farm) as the direction of wanted development. This remains the traditional path of progress followed by most European and OECD countries. Labor turned away from the countryside and ran down supply chains. In the EU or USA, there is now greater employment in catering than on farms, although the International Labor Organization predicts that 1.3 billion men, women and children remain employed in agriculture, 450 million of them in the form of waged labor (International Labor Organization). For years, not least promoted by the IMF, World Bank and other developmental programs, policies have promoted a reduction of work in agriculture and farming. A further reduction in rural development has increased urbanization. Most people around the world today live in towns or cities (UN Habitat, 2010). One weakness of the Green Revolution was that it promoted this shift by calling out only to those with access to credits, in that way leaving out small, independent farmers. More recently a counter wave has come forward, thanks to advocacy organizations such as Via Campesinain addition to the World Bank and FAO's IAASTD.

This champions for small--scale farmers and their importance for land management and responsible utilization; that small-scaled and female--run production activities per hectare can be significant; and that there is a greater social gain in raising their output to higher levels than in removing them from the land, adding to already fast--growing conurbations. This strengthens a traditional component in classical economics: how efficiency is defined. Should this definition focus on capital or ecological terms? Or rather in output per unit of labor or per land space (hectare)? If, as the Millennium Eco Assessment argued (Millennium Ecosystem Assessment (Program), 2005), peoples' future depends on investing in eco-systems strength, what can a labor process for a sustainable food system translate into? The degree of efficiency from work in a conventional capitalist point of view might not be the same as efficiency targeted at outcomes from sustainable developments.

THE ROLE OF BIG BUSINESS IN FOOD PRODUCTION

At the beginning of the 2000s, the Big Food business along with the World Bank and International Monetary Fund (IMF) began exploring the food system of for 20 years in the future. Regardless of its connections to 'hard-headed' neo-liberal and market-led initiatives, said lobbyists started to push for longer and minimally ideological points of view (World Bank and World Health Organization 2003; World Bank/International Finance Corporation 2006). In tandem, large food companies investigated non-economic risks to their long-term targets and business plans and started to identify the requirement for novel ones, often in partnership. In 2002, the Sustainable Agriculture Initiative (SAI) was set up by Danone, Nestlé and Unilever, and currently also covers Kellogg's, Kraft, McDonald's, PepsiCo and Sara Lee (SAI, 2008). The SAI has two main objectives: the support of sustainable agriculture internationally, and to disseminate the issues across the food sector. In 2010, the World Economic Forum, the annual meeting of big business interests in Davos, Switzerland, established a policy plan for international agriculture, developed by McKinsey. This highlighted an absence of governmental guidance and clarity of ways forward (World Economic Forum and McKinsey & Co., 2010). These worrying aspects are not entierly entirely novel to big food corporations, and emphasize a branch of macro-research of human populations and environmental challenges on food set out, for instance, by the 1972 Club of Rome report (Meadows and Club of Rome, 1972).

A current paradox in the food policy world exists: organizations, often described as being strongly against environmental and social justice, are currently becoming engaged. To some this may be regarded as 'light green' or 'greenwash', to others this engagement is essential (Monbiot, 2000; Porritt, 2005). It can this be said that Big Food is so reasserting its social responsibility as part of overall food security, an aspect that has been kept at bay in the global economic crisis by the government strives to keep banking liquidity and consumer capitalism. With these steps, it can be argued that Big Food is driving a weak versions of the sustainable development agenda which emerged in the 1970s and 1980s, through the 1980 North–South Commission headed by former West German Chancellor Willi Brandt (Brandt, 1980) – in which there was a call for financially supporting transfers from developed to developing countries – and the environmental focus of the 1987 Brundtland Commission chaired by Gro Harland Brundtland (the former Norwegian Prime Minister, public health doctor and later the WHO Director--General). Brundtland had stated that economics required a transformation in the context of sustainable development, with well--being and sustainability reintegrated to provide the world with a clearer and fresher political orientation (Brundtland ,1987). Ironically, the early 21st-century merge of big business and sustainable development translates into the social analysis of food systems, especially through the discussion of ethics and social standards of food production. It is yet to be established how strongly corporations will chance change ethical, social and environmental standards in addition to those required by the State.

CONSUMPTION AT WESTERN LEVELS

Innumerous recent reports on food security, it has been regularly assumed that Western levels of food intake are acceptable, will continue to be and are positive targets for the 21st century. Modern Western-style supermarkets with approximately 30 thousand items available offer choices at levels previously unheard of. They illustrate a fundamental change in food culture from one centered on the necessity and limited choice (established by seasons and availability locally) to one centered around desire and choice (guided by retailer contracts and price) (Burch and Lawrence, 2007). A criticism of this unlimited food selection as a targeted public policy objective has come forth from the public health point of vicw regarding a nutrition transition. This is the name used to describe the dietary modifications that emerge from a consumer shift from traditional foods to more western style eating habits, and as they trade 'up' their wants from simple to more complicated eating, mainly symbolized by consuming a larger quantity of highly processed foods.

The nutrition transition is symbolized by the intake of larger quantities of meat, dairy and soft drinks (Popkin, 2009a, 2009b; Popkin and Nielsen, 2003). This has significant public health consequences, in addition to extra ecological stress by needing more land, water and grain utilization in the form of animal feed (Steinfeld et al. 2006). The European EIPRO research group reported that food, drink, tobacco and narcotics made up for approximately 20–30% of the environmental impact of the entirety of consumption by Europeans. Meat and meat products (including meat, poultry, sausages or similar) were the largest contributor, accounting for 4–12% of the impact on global warming of all consumer products (Tukkeret al. 2006). The Stern report estimated that agriculture and food are considerable sources of greenhouse gas emissions (GHGs) (Stern, 2006). At an international level, farm animals are estimated to be responsible for 31% of GHGs, and fertilizers for 38% of nitrous oxide (N2O). Although the methane effects originating from farm animals have been notoriously identified, the impact of fertilizers in turn have not been given sufficient attention. The discussion regarding future intake habits is currently being dragged into a discussion about whether Western habits are to be replicated internationally and the degree to which this will damage the World.

DIETARY SUSTAINABILITY

For writers of policy, the previously mentioned points are delimiting the challenge. What constitutes a favorable diet and how can the food system aid in the development of human and environmental health (UN 2011)? The productions ancient paradigm allowed for a culture of selection molded by price. Price The price reduction was the target. The new plan, however, focuses on the importance of addressing other factors of equal importance, however, if climate change, water stress, pressures on land utilization, social justice and so on are to be added into the food system, they would be modified drastically, and probably turnpricier (Lang, 2010b; Lang et al. , 2011). Over the 2000s, there were various efforts made to tackle these issues. The majority of them revolved on around whether nutrition could be tied to environmental considerations and still be translated into sound public health advice. The available evidence for regular fish intake, for example, is significant, yet also the environmental evidence for either consuming a limited amount or only some not--at--risk types of seafood exists(Royal Commission on Environmental Pollution, 2004).

The Swedish National Food Administration and Environment Agency became the first to give out formal guidance on how to maneuver this and similar points (National Food Administration (of Sweden), 2008). The UK Government's Sustainable Development Commission debated that the evidence from a nutrition perspective for limiting fats, sugars and processed foods matched correctly with environmental issues (Sustainable Development Commission, 2009b). The Netherlands also generally followed suit (Health Council of the Netherlands, 2011). The sustainability of overall diets – not limited to specific products – highlights key policy challenges: is a sustainable diet the same all over the world? Or will it differ by region? Can 'soft' policy guidelines, for example, labeling and information for the consumer, help solve multi factorial issues including water protection and the cutback on non-essential 'virtual' water utilization that are part of the food supply chains? Part of the world's biggest food companies have already strengthened specifications for their lines of products, considering carbon specifically (Carbon Trust, 2008). In this way, they are specifically selecting the food products in terms of their environmental impact, prior to the arrival of products to the supermarkets and limiting consumer options of opting for the 'wrong thing'. This surpasses practices of 'nudging', which carry some engagement with conscious consumers. With this practice, the behavior modification is being made prior to the consumer making a product selection as part of their overall diet.

Box 4. Wild foods.

Besides being better for our planet, wild fruits and vegetables offer more nutrition—with an intense and fuller flavor—versus conventionally grown produce. Wild foods generally contain greater amounts of vitamins and minerals, antioxidants, and other health-promoting chemical constituents such as essential oils. Because wild foods haven't been bred to create a uniform crop, they tend to be packed with more nutrition and flavor.

These wild foods are collected by foragers or harvested by wild farmers. To confuse matters, most of the time wild foods are simply wild. But they can also be organic, depending on how the farmer chooses to farm his land—both organic wild rice and organic wild blueberries, for example, are available. If you're comparing straight wild to straight organic, both are very good for you, but wild foods may pack more flavor and nutrition than organic.

Some of these wild foods (for instance, wild rice from Lundberg and wild blueberries from Wyman's of Maine) are sold at your local supermarket or natural grocer—and others you'll need to pick up from a local farmer's market or trusted forager. When not shopping at a grocery store, it's extremely important to purchase from an experienced and conscientious source so you know you have the right species that has been harvested at the right time of growth and that the foraging is done with ecosystem health in mind.

WHAT IS A SUSTAINABLE FOOD SYSTEM?

A Food System refers to all of the components and activities taking part in the production, processing, distribution, consumption and disposal of food that result from agriculture, forestry or fisheries; food systems also include the economic, social and natural environment in which these activities are carried out.

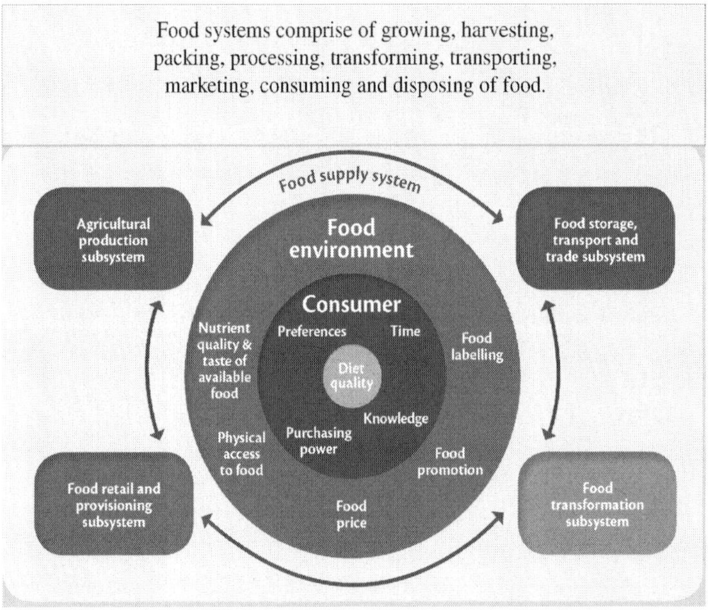

Figure 3. Food systems and diets.

Food systems include the inputs needed and outputs generated at each step. A food system operates within, and is influenced by, social, political, economic and natural environments. Consumers are central to food systems. The quality of an individual's diet is influenced by consumer purchasing power, knowledge, preferences (including values, beliefs, social norms) and time.

In turn, food systems influence the diet quality of consumers by shaping the 'food environment' that provides the food options from which people make purchasing decisions. Underpinning these food environments are food supply systems. Often referred to as the 'food supply chain' or 'food value chain'" they are made up of four interlinked and interacting subsystems covering everything from agricultural production to retail. From a policy perspective, the distinction between promoting 'healthy diets', rather than promoting nutrition per se is important, as healthy diets underpin the solution to malnutrition in all its forms.

A healthy or high-quality diet is one that includes a diversity of foods that are safe and provide levels of energy appropriate to age, sex, disease status and physical activity, as well as essential micronutrients.

Food systems are made up of subsystems including:

- Farming system
- Waste management system
- Input supply system

As well as their interactions with additional systems such as:

- Energy system
- Trade system
- Health system

Due to this complexity, a change in the entire system might develop from a modification of any of the subsystems or their components in turn. For example, changes in import tariffs may create a reduction in the availability of certain food items.

A sustainable food system (SFS) is the term used for a food system that "delivers food security and nutrition for all in such a way that the economic, social and environmental bases to generate food security and nutrition for future generations are not compromised." (FAO, 2018).

Additionally, a SFS:

- Is profitable throughout (referring to economic sustainability)
- Presents broad benefits for society (social sustainability)
- Impacts the natural environment in a positive or neutral way (environmental sustainability).

Biodiversity at an agricultural level is a key factor in setting up and maintaining a food system that is sustainable. If agricultural biodiversity does not exist, a food system is not considered sustainable.

Only three crops – rice, wheat and maize – represent over 50% of the World's plant-derived energy (calories) for consumption. Yields of said crops have stagnated. Thousands of alternative crops are able to replace and complement these staples. Sorghum, millets and quinoa are some similar cereals that can grow in testing locations, carry a high nutrient density and have the capacity to provide increased yields. Solutions based on biodiversity are at the center of agro ecological production, which increases the output while lowering environmental stress.

Numerous species exist in the wild and now on farms. Part of these species represents in turn millions of varieties with the ability to spice up eating practices, improve nutrition and carry less environmental impact than conventional food selection. In India for example, there are over 1,000 varieties of mango fruits.

- Trees that give fruits, legumes, vegetables, cereals, chicken and other small livestock, as well as seafood varieties, can be put together in portfolios to give year-round harvest of healthy, nutrient-rich foods, which cover hunger gaps and target specific nutrient requirements.
- The nutrient composition across different species, or different varieties, sometimes varies significantly. For example:
- Consuming a single To'o banana covers the daily recommended intake of vitamin A for women and children. In order to do the same with Cavendish bananas, the type that are is most often found in on supermarket shelves, one would need to eat an entire kilogram!
- Certain local fish varieties, for example, mola and darkina in Bangladesh, contain much higher quantities of essential micronutrients when compared to commonly consumed fish, as is tilapia.
- Local and free-growing plants, fruit-baring trees and animal species are regularly higher innutrients than their more popular international counterparts. In Brazil, for example, the fruit of Amazonian fruit trees buriti, pupunha and tucuma have greaterquantities of beta-carotene. Brazil nut, caburi, assai and uxi also provide a significant array of minerals and phytonutrients.

Favorable diets must be available, accessible, affordable and acceptable. Quinoa, one of the world's favored grains, used to be avoided by city dwellers in the Andes. These daysquinoa is known for being anutrient that is -highly desirable.

Employing agricultural techniques focused on biodiversity – genetic, varieties, species, soil and landscapes – may increase outputs, and lower waste and reliance on external inputs.

- The erosion of soil may be limited by employing agricultural biodiversity techniques, including hedgerows, cover crops, agro forestry or intercropping. In Indonesia, intercropping coffee plants with vegetables in hilly areas produced a 64% lowering of soil erosion, with no reduction in coffee output.
- It is possible to control pests and diseases by opting for plants that increase the number of pest predators, or by selecting varieties that are pest or disease resistant. Scientists in Uganda investigating a type of common bean reported that combining 50% of traditional resistant varieties in a plot turned them more resiliant resilient to common diseases.
- Stronger landscape diversity– with tree patches, wild vegetation, flowers – allows for greater diversity in pollinators. Organic fields all over the world have been found to host a 70% greater amount of bees and 50% greater diversity of bees than conventional fields.
- The diversification of crops, greater diversity in vegetation and specific agro ecological methodologies strengthen natural biodiversity conservation. In Costa Rica, double the number of birds and types of birds were observed in dynamic coffee and cacao agro forests when compared toless complex pastures and sugarcane fields.
- Quality of soil. Crop production with strong agricultural biodiversity from the rotation of crops, shows higher levels of soil carbon (28%–112% more) as well as nitrogen (18%–58% more) when in comparison to those with less agricultural biodiversity.
- Yield. The diversification of corn and soybean crops with the implementation of crop rotations in combination with a reduction of tillage augmented yield by 7% and 22% respectively. In Ethiopia, research has demonstrated an increase of between 415kg/ha and 1,338kg/ha in barley for each increase in a form of diversity.

Diversification between and across species augments resilience to environmental changes since they respond differently to modifications or create beneficial synergies.

In 2014 , at the Food and Agriculture (FAO) International Symposium, 'Agro ecology For Food Security and Nutrition', Professor Stephen Gleissman showed some research detailing the transition stages that food systems progress across as they slowly take up agro ecology and develop in a sustainable manner, summarized below:

1. Augment the efficiency of industrial/conventional methodologies while at the same time reduce the dependence on external inputs that may be more expensive and carry a higher negative environmental impact. As a way to illustrate this, it is possible to look at multi-cropping and the optimization of crop spacing to reduce the land available for the growth of weed, hence lowering the requirement for agrochemical spray. Higher productivity is an additional perk.
2. Change industrial and/or conventional inputs for other practices that beneficially work together with the environment and cause no harm to farm employees or consumers. It is possible to achieve this through the employment of synthetic fertilizers (which may lead to waterway pollution and the acidification of the soil) with a cover crop to fix nitrogen and/or the rotations of livestock.
3. Replace the basic structures and working relationships of the agro-ecological system in a way that it functions on a new collection of ecological processes. In this way the true process can begin to take place. "Externalities" are avoided by way of prevention. The system is intuitively modified to function with coherence in accordance to the seasons, conditions of the soil, topography, among others. All sorts of influential factors such as the energy use (e.g. gravity-fed watering troughs) to agro biodiversity (e.g. diversification of cropping systems) is are taken into account.
4. The setup (or re-establishment) of direct links across those who produce food and those who eat the produced food. This needs a significant amount of time investment off-farm and a stronger change in thinking from both the producer and the consumer. Both sides are required to display a willingness to take part in local food networks, to begin with—international food networks are a follow-up concern. Local food communities are the social and economic basis of agricultural practices that are more sustainable, driving long-term modifications through the economic and social attractive points offered by food citizenship. Farmers markets, agriculture supported by the community, agriculture through generative practices, permaculture, companies in the hospitably business that are tightly working with farmers, producers of wine

and coffee producers—everyone including artists may be key in easing the transition.

5. From the synergy of the four previously mentioned efforts, an international food system based on equity, participation and justice is constructed. The life-support systems of Earth are inherently renewed and protected. Reaching this stage is still far off—even though there are some participants of the agricultural industry that are managing part of this at a collective, international level crossing multinational boundary boundaries. Specialty chocolate, through trading it directly, is one such good. Biological wine is another example. These two products are based on sustainable farming practices, transparent and closely linked to supply and demand routes, differentiation and citizenship—at first locally and then globally. Yet these still represent just a minimal part of their respective areas of work and the food system in its wholeness.

These intermediary levels of development can appear unclear. They're not a formula but they're as detailed as it is possible to get to for the time being to an internationally-relevant process for agroecology.

Sustainable Diets

Two of the most impactful issues we are currently faced with include malnutrition in all its forms and the environmental degradation of natural resources. These two issues are occurring at a fast rate. Over 820 million individuals go to bed hungry daily. In 2018, it was estimated that 1.3 billion individuals went through food insecurity of moderate level, that is, they did not have constant access to enough and nutritious food. Overweight and obesity and their connected diet-related non-communicable diseases (NCDs) are adding to approximately 4 million deaths worldwide. Currently, approximately 2 billion adults and more than 40 million children under the age of five are considered to be overweight. In addition, more than 670 million adults and 120 million girls and boys between that the ages of 5-19 years of age are considered to suffering from obesity. Malnutrition is demanding on the health of people, their overall wellbeing and productivity. Malnutrition additionally carries strong socio-economic costs for communities in all regions of the world.

Lacking diets are a key determining factor to in the increasing rates of malnutrition in all its presentations. Additionally, unfavorable eating practices and malnutrition are in the top ten risk factors adding to the burden of disease internationally. Moreover, the way food is grown and eaten is creating a dip in the environment and natural resource pool. To illustrate this point, the production of food uses up approximately 48 to 70 percent of land and freshwater resources internationally.

Other factors are also adding to the dynamic ways of life as well as eating patterns of today, including social, demographic and economic factors. These in turn put stress on resources for the production of food. Considering the damaging environmental impact of modern food systems, and the worries raised regarding their sustainability, there is a pressing requirement to champion eating practices that are favorable for health and have less effects on the environment. These eating practices also require socio-cultural acceptability and to be economically accessible for the individuals.

Food systems are in tandem a leading cause of degradation of the environment and depletion of natural resources. It is estimated that today food systems are the cause of a significant portion (20-35 percent) of greenhouse gas (GHG) emissions, and are a the main reason of for land conversion, deforestation and biodiversity loss. Agriculture alone is responsible for approximately 70 percent of global withdrawals of freshwater, in addition to causing water contamination (Sofi, 2010). With the global population predicted to reach 9.7 billion people by 2050, this stress on the environment does not allow for the sustainability of the current food systems. The Intergovernmental Panel on Climate Change (IPCC) in their latest report stated that "Consumption of healthy and sustainable diets presents major opportunities for reducing GHG emissions from food systems and improving health outcomes" (Springmann, 2018).

Additionally, the effects on the environment of agricultural practices are a contributor to morbidity and mortality. In 2014, the FAO/WHO Second International Conference on Nutrition (ICN2) recognized that: "current food systems are being increasingly challenged to provide adequate, safe, diversified and nutrient-rich food for all that contribute to healthy diets due to, inter alia, constraints posed by resource scarcity and environmental degradation, as well as by unsustainable production and consumption patterns, food losses and waste, and unbalanced distribution" (Trichopoulou, 2003). Hence, shaping food systems to develop healthier eating practices also requires attention to the environment.

In addition, modern food systems are known for their inequitable power concentration and imbalance, with certain parties involved profiting strongly while others stay deep in poverty. Said systems are not able to deliver equal benefits for all and are leaving the most vulnerable behind.

Internationally, food systems are intertwined with unique historical, religious, social, cultural and economic backgrounds, and are hence highly diverse. Although healthy diets are characterized through dietary targets defined through nutrient suitability, or the targeted consumption of specific food groups, or following as a specific dietary pattern, eating practices are more than the collection of nutrients and foods eaten or the dietary patterns linked to them.

Sustainable diets are dietary patterns that promote all dimensions of an individual's health and wellbeing; have low environmental pressure and impact; are accessible, affordable, safe and equitable; and are culturally acceptable. The main aim of a sustainable diet is to achieve optimal growth and development of all individuals and support functioning and physical, mental, and social wellbeing at all life stages for present and future generations; contribute to preventing all forms of malnutrition; lower the likelihood of developing diet-related non-communicable diseases; and strengthen the preservation of biodiversity and health of the planet. Sustainable eating practices must connect all the aspects of sustainability to prevent unintended consequences.

It is extensively known that establishing a food supply that meets the definition of sustainable diets will be difficult and will certainly require compromises. Some of the factors to consider in establishing the definition of a sustainable food system include:

- Nutrition – providing a favorable eating plan made up of sufficient energy, macronutrients and micronutrients, with acknowledgment of lifestyle; facilities for food preparation; accessibility; affordability; individual requirements and health status; knowledge of nutrition, as well as religious and cultural beliefs and values.
- Environment – the level and types of greenhouse gas emissions linked to different forms of food and varying methods of production for a specific food; efficient utilization of fertilizers and pesticides; biodiversity of animals and plants; fish stocks and

marine ecosystems; efficient use of resources (including energy, land and water inputs required for production); crop resistant to climatic events (including droughts and floods for example), pests (such as locusts and beetles) and diseases; value from an aesthetic perspective and cultural/religious value of nature.

- The supply of food and the economy – Infrastructure and facilities for food trade; the transportation of food, storage and distribution; the added value of agricultural products (such as local and/or organic); employment; terms of trade and subsidies (such as fair trade, EU common agricultural policy); standards for food production and food safety.
- Ethics and society – standards for work conditions; ethics and welfare of animals; new technological impacts; food acceptability from a cultural perspective; preferences of the individualas well as personal requirements (for example vegan and coeliac tailored eating plans); trends in dietary patterns (such as a reduction of meat and animal product intake, high fat-eating plans).
- Additional factors –infectious diseases linked to agriculture; environmental health risks; occupational injuries.

Selecting a more Sustainable Way of Eating

By modifying the kinds of food items we consume and their frequency of consumption, we can alleviate the impacts on the food system worldwide, while keeping to a favorable eating plan.

Opting for a more plant-based way of eating such as those described in dietary guidelines of various countries is a possible way in which to manage this. Certain researchers have gone a step ahead. In accordance to research by the EAT-Lancet Commission, in order to prevent a potentially catastrophic degradation of the planet and healthy food for all by 2050, world intake levels of foods including red meat and sugar must be reduced by approximately 50%, while intake of fruit, vegetables, nuts and legumes must double, in addition to significant lowering of food losses and waste and strong improvements in agricultural practices worldwide.

The Planetary Health Diet

	Macronutrient intake grams per day (possible range)	Caloric intake kcal per day
Whole grains		
Rice, wheat, corn and other	232	811
Tubers or starchy vegetables		
Potatoes and cassava	50 (0–100)	39
Vegetables		
All vegetables	300 (200–600)	78
Fruits		
All fruits	200 (100–300)	126
Dairy foods		
Whole milk or equivalents	250 (0–500)	153
Protein sources		
Beef, lamb and pork	14 (0–28)	30
Chicken and other poultry	29 (0–58)	62
Eggs	13 (0–25)	19
Fish	28 (0–100)	40
Legumes	75 (0–100)	284
Nuts	50 (0–75)	291
Added fats		
Unsaturated oils	40 (20–80)	354
Saturated oils	11.8 (0-11.8)	96
Added sugars		
All sugars	31 (0–31)	120

Figure 4. The Planetary Health Diet.

In the process of making a food choice, judging the degree of sustainability of a specific food unveils to be more complex than the average consumer might expect. As a way to illustrate this point, local and imported foods do not always vary significantly in terms of their carbon footprint. The effect on the environment of a particular food is connected to many factors apart from transportation-related emissions; this includes packaging, seasonality and the farming system used for its production, which in turn includes water usage, required heat, fertilizers and other inputs. There is also a wide variation in resource efficiency according to farming practices and a need to consider local environmental conditions when assessing land use. For example, in the UK, most of the land used to raise sheep is unsuitable for other agricultural practices.

While the need for diversification of land use is less pronounced for staple crops, including wheat, rice and maize, the environmental impact among different producers may still vary significantly when considering greenhouse gas emissions, land and water use, as well as acidification and eutrophication effects (excessive plant and algal growth affecting aquatic ecosystems).

Beyond Emissions

In this context, the social and economic impact of food choices is not to be neglected. To illustrate this point: green beans are a the main trading good commodity in Kenya, with approximately 50,000 smallholder farmers earning their income from this crop, as well as from related jobs further down the supply chain of this crop. A reduction in demand for off-season imported foods to countries such as the UK and Germany, because of the growing environmental concerns this practice carries, is likely to have a strong impact on the quality of life of producers.

What is the importance of a sustainable food supply?

Currently, over three billion people are experiencing malnourishment and many of the World's 7 billion people consume diets lacking quality. Simultaneously, the number of people in the World is growing rapidly, and it is theorized that there will be almost 10 billion people on Earth by 2050. When discussing food sustainability, the target is to secure a future when this developed population has both sufficient food at reach and access to quality food.

Envisioning a successful future for food must consider the earth as a full system, as opposed to simply looking at local levels. The "Anthropocene" is a name given to describe the modern geological epoch, a time period characterized by humanity being the main driver of development in atmospheric, geologic, hydrologic, biospheric and other systems on Earth. The influence of humanity is at its peak point in the history of Earth. The term "anthropogenic" is an adjective that denotes "originating in human activity."

When referring to anthropogenic activities, agriculture is the strongest cause of modification of the worldwide environment. Such modifications may change include climate change, deforestation, desertification, and damage to coastal reefs and marine ecosystems.

- Food production:
  - Produces approximately 30% of global greenhouse gas emissions, and the livestock sector alone represents almost half (14.5%) of these emissions (Vermeulen et al., 2012; FAO, 2014).
  - Takes up approximately 40% of global land (Foley et al., 2005).

- Utilizes approximately 70% of freshwater (IWMI, 2007).
- Is the strongest threat to endangered species (Tilman, 2017).
- Leads to nutrient overload zones and dead zones in lakes and coastal areas (Diaz, 2008).
- Has led to most (~60%) of the world's fish stocks to be completely fished or overfished (33%)(FAO, 2018).

These types of environmental changes of at global scales augment the likelihood of irreversible and catastrophic changes in the Earth's system characterized by increasing human mortality, morbidity, conflict, and reducing food security (Oppenheimer, 2014). Agriculture ,as it is practiced today, is at the same time a cause of global environmental change and a result of changes in environmental conditions (Springman, 2016). Left alone, the World is likely to fail to meet the UN Sustainable Development Goals and the Paris Agreement. In other words: global food systems are not unsustainable. The way in which we consume foodmust be reconsidered as must be the way in which food is produced.

Considering Meat and Dairy Consumption

Most will concur with the opinion that meat and dairy products are linked to greater greenhouse gas emissions than plant-based foods, even though the quantities may vary with the kind of farming practices implemented. Specifically, the meat of cattle and sheep origin has a greater environmental impact than chicken and pork, originating from the methane production by ruminant animals during digestion, as well as to the larger amount of land needed for rearing these animals. Nevertheless, modifications to agricultural practices, as well as altering the feed of animals, can make it possible to lessen some of these effects.

Certain research has reported that dietary patterns that limit the intake of foods of animal origin, as well as suggest changing some ruminant meat by monogastric (chickens and pigs) types of meat, may lower diet-related greenhouse gas emissions, land utilization and, sometimes, water requirements, in comparison to modern dietary habits in developed countries. Data from over 55,000 people residing in the United Kingdom suggested that eating <50 g/day of meat, in comparison to >100 g/day, was linked to 35% fewer greenhouse gas emissions. Thosc choosing a vegetarian (47% less emissions) or vegan eating plan (60% less emissions)had even less diet-related emissions. Nevertheless, the selection of meat replacement foods is key and the nutritional suitability of diets must be taken into account.

A well-designed and diverse vegetarian or vegan eating plan can be nutritious and favorable for health. Nevertheless, anyone cutting out foods of animal origin should ensure that they consume a diversity of foods providing important nutrients including calcium, iron, zinc, vitamin B12 and iodine. Supplementing vitamin B12 is often recommended for those taking up a vegan lifestyle, as this vitamin is usually only found in foods of animal origin.

Even though dairy and meat products tend to score poorly in regard to their environmental impact, they make up significantly nutrient-dense, and widely available sources of many micronutrients, in addition to protein. In the typical eating pattern found in the United Kingdom, meat is a key contributor to dietary consumption of iron (21%), zinc (34%) and selenium (32%) for adults, while dairy foods make up a significant proportion of calcium and iodine (both 34% of the total). Additionally, oily fish is the main dietary source of long-chain omega 3 fatty acids and vitamin D. It is hence important to think of and balance these factors when analyzing the overall impact of foods of animal origin.

Eating plans do not have to eliminate whole food categories to be sustainable – research has identified eating plans that are nutritionally suitable, while maintaining food diversity, tolerating certain quantities of meat and dairy foods, and having less environmental impact.

Considering Organic Farming

Organic agricultural practices are generally seen as beneficial for the environment, even though their greater sustainability and overall environmental benefits when compared to conventional farming practices remains debatable. Although organic farming practices may protect the 'ecosystem services' (including land, water, soil, biodiversity) to a greater extent, something key to food production, yields maybe 5-34% less when compared to conventional techniques, depending on the kind of crop being farmed as well as to the local conditions. This has made the basis for the debate on the feasibility of the extensive adoption of organic farming practices. Nevertheless, in economic terms, smaller yields may be compensated by the increased price consumers are likely to pay for organic products in richer countries, making organic production systems highly profitable for producers, regardless of any ecosystem effects. It is possible that a mixture of organic and other innovative farming techniques will be required in order to feed the World's population, without putting at risk the health of the ecosystems upon which agriculture depends.

Organic farming is eco-friendly from many different standpoints. The avoidance of mineral nitrogen fertilizer use, as well as limiting per hectare livestock herd sizes and livestock manure use to the scope necessary for crop plant nitrogen needs, creates virtually hermetic nutrient cycles. The farm's livestock manure is used to grow its own crops and can be readily uptaken by the crops. Nutrient surpluses resulting from purchased fodder and mineral fertilizer use are thus avoided. This above all protects surface water bodies and groundwater, by virtue of the fact that organic farming often generates a lower level of nutrient deposits (particularly nitrates) than is the case with conventional farming; plus the fact that avoiding the use of chemical pesticides contributes to water body conservation.

Organic-fertilizer use and cultivating nitrogen-fixating protein crops (legumes) promote humus formation and soil fertility, engender conditions that enable soil organisms to thrive, and create stable soil structures by virtue of their activities. Catch-cropping and under sowing reduces the risk of erosion, because the ground is covered virtually year round.

Organic farming also promotes farmland flora and fauna biodiversity via extensive crop rotation and catch-cropping, and the avoidance of pesticide use. Species-appropriate livestock farming, sufficient exercise and pasturing, fresh air, longer fattening periods, and reduced antibiotic use promote animal welfare, as well as acceptance on the part of the general public.

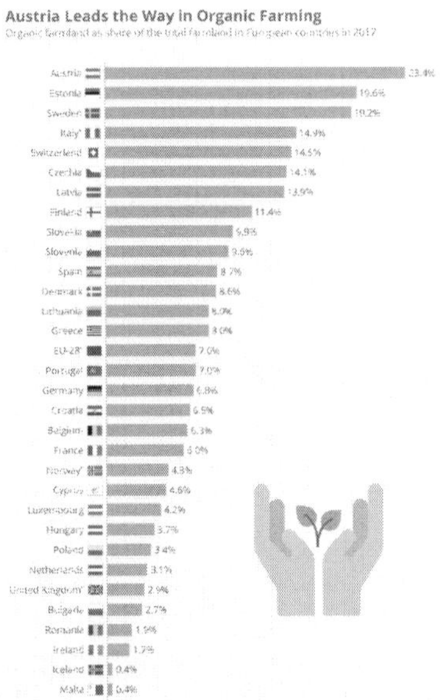

Figure 5. Organic farming in the European Union.

Organic Food Production

Organic production is an overall system of food production and farm management that makes use of the best available environmental practices with a high level of biodiversity, natural resources preservation, and high animal welfare standards. The key principles of organic food production include:

- The use of chemical pesticides and synthetic fertilizers is prohibited.
- The use of antibiotics is severely restricted.
- Genetically modified organisms are banned.
- Crop rotation is applied.

European regulations for organic food production

European regulations regarding organic food production and labeling of organic products makes certain that the same high quality standards are kept all over the EU. Said regulations cover agriculture and aquaculture farming practices, food processing and labeling, certification procedures for farmers in addition to the import of non-EU organic products.

Organic farmers in the European Union make use of energy and natural resources in alignment with best practices, promote the health of animals for food consumption and contribute to maintaining biodiversity, ecological balance and the quality of water and soil.

At a European level, organic food production practices must cover:

- Crop rotation for an efficient use of resources
- A ban of the use of chemical pesticides and synthetic fertilizers
- Very strict limits on livestock antibiotics
- Ban of genetically modified organisms (GMOs)
- Use of on-site resources for natural fertilizers and animal feed
- Raising livestock in a free-range, open-air environment and the use of organic fodder
- Tailored animal husbandry practices

The EU's organic logo on food products is a visual guarantee that EU rules on organic production have been followed in the development of the said item. In the case of processed food, it means that at least 95% of the ingredients of agricultural origin are organic. Supermarkets and other food sellers can label their products with the term organic only if they comply with these rules.

Figure 6. European organic food production in 2016.

In 2010, the organic food market in Europe was estimated to be at €19.6 billion (US$26.5 billion), with the largest individual market being German, which had an approximate turnover of €6 billion [US$8.1 billion], followed by the Freanch market (€3.4 billion [US$4.6 billion]) and the United Kingdom (€2 billion [US$2.7 billion]) (Willer &Kilcher, 2012). For the European market, the key reason to buy organic food is the perception that organic food is more beneficial for health (Willer &Kilcher, 2012).

At least for Europe, the obstacles to buying organic produce are likely to branch off more from the structural components of the community including the access, availability, and affordability of the supply; than from a preference or lack of nutritional knowledge.

The Food Gap and its Impacts on Food Security, Ecosystems, and Greenhouse Gas Emissions

The global agricultural system is standing at the edge of a great precipice. To cover diverse human requirements, by 2050 it must at the same time produce far more food for a number of people expected to be at about 9.6

billion, represent economic opportunities for the various millions of rural paupers who rely on agriculture for their living, and lower environmental stress, such as ecosystem degradation and high greenhouse gas emissions.

Scope of the Food Gap

Over 800 million people currently experience food insecurity, meaning they are regularly hungry. In accordance with existing projections, the world is facing a 69 percent gap between the production of calories during 2006 and those most likely needed for 2050. To reduce this gap via agricultural production rises only, overall yields would need to augmentin ata much greater level between 2006 and 2050 than in the equivalent number of years from 1962 to 2006—an 11% greater increase. Over the same time, milk and meat production from pasture will be required to augment 40 percent more than what happened from 1962 to 2006. If the globalrich population ate less meat and other resource-demanding foods, the food gap is also likely to reduce. Nevertheless, since the rich outdo the poor when food supplies are limited, global paupers would experience the consequences of any gap between supply and demand in a more acute fashion.

The Challenge of Development and Poverty

Approximately 2 billion people work in agriculture, the majority of them are poor. To eradicate poverty, agriculture hence must grow in forms that allow for economic opportunities to populations in and at risk of poverty. The female part of the population makes up most of the agricultural workers in several developing countries. Increasing women's income has disproportionate beneficial points for easing hunger, hence helping female farmers is a specifically effective strategy for the reduction of poverty and enhancement of food security.

The Challenge of Land Utilization and Biodiversity

Land used for crops and pasture takes up approximately half of the worldwide land that is not covered by ice, water, or desert. The continuous expansion of land used for crops and pastures is the main source of degradation and biodiversity loss of the ecosystem. Between 1962 and 2006, land used for crops and pasture grew by approximately 500 million hectares—an area equivalent to about 60 percent of the United States. The transformation of forests, savannas, and peat lands into land used for agriculture makes up approximately 11 percent of worldwide greenhouse gas emissions.

The Challenge of Crop and Pasture Yield

On average, yields of crops would need to grow by 32 percent more from 2006 to 2050 than they did from 1962 to 2006 in order to reach the estimated requirements for the near future without expanding the yearly harvested area size. Even though the significant potential for yield increases exists, boosting yields at an even faster rate in the future is a tall order. From 1962 to 2006, the majority of farmers worldwide took up scientifically bred seeds and fertilizer, and the irrigation areas doubled. Currently, a limited amount of water remains to expand irrigation, and no similar dominant novel technologies seem to be available. Climate change is likely to also reduce yields significantly, turning gains even more elusive.

The challenge being faced by land utilization covers pasture, which makes up over two-thirds of agricultural land worldwide. Pasture expansion at least equals cropland expansion as a reason for forest and woodland conversion. To reach the estimated requirements for milk and meat from cows and sheep without increasing pasture, the annual output from pasture lands per hectare will need to grow more than 80 percent by 2050.

The Challenge of Climate Change

Crop growth and animal husbandry practices employed in modern times releases approximately 13 percent of worldwide greenhouse gas emissions, or approximately 6.5 gigatons (Gt) of carbon dioxide equivalent (CO2e) annually, without considering land use modifications. Assuming certain augments in the carbon efficiency of agriculture, emissions may possibly increase to 9.5 Gt of CO2e by 2050. When in combination with ongoing emissions from land use modification, global agriculture-related emissions could go up to 15 Gt by 2050. In contrast, to hold global warming at less than 2° Celsius, global yearly emissions from pooled sources would be required to fall to about 21-22 Gt by 2050 in accordance with conservative estimates. To manage these levels, agricultural practices must significantly reduce their greenhouse gas emissions— even while increasing production.

The Fishery Challenge

Wild and aquaculture originating fish contributed to approximately 16 percent of the global protein of animal origin in 2009 and are the main source of protein of animal origin for about 1.3 billion people. Nevertheless, 57 percent of wild marine fish stocks are utilized to their full potential, with an additional 30 percent being overexploited and at risk of declining in the future, unless significant improvements in fisheries management are out put into place. Internationally, the wild fish catch peaked in the 1990s, has declined modestly since, and will need to be reduced even further for at least a temporary time frame if fisheries are to heal sufficiently to allow for present catch levels to be maintained.

The Combined Challenge

These numerous challenges are presented in combination. Overfishing lowers attainable fish catch. Deforestation can lead to harsh regional as well as global consequences for food production. Left unattended, climate change is likely to cause severe alterations to the global food supply. Even relatively small warming is likely to have a harsh impact on the most food-insecure countries.

Box 5. Global sustainable fishing initiative 2020.

Governments responsible for 40% of the world's coastlines have pledged to end overfishing, restore dwindling fish populations and stop the flow of plastic pollution into the seas in the following 10 years.

The countries – Australia, Canada, Chile, Fiji, Ghana, Indonesia, Jamaica, Japan, Kenya, Mexico, Namibia, Norway, Palau and Portugal – will end harmful subsidies that contribute to overfishing, a key demand of campaigners. They will also aim to eliminate illegal fishing through better enforcement and management, and to minimizes bycatch and discards, as well as implementing national fisheries plans based on scientific advice.

Each of the countries, members of the High Level Panel for Sustainable Ocean Economy, has also pledged to ensure that all the areas of the ocean within its own national jurisdiction – known as exclusive economic zones – are managed sustainably by 2025. That amounts to an area of ocean roughly the size of Africa.

Research has found that if oceans were sustainably managed, they could provide six times more food than today, when many species are fished up to and beyond their recovery limits. Economists also calculate that for every $1 invested in sustainable oceans, there is about $5 return in economic, social, environmental and health benefits, and that sustainably managing the world's oceans would create about 12m new jobs.

Their commitments also include: a global target to protect 30% of the world's oceans by 2030, alongside setting out national plans by 2025 that would ensure local sustainability; to use technology to improve the monitoring of fishing; to eliminate the discarding of "ghost" fishing gear; to invest in sewage and waste management infrastructure in developing countries; to place national targets on decarbonizsing shipping transport; and to scale up environmentally responsible forms of fish farming.

Some of the work of restoring health to the oceans must also take place on land. In a report, the leaders set out the case for shifting to a "circular economy that would prevent plastic pollution from reaching the sea, and improving agricultural regulation on land to halt the spread of "dead zones" from fertilizer and manure runoff.

Sustainable Development Goals

The Sustainable Development Goals (SDG) were adopted by all United Nations Member States in 2015 as a global call to action to end poverty, protect the planet and ensure that all people enjoy peace and prosperity by 2030 (United Nations, 2015). The comprising 17 goals are a synergic movement, meaning that action in one area will affect outcomes in another, and that development of each and all goals must consider social, economic and environmental sustainability. The creativity, know-how, technology and financial resources from all of society are required to achieve the SDG in every context.

Figure 7. United Nations Sustainable Development Goals.

(United Nations, 2015).

Goal 9: Industry, innovation and infrastructure

Investment in infrastructure and innovation are crucial drivers of economic growth and development. With over half the world population now living in cities, mass transport and renewable energy are becoming ever more important, as are the growth of new industries and information and communication technologies.

Technological progress is also key to finding lasting solutions to both economic and environmental challenges, such as providing new jobs and promoting energy efficiency. Promoting sustainable industries, and investing in scientific research and innovation, are all important ways to facilitate sustainable development.

Over 4 billion people still lack access to the Internet, and 90 percent are from developing countries. Bridging this digital divide is crucial to ensure equal access to information and knowledge, as well as foster innovation and entrepreneurship.

In many parts of the World, farming is an indispensable part of the rural economy, accounting for 29 percent of GDP and 65 percent of all employment. To secure the livelihoods of rural populations, generate a decent income and provide a basis for inclusive growth and poverty reduction, we will need to support farming systems that are viable in the long term – particularly for smallholder farms.

Today, agricultural systems across the World are challenged by climate change and other threats such as increased energy costs. Within such a context, sustainable, resource-efficient agricultural practices help farmers adapt to change, sustain their lives and lower greenhouse gas emissions from farm activities. Sustainable food production also necessitates the development of sustainable food value chains in order to offer innovative pathways out of poverty, e.g. by local value addition through local processing, and by linking farmers directly to higher-value export markets. Food waste reduction represents an important but often overlooked component of sustainable food systems. Globally, up to 33% of all food harvested is wasted. Addressing food waste offers a major opportunity to improve food security and minimize the environmental footprint of agricultural systems throughout the supply chain.

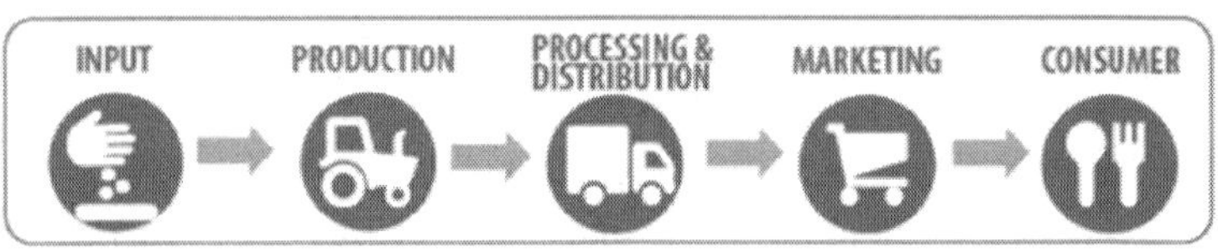

Figure 8. Greening the food value chain.

The implementation of sustainable food value chains can offer important development pathways for millions of poor households in developing countries. However, food value chains are complex and intricate systems, in which the root causes for unsustainability may not always be apparent. Typically, we need to address multiple challenges in concert in order to break the vicious poverty cycle. This of course necessitates a high degree of alignment and active cooperation among multiple value chain actors, including farmers, agribusinesses, governments and civil society groups. Around the world, decision-makers and practitioners in public, private and non-governmental organizations are collaborating to design and implement innovative solutions to address such challenges and achieve lasting impact in terms of improving the system at scale and in a sustainable manner. In the process, valuable lessons are learned.

The life cycle of foods covers all aspects ranging from agriculture, manufacturing, packaging, distribution, use and disposal. Outputs from agricultural practices tend to be the greatest contributor to the life cycle consequences of food, usually more than 50 percent of the environmental footprint. Generally, food processing is the second strongest contributor to effects on the supply chain. Effects from packaging tend to be extremely narrow compared to other factors of the supply chain but may reach up to 20 percent because of the energy required to make the package or when packaging products with a lighter weight. The transportation of consumers to purchase food may also represent a significant impact, and consumer utilization of the food is also likely to add to the life cycle effects.

Agricultural Practices

Agricultural practices are the largest source of environmental effects from food and drinks. Production from agriculture is projected to be the cause of approximately one-third of the human-induced greenhouse gas (GHG) emissions and approximately half of the food system's GHG emissions. It has been estimated that in the U.S. about 70 percent of river and stream contamination is caused by agriculture from chemicals, silt, and animal waste. What is more, agricultural practices are the largest utilizes of water worldwide, and only about 45 percent of the irrigation water is used effectively.

To mitigate the effects of agriculture, aiming for more responsible methods is key. When animal-based products are employed, it is better to opt for sources with less-intensive feeding and raising needs. It is estimated that about 70 percent of antibiotics used in the United States are given to farm animals for the artificial promotion of growth and to make up for unfavorable living conditions. As a consequence, businesses should support and procure products of animal origin raised humanely and less intensively. To illustrate this point, Del Monte Meat Co., Inc. provides meat products made with strict humane standards and reared on sustainable farms and ranches.

Consolidation of farms has made way to a centering of wealth, lowering rural population, reduction of infrastructure in communities dedicated to farming and lessening of small farms, providing for more foods that are more nutritionally dense and employing more environmentally friendly production methods. Nevertheless, fair prices must be offered to small-scale farmers to avoid further consolidation. To provide markets and wages that are fair, greater choice, and more environmentally preferable options, diversification of sourcing from growers and suppliers must be practiced. Some businesses have opted for to work with programs like Fair-trade to strengthen this effort.

Manufacturing

Food processing is generally the second-largest source of environmental impact from food and drink products and is usually the area targeted by the food industry for its sustainability efforts. Food processing makes up for approximately 25 percent of all water utilization worldwide and 50-80 percent of all water required by industrial countries. In addition, it is estimated that 7 percent of the food supply is wasted through processing.

Minimally processing food in terms of water, raw materials and energy is likely to lower the total impact of food processing. Further, processors should target the preference for renewable energies or process wastes to produce energy.

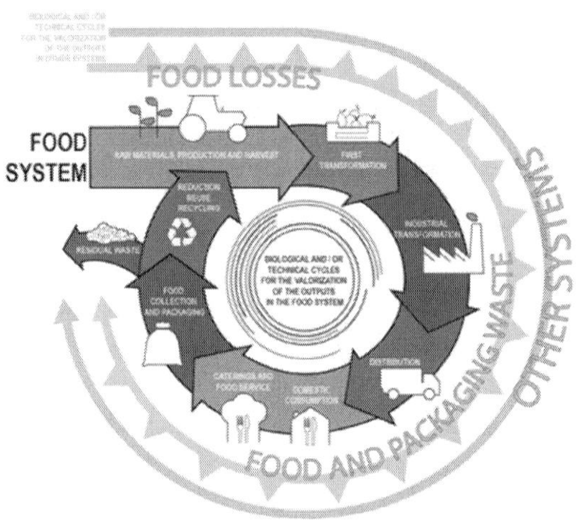

Figure 9. Food and Packaging Waste.

The word sustainability is increasingly becoming a catch-all term referring to a number of things, such as using recyclable materials, minimizing greenhouse gas (GHG) emissions, partnering with community groups and NGOs, transparency, protecting farmers and farmland, water conservation, reducing emissions, increasing energy efficiencies and more. Oxfam, an international group of charitable organizations, recently ranked food and beverage companies based on a "scorecard" comprising seven themes, which are corporate transparency, addressing women's issues, protecting workers, protecting farmers, land issues, water issues and working to minimize climate change.

The Grocery Manufacturers Association released the 2016 Environmental Success Stories report based on three defined areas of environmental sustainability: air, waste and water. According to the GMA's criteria, food and beverage companies' success stories that were selected "demonstrate some or all of the following virtues: innovation in the system or product design; monetary savings or quantifiable return on investment; reduction or improvement in the efficiency of environmental factors; interaction or collaboration with stakeholders; successfully executed and completed—not proposed or planned."

Food Engineering has its own set of criteria with the focus being on projects and/or programs that reduce, reuse and/or recycle in the plant and help progress environmental stewardship. Plants do not necessarily have to be certified by LEED, Green Globes or any other organization. However, they should demonstrate either some or all of the following characteristics:

- preventing pollution as well as protecting the environment;
- use of creativity and innovation;
- improving conservation efforts (water, energy, chemicals, etc.);
- fostering a work culture of environmental friendliness;
- return on investment;
- cost-effectiveness.

To source food ingredients produced by best practice, reducing food loss in the processing line and implementation of new technologies are some examples of changes in the management in the food and drink sector that may offer advantages from a sustainability perspective.

Food processing provides added value to final products by enhancing their functional, nutritional, sensorial and safety properties. At the same time, these processing steps face various challenges with regards to the sustainability of food systems such as environmental concerns (e.g. climate change, biodiversity, waste management, water and soil quality preservation), and encompassing a range of issues such as security of supply, health, safety, quality, and affordability. Food production needs to increase;

globally approximately 795 million people go hungry and about 2 billion people are malnourished. It is projected that the world food supply will increase by 70% to feed almost 10 billion people by 2050. Simultaneously, approximately 30% of the global adult population is overweight or obese, and circa 30% of food produced worldwide is lost or wasted. The food sector has been reported to account for around 30% of the world's total energy consumption and around 22% of total Greenhouse Gas emissions(UN Sustainable Development Goals, 2018). Greenhouse gas emissions of the food supply chain have been calculated to be mainly due to the agriculture stage (70%), as has been reported for single food items (Corson and van der Werf, 2012), followed by food manufacturing (10%), logistics (about 7%), packaging (5%), use (5%), and waste disposal (4%) (Notarnicola et al., 2017).

Life Cycle Thinking, i.e. going beyond the traditional focus on the production site and the manufacturing processes per se, to include environmental, social and economic impacts of a product over its entire life cycle and value chain, is recognized as fundamental for addressing the sustainability of food systems (Notarnicola et al., 2017). In addition, the Environmental Management standard (ISO 14001:2015, 2015), substituting (ISO 14001:2004, 2004), require that organizations identify environmental aspects of activities, products and services that it they can control and curb, taking into account a life cycle thinking, and measure those having a significant environmental impact using established methods. The new version of the standard has also sharpened its requirements urging organizations to take into account other stakeholders' potential interests and needs. This change will require organizations to look at the environmental impact of their activities oin a broader perspective than before. This increases the need for tools that can provide a quick and easy evaluation of the sustainability aspects of supply chains and product portfolios.

Box 6. Life cycle thinking.
Life cycle thinking takes a holistic view of the production, consumption, reuse/recycling and disposal of the residuals of a product (for example, biofuel) to evaluate its environmental impacts throughout its entire life cycle. Life The life cycle approach for a product is illustrated in Figure 8 below where raw materials required for the products are extracted from the natural environment and then converted to useful products in the design and development phase where they are developed according to their final usage requirements.

They are then distributed to locations (for example, gas pumps for biofuel and homes for electricity) for their intended use. After their usage and at times usage after maintenance, they are subjected to disposal where they could be sorted out and reused in some other ways, which is mainly applicable in the case of physical products. Some components of the disposed of product could be recycled to be used in the production process, or some materials could be recovered. Those without any possibility for reuse, recycle or recover are forwarded to landfill or incineration.

Along with the product life cycle, there could be potential wastes and emissions during each step in the cycle. Thus resource and energy consumption at each life cycle stage along with potential environmental pollution creates impacts from cradle-to-grave. Life cycle thinking is explained, in conjunction with the figure below, where raw materials from natural resources are recovered, reused and recycled as much as possible before disposing of it to landfill or incinerated.

LCA practice along with life cycle thinking will help practitioners understand the potential emissions, and recovery, reuse and recycle of the components, minimize negative impacts and achieve maximum benefits with minimal environmental impacts leading to the development of sustainable strategies for a product or system (UNEP, 2012).

Life Cycle thinking - sometimes known as the "cradle-to-grave" approach - has become a central feature of modern environmental management and of the developments which underlie the protean concept of Sustainable Development. The basic idea is simple enough (and is closely related to Life Cycle Costing): it is not sufficient, in assessing the environmental performance of a product, merely to look at its use; it is necessary to ask where the materials come from, what energy and other resources are used to make the product; and what happens to it after use.

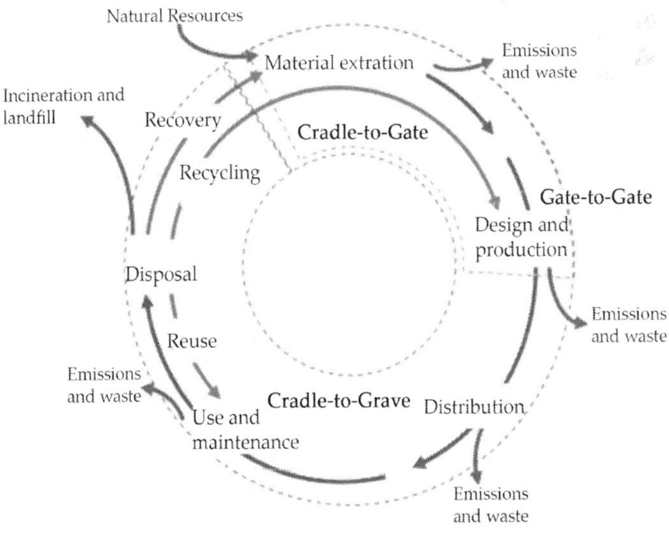

Figure 10. Life cycle approach.

Packaging and Disposal

Packaging aids in the safe delivery of food and has had a minimal contribution to the overall environmental impact of food production. Nevertheless, it has been reported that over 95 percent of the environmental impact originating from packaging is in the process of producing said packaging. The rest is from the disposal of the packaging. Hence, improvement of packaging should focus on lowering the material required and using recycled content. As an example, Kellogg Co. uses recyclable cartons with 100 percent recycled content and a minimum of 35 percent post-consumer material in its cereal boxes, lowering the total energy needs to produce the package.

One of the largest culprits when it comes to a company's impact is packaging materials and accessories. The lifecycle concept must consider the shipping of a product from the producer, through the retailer, and onto the consumer—a chain of steps which that generally includes significant amounts of expensive packaging materials. This has conducted to strong efforts in the innovation of new eco-friendly alternatives to traditionally used packaging materials. From recyclable plastics to biodegradable containers, there is apparently no limit to the options within reach of the environmentally aware business. Here are some to keep in mind:

1. BIODEGRADABLE PACKING PEANUTS

The city of New York has in recent years reinstated a ban on Styrofoam, the light, airy material employed for takeaway cartons and loose-fill packaging. It adds to a number of other U.S. cities also banning this material, also known as EPS (expanded polystyrene foam). EPS is neither biodegradable nor is it economically recyclable, regularly making its way into bodies of water where it can have harsh negative impacts on marine life.

Styrofoam has been a regularly used material in loose-fill packaging for delicate or otherwise sensitive goods, aiding in the prevention of movement and cushioning against sudden forces. For companies searching for the closest thing to this often-used material, biodegradable air peanuts are now an option. These work similarly to their Styrofoam brethren, minus the lingering eternal effectcontaminating the environment. They are also financially competitive.

2. CORRUGATED BUBBLE WRAP

Bubble wrap packaging is familiar to most, often a favorite of children which aids in the protection of fragile goods during transportation. It is not the most eco-friendly material, nevertheless, originating from plastic. Several alternatives are currently under development. One such alternative is a wrap produced from up-cycled corrugated cardboard. Instead ofdiscarding or recycling post-consumer waste from cardboard, it receives the opportunity for an additional life as a support material. Minimal cuts are created on it to produce a concertina-type effect that shelters against shocks similar to the way done by using bubble wrap.

3. AIR PILLOWS MADE OF RECYCLED MATERIALS

Another eco- and cost-saving alternative to Styrofoam or bubble wrap are is air pillows. Found in an array of dimensions, they are perfect for taking up the void space in boxes or providing cushioning surrounding packed goods. They are small bags, which may be inflated, and hence, when used as packaging, are made up mostly of air. This reduces the quantity of plastic utilized in their production and means they may be shipped with minimal packaging when in comparison to other materials used for protection. What's more, they can be reused, recycled, and are even biodegradable.

4. CORNSTARCH PACKAGING

Cornstarch is a plant-based material that has penetrated the eco-friendly packaging industry. Originating from the corn or maize plant, it carries properties similar to plastic, which can be employed in numerous manners that have traditionally made use of plastics. From bottles to molded forms and loose-fill packaging, packaging made from cornstarch provides numerous additional uses to this staple crop. Although it is a more environmentally sustainable alternative to petroleum-based plastic packaging, cornstarch also presents some challenges. As it is derived from the grains of corn, it indeed competes for use as part of the human and animal food supply, possibly increasing the price of a dietary staple.

5. MUSHROOM PACKAGING

Another cost-effective, green packaging option that can be employed to support goods of small size can de produced from mushrooms. It makes use of cleaned and pulverized leftover products from agriculture, which is then combined by a matrix of mushroom roots, also called mycelium.

The agricultural leftovers are just that — waste —and hence would not be utilized directly as a food source for humans or feed for animals. It ,therefore, avoids the possible controversy connected to packaging made from cornstarch. The raw material can be shaped as required, dried, and thus turned into sustainable packaging. Not only does this material prevent the use of petroleum and food sources as raw material, but it also decomposes at an incredible rate. Packaging made from mushroom may be composted at home, thus being broken down into organic matter that is non-toxic.

6. SEAWEED PACKAGING

The gelatinous substance known as agar, naturally found in numerous types of seaweeds and algae, is starting to be used in several applications. This is ,in particular, being done in the food industry, where such a component may be used as a thickener or a plant-based alternative to gelatin. Recently a design team has received an award for prototyping its employment as an alternative material for packaging. Developed from a plentiful and sustainable starting material, packaging made from seaweed may be the next big thing in sustainable packaging options.

7. RECYCLED CARDBOARD AND PAPER

Cardboard boxes are the industry standard for the storage of filler material. While cardboard and paper are indeed organic matter, when sourced unsustainably, their use has a large negative impact on the environment. Fortunately, paper and cardboard are two of the most recyclable materials at hand. To secure that the a packaging is as sustainable as possible, opting for post-consumer or post-industrial recycled paper and cardboard is a good option. As another option, materials labeled as FSC-certified are sourced from sustainably managed forests and might be an even better option under certain circumstances.

8. ECO-FRIENDLY PLASTIC AND RECYCLED PLASTICS

For not the fact remains that some shipping requires a tough and reliable material that will not break and is able to support heavy loads. While several of the plant-based alternatives may be great for supporting or filling, there remain sometimes when only plastic will do. However, it is not necessary to cut back on sustainability efforts in these cases, as numerous plastic shipping materials and tools are currently made from 100 percent recycled plastic. From drums, spill trays, and spill control pallets, it is possible to opt for eco-friendly shipping materials for most shipping requirements.

9. ORGANIC FABRICS

A main player on in the negative impact of on the environment are is the plastic bags. A significant portion of companies uses plastic bags that finish as contaminants of the environment. A more sustainable optionare is inclusive of organic fabrics. Various organic fabrics are available in the market today such as hemp, organic or recycled cotton, tapioca, palm leaves, and several others. These alternative materials arebiodegraded in around 100 days compared to the 10,000 years needed for a plastic bag to decompose. Several other uses for these fabrics apart from bags can be thought up as an additional benefit for the switch from plastic.

With communities all over the World starting to prohibit the use of specific materials derived from fossil fuels, it is possible that the tide is beginning to turn on plastics. With so many more sustainable options at competitive prices, more companies are beginning to see the opportunities in making the switch. Environmental sustainability is becoming mainstream, and smart business owners throughout the World are making the change to ensure they are a step ahead.

Logistics and Utilization

The contribution of logistics and utilization on the environmental impact of food fluctuates greatly. Important factors include distance and form of transport of the food item and the quantity of energy required to keep and process the food for intake. Logistics ought to be as efficient as possible. Air movement of food is the least efficient option for distribution, and options must be found. As an example, General Mills distributes approximately 80 percent of its shipments to the United Kingdom by sea, usually the least energy-intensive distribution alternative. Logistics and operations systems should also weight out new technologies and remodel distribution routes to find further efficiencies. As an example, Nestleuses dual-temperature vehicles to lower transportation by 7 percent in its operations in Argentina.

Delivering safe and nutritious food is still a keygoal of the food industry. These issues surge in tandem with the life cycle considerations previously mentioned. As an example, food safety is connected to agriculture, with factory farming and high-speed processing of products of animal origin linked to foodborne pathogens.

Applying this type of sustainable practices has several upsides. The World Business Council for Sustainable Development has reported that companies which that incorporate sustainable practices have bigger financial success with less production costs, improved product function and quality, greater market share, better environmental performance, improved relationships with stakeholders, and smaller risks. In addition, research has found that businesses committed to sustainability did financially better by about 15 percent over the six months from May through November 2008—a noteworthy point considering the recent economic turmoil. Consumer demands for environmental sustainability is are increasing. Consumer interest in sustainable products increased from around 50 percent in 2007 to 70 percent in 2010. As an outcome, a life cycle approach to sustainability is likely the best path to protect a businesses' value as well as the future generation's food security.

Goal 11: Make cities and human settlements inclusive, safe, resilient and sustainable

Substantial progress has been gained in lowering the proportion of the international urban population living in slums, though more than 1 billion people continue to live in such situations. Urgent action is needed to reverse the current situation, which sees the vast majority of urban residents breathing poor-quality air and having limited access to transport and open public spaces. With the areas occupied by cities growing faster than their populations, there are profound repercussions for sustainability.

Cities are hubs for ideas, commerce, culture, science, productivity, social, human and economic development. Urban planning, transport systems, water, sanitation, waste management, disaster risk reduction, access to information, education and capacity-building are all relevant issues to sustainable urban development. Given the importance of this topic to global development efforts, recent movements pushing to address sustainable development from an urban perspective have taken place throughout the world.

Sustainable cities, urban sustainability, or eco-city (also "ecocity") is a city designed with consideration for social, economic, environmental impact (commonly referred to as the triple bottom line), and resilient habitat for existing populations, without compromising the ability of future generations to experience the same. These cities are inhabited by people who are dedicated towards minimizing required inputs of energy, water, food, waste, output of heat, air pollution - CO2, methane, and water pollution.

Ideally, a sustainable city creates an enduring way of life across the four domains of ecology, economics, politics and culture. Goals The goals of a sustainable city are to be able to feed itself with a sustainable reliance on the surrounding natural environment and have the ability to power itself with renewable sources of energy. The central focus of this topic is to create the smallest conceivable ecological footprint while also producing the lowest quantity of pollution achievable. All of this is to be accomplished by efficiently using the land in ways such as composting used materials, recycling, and/or converting waste-to-energy. The idea is that these contributions will lead to a decrease of in the city's impact on climate change.

Sustainable Cities

For years, cities have been at the center of the arts and culture scene, successful businesses, and innovative ideas. More than ninety percent of urban zones are coastal, which translates into most communities on the planet are very vulnerable to the consequences of climate change as sea levels increase, polar ice melts, and powerful storms sweep across these zones.

Simply the number of individuals who live in cities these days and who are likely to move into them in the future years is grandiose. Over half of the world's peoples are predicted to live in an urban zone by 2050, which means there are additional financial implications when extreme weather like unexpected storms and flooding lead to financial and governmental disruptions.

The upside is that while cities are especially likely to suffer from a climate crisis, they are also likely to lead some of the most influential solutions. Below are examples of leading sustainable cities and the way in which they are leading the path towards clean energy and climate solutions.

1. COPENHAGEN, DENMARK

Copenhagen is regularly listed as one of the greenest cities on Earth. To begin with, in 2009 the city set the target to become the world's first carbon-neutral capital by 2025 as part of its CPH 2025 Climate Plan. Copenhagen has aimed to reduce energy consumption in a number of manners, including using an energy-efficient district system for heating that links to nearly every household and innovative cooling systems that save around 70 percent of the energy compared to the normally used air conditioning.

Copenhagen has also targeted the reduction of emissions and improving the health of the people living there by improving transportation, integrating mobility, and building what is called super cycle highways. Super cycle highways and similar bike lanes around Copenhagen have led to 45 percent of the residents moving by bike daily.

2. SAN FRANCISCO, CALIFORNIA

It's well known that San Francisco and the surrounding Bay Area are a leading tech-hub and home to some of the most innovative businesses in the world, including Sales force, Airbnb, Uber, and Twitter. Technology innovations to make energy usage more efficient in buildings and enhance its mobility system hasve turned San Francisco into a leader in sustainability and clean energy. Considering San Francisco's public transportation system: it's not unusual to spot hybrid-electric buses moving down the city's streets and over half of all buses and light produce no emissions.

The Bay Area has also reduced its water utilization significantly recently. Since California has been facing serious droughts, San Francisco has lowered its water utilization to approximately 49 gallons of water per day (the average nationwide is 80-100 gallons per day).These changes in strategy and similar developments in sustainable food, recycling, and composting are likely to help San Francisco meet its target of becoming zero waste by 2020.

3. VANCOUVER, CANADA

Vancouver has been at the leading front of environmental activism for years. In 1990, it turned into one of the leading North American locations to directly tackle the climate crisis by publishing a report called "The Clouds of Change." This was simply the start of an environmental plan that Vancouver published years later in 2012, the Greenest City Action Plan, which established 10 goals to achieve by 2020, including augmenting green jobs, lowering community-based greenhouse gas emissions, and further developing green buildings around the city.

In addition, Vancouver has promised to get100 percent of its energy from renewable by 2050. This target is especially ambitious given that it focuses on all forms of energy in the city—including heating, cooling, and transport—not simply electricity. Vancouver's eye on green energy and sustainable policies has led it to report the smallest greenhouse gas emissions per individual of any large North American city. Between prioritizing sustainable sources of energy consumption, striving for zero waste, and aiming to meet its Greenest City Action Plan, the City has set the stage for companies and residents to work collectively to be one of the greenest and most climate change prepared cities on Earth.

4. STOCKHOLM, SWEDEN

Stockholm is a developing city that looks to be a hotspot for newcomers and do good for the environment collectively. Awarded the first "European Green Capital" award by the European Commission in 2010, Stockholm targets to be fossil-fuel free by 2050.

And how does Sweden aim to meet its targets? One possibility is to change from oil to "district" heating, which translates into the country using heat from centralized sources (including as a power station) to heat and cool its buildings more efficiently. District heating on its own makes up for more than 80 percent of heating and hot water in flats today and is a the main component in how Sweden has lowered its greenhouse gas emissions recently.

Another key to Stockholm's success with sustainability is its people, who take pride from being "climate-smart." Eight out of 10 residents consider the city should require citizens to live more sustainably and think creating a climate-smart place to live should be a natural part of city living.

5. SINGAPORE

With demographics of over 5 million people, Singapore is regularly seen as one of the furthest future-thinking sustainable cities in Asia. The city-state has created a Sustainable Development Blueprint, which highlights sustainable development targets leading up to 2030. The targets include bettering energy efficiency by 35 percent, securing that 80 percent of the buildings are green certified, and having 80 percent of households be reachable under 10-minutes walking from a train station.

The city has also upped its sustainability game by creating strong modifications in transportation. The city-state has a limit on car ownership for its residents and has developed effective public transportation systems, which is helping with lowering pollution and crowds on streets and highways. Singapore's transportation system allows residents to navigate the city, in tandem with cycling and walking.

Eating in a more Sustainable Fashion

The non-simplicity of the challenges around sustainable practices in the global food system seems to turn it almost impossible for people to understand, at the point of selecting a food item at the store, what its effect on the environment to date has been. Nevertheless, there is sufficient knowledge to back up some general guidelines that can be adopted in order to eat more sustainably:

- Follow a more plant-based eating plan
- Opt for more sustainable fished seafood
- Reduce food waste in the home

Eat a More Plant-based Diet

A favorable, plant-based eating plan has the goal to increase consumption of nutrient-dense plant-based foods while keeping to a minimum all processed foods, oils, and foods of animal origin (including dairy products and eggs).

It champions for the intake of lots of vegetables (cooked or raw), fruits, beans, peas, lentils, soybeans, seeds, and nuts (in lesser quantities) and is generally minimal in fat (although this last point is changing). Supporters of this way of eating have diverse opinions as to what makes up the best plant-based diet. Ornish et al., have recommended permitting products of animal origin including egg whites and reduced-fat milk in minimal amounts for the management of diverse health conditions.

Esselstyn, who directs the cardiovascular prevention and reversal program at the Cleveland Clinic Wellness Institute, suggests complete avoidance of all foods of animal origin in addition to soybeans and nuts, especially if severe coronary artery disease is present.

Regardless of these minimal variations, there is research that suggests that a widely defined plant- based eating plan has strong benefits for health. It is important to highlight that the term plant- based is often used interchangeably with vegetarian or vegan. Vegetarian or vegan lifestyles taken up for ethical or religious justifications may or may not be favorable for health. It is hence key to understand the detailed definitions of similar eating plans and to ensure the specifics of a patient's eating plan instead of assuming how healthy it is.

Below is a brief overview of classic diets that limit products of animal origin. A The main difference is that even thoughthe majority of these eating plans are characterized by what they avoid, the plant-based eating plan is defined by what it covers.

Vegan (or strict vegetarian): Avoids all products of animal origin, particularly meat, sea- food, poultry, eggs, and dairy products. Does not need intake of whole foods or restrict fat or refined sugar.

- Raw food, vegan: Same exclusions as veganism as well as the exclusion of all foods prepared at temperatures over 118°F.
- Lacto-vegetarian: Excludes eggs, meat, seafood, and poultry and allows for milk products.
- Ovo-vegetarian: Avoids meat, sea- food, poultry, and dairy products and allows eggs.
- Lacto-ovo vegetarian: Avoids meat, seafood, and poultry and allows eggs and dairy products.
- Mediterranean: Similar to whole- foods, plant-based diet but permits limited amounts of chicken, dairy products, eggs, and red meat sporadically. Fish and olive oil are encouraged. There is no

fat restriction.

- Whole-foods, plant-based, low-fat: Focuses on plant-based foods in their whole form, specifically vegetables, fruits, legumes, and seeds and nuts (in limited amounts). For maximal benefits for health, this diet keeps animal products to a minimum. Total fat is usually limited.

Setbacks of a plant-based diet:

Protein

Overall, people following a plant-based diet are not at risk of protein deficiency. Proteins are composed of amino acids, some of which, known as essential amino acids, are not able to be created by the human organism and must come from the diet. Essential amino acids are part of meat, dairy products, and eggs, in addition to various plant-based foods, including quinoa. Essential amino acids may also come from consuming specific combinations of plant- based foods. Examples can be brown rice with beans, and hummus with whole wheat bread. Hence, a well-balanced, plant-based eating plan can combine suitable quantities of essential amino acids and avoid protein deficiency.

Iron

Plant-based eating plans include iron, yet the iron from plants is less bioavailable than the iron in foods of animal origin. Plant-based foods that are high in iron are kidney beans, black beans, soybeans, spinach, raisins, cashews, oatmeal, cabbage, and tomato juice. Iron stores may be small in people on a plant-based eating plan and eat little or no animal products. Nevertheless, the American Dietetic Association reports that iron-deficiency anemia is not common even in people who follow a plant-based eating plan.

Vitamin B12

Vitamin B12 is required for the synthesis of blood and cell division. Vitamin B12 insufficiency is a very serious issue and can give way to macrocytic anemia and irreversible damage to the nerves. Vitamin B12 is a result of bacterial infection, not plants or animals. People who are on a plant-based eating plan that has no animal products may be lacking in B vitamins and require supplementation with vitamin B12 or foods enriched with vitamin B.

Calcium

Calcium consumption can be achieved in a carefully designed plant-based eating plan. Individuals who do not consume plants that have large quantities of calcium can represent a risk for impaired bone mineralization and fractures. Nevertheless, research has found that the risk of fracture was quite close for vegetarians and non-vegetarians. The main point to ensure bone health is suitable calcium consumption, which seems to be independent of dietary selection. Certain important foods rich in calcium are tofu, mustard and turnip greens, bok choy, and kale. Spinach and some other plants include calcium that, although plentiful, is linked to oxalate and hence is weekly absorbed.

Fatty Acids

Key fatty acids are fatty acids that people have to eat for adequate health since the human body does not make them. Just two kinds of essential fatty acids are known: linoleic acid (an omega-6 fatty acid) and alpha-linolenic acid (an omega-3 fatty acid). Three additional fatty acids are justpartially essential: palmitoleic acid (a monounsaturated fatty acid), lauric acid (a saturated fatty acid), and gamma-linolenic acid (an omega-6 fatty acid). A lack of essential fatty acids can show up as skin, hair, and nail abnormalities.

The fatty acids that people following a vegan lifestyle are most likely to be lacking in are the omega-3 fats (n-3 fats). Intake of the plant version of omega-3 fats, alpha-linolenic acid, are is also limited among people following a vegan lifestyle. Suitable consumption of n-3 fats is linked to a lowered incidence of heart conditions. Foods that are rich sources of n-3 fats must be highlighted. These are ground flax seeds, flax oil, walnuts, and canola oil.

A plant-based diet that is favorable for health requires planning, reading labels, and discipline. The guidelines for people who want to start on a plant-based diet can include consuming a diversity of fruits and vegetables that can include beans, legumes, seeds, nuts, and whole grains and cut back on products of animal origin, added fats, oils, and refined, processed carbohydrates. The main up point for people who decide to follow a plant-based eating plan are is the likelihood of lowering the amount of medicine consumed to manage a diversity of chronic conditions, reduce body weight, lower the likelihood of cancer, and a lowering of their risk of death from ischemic heart conditions.

A plant-based eating plan is not an all-or- nothing way of life, but a lifestyle that is personalized to each individual. It may be particularly good for those experiencing obesity, type 2 diabetes, high blood pressure, lipid disorders, or cardiovascular conditions.

Choose fish from sustainable stock

Sustainability is turning into a highly pressing issue for people who are aiming to buy seafood with a more responsible precedence - but why is this important? Most of the time, consumers can opt to make a true difference. As a consumer, one can influence the demand for sustainability in seafood, by selecting fish exclusively from healthy, responsibly managed sources, and fished or farmed in ways which that reduce harm to the aquatic environment. Here are some key tips from the Marine Conservation Society (MCS), the UK Charity for seas, shores and wildlife, to help the consumer make the best sustainable choice when selecting seafood.

1. Become more informed

Regularly consulting the MCS website and learning all that is possible regarding the issues affecting seas and oceans and the way in which it is possible to make a difference. Find out where the seafood originates from and why selecting it carefully is important.

2. Track detailed rankings of sustainability

The Good Fish Guide is for people interested in sustainably consuming seafood. It has more than 650 ratings and sustainability information for more than 150 types of seafood most commonly consumed.

3. Obtain an MCS pocket guide or download the app.

Consulting an MCS pocket guide or downloading the smartphone app to inform you of these rankings while being out and about or using it for the creation of a personal shopping list. These practical recommendations include the top options for purchasing seafood.

4. Sharing is caring

Communicating with others regarding the importance of selecting sustainable seafood and highlight them in the direction of the MCS website to learn more.

5. Variety is key

This is particularly the case regarding seafood consumption. Most people are heavily dependent on the "Big 5" (Cod, Haddock, Tuna, Salmon and Prawns). Numerous fantastic options exists, including hake or coley to substitute for cod and haddock, rainbow trout to replace salmon, and herring or sardines rather than tuna –perfect alternatives to get secure adequate levels of omega 3.

6. Selecting seafood gathered using methods with less damaging environmental effects

Consuming seafood fished in a more environmentally sustainable manner - hand line, pole and line, pot or trap or dive caught - or from companies using best approaches to minimize discards and habitat impacts. These techniques usually have lower effects on other species.

7. Regarding food labels

In the European Union, retailers and brands are required by law to declare the species of fish, production method (wild caught/farmed), fishing location and capture method for unprocessed seafood products. If the details ofn them are not enough to make an informed decision, it is important to request more details from the fishmonger/waiter, particularly where the fish is caught and how. If a generic reference is given for the name of the fish e.g. "skate" or "tuna" the specific details regarding the species must be found out.

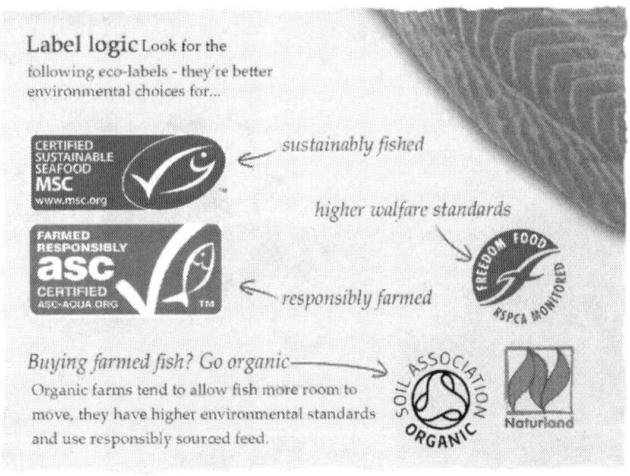

Figure 11. Sustainable fishing labels.

Source: Marine Conservation Society.

8. The logo of the Marine Stewardship Council (MSC)

Products of marine origin stamped by this logo may be found in the frozen and fresh counter sections of supermarkets and are turning ever more popular in restaurants. They identify the product as originating from well-managed companies and are entierly entirely traceable.

9. Go Organic

Organically produced seafood originates from farms with smaller stocking densities, higher standards of sustainable practices and are fed with feed sourced in a more environmentally friendly manner.

10. Avoid the red list

The red seafood list (rated 5 on the Good Fish Guide) identifies seafood from the most unsustainable companies and fish farming methods. It covers endangered species such as European eel and wild northeast Atlantic Halibut in addition to seafood from harmful fishing and farming techniques that require significant improvement. Fortunately, there are several certified sustainable and MCS green rated (Best Choice) options available.

Reducing food waste in the home

Most people don't realize how much food they throw away every day — from uneaten leftovers to spoiled produce. The Environmental Protection Agency of the United States estimates that in 2018, about 68 percent of the wasted food we generated—or about 42.8 million tons-- ended up in landfills or combustion facilities. By managing food sustainably and reducing waste, we can help businesses and consumers save money, provide a bridge in our communities for those who do not have enough to eat, and conserve resources for future generations.

Top 5 tips on reducing food waste:

1. Limit food waste by planning ahead

As much as possible, aim to have a weekly meal plan. With a developed meal plan, food waste is more likely to be kept to a minimum.

2. Buy smart

Checking the "best-before" and "packaged on" dates when buying food is one of the best steps to take towards food waste reduction. Unless they will be consumed right away, it is best to avoid foods with a short shelf life left.

Below are some additional ways to minimize food waste when buying groceries.

Foods that can go bad:

- Foods such as meats, poultry, fish, milk, cheese and yogurts should be selected towards the end of the shopping trip as this maintains them cold for the longest possible time period.
- Avoid cross-contamination by maintaining items such as meats, poultry and fish separate from other groceries in the shopping cart.
- Think about bringing a cooler on warmer days to make sure food stays fresh when not going directly home after shopping.

Produce

- Maintain fresh produce away from other foods to prevent bruising. Bruising leads to fresh foods spoiling faster.
- Canned, packaged and boxed items
- Do not buy canned, packaged and boxed items that are open or have a broken seal. Avoid cans that are damaged as they are likely to become contaminated faster.

3. Store foods properly to reduce food waste

Place perishable items in the fridge or freezer. Ensure cool air can circulate with ease around the food to maintain it for longer.

4. Fill the pantry

Keep all unopened non-perishable food items in a clean, dry place at room temperature. Maintain your pantry fully stocked with key, non-perishable items that can be used in a diversity of meals. Examples of pantry items are:

- Grain products: Whole grain pasta, brown rice, quinoa, couscous, kasha and quick cooking polenta
- Canned vegetables and fruits: canned tomatoes low in salt, corn, carrots and mushrooms, canned peaches, mandarin oranges and pineapple packed in water or light syrup
- Dried or canned beans: Chickpeas, beans and lentils
- Canned fish: Low sodium canned tuna and salmon
- Cooking oils: Extra-virgin olive oil, canola oil and sesame oil

- Vinegars: White or red wine vinegar and balsamic vinegar
- Baking products: Flour, white and brown sugar, baking soda, baking powder, corn starch, plain oats and wheat bran
- Unopened condiments: Dijon mustard, salad dressing and ketchup

Use the "First In First Out" rule. When filling up the pantry, circulate items in order to consume the oldest first. Ensure to consult best-before dates prior to using the food items. Consult food labels on packaged, canned or bottled items that might require cooling after opening, such as soy sauce.

5. Use leftovers mindfully

Consume leftovers to prepare weekly meals and minimize waste. Use these ideas to use leftovers in a creative way for different preparations.

Minimizing food waste can happen with certain forethought and maintenance practices. Maintain these various ideas in your head to aid manage your food budget while ensuring the safety of all.

The good news is that a sustainable diet is an easy road to take. You just need to follow a few simple rules:

- Choose plant-based foods: this is brilliant advice not just for health reasons, but also because it points to a sustainable diet, greatly reducing the environmental impact of food production.
- Eat a varied diet: filling plates with color helps ensure a variety of foods reach the table. A varied plate on the table means variety in agriculture.
- Eat five portions of fruit and vegetables every day, not just as a side dish. In a healthy, sustainable diet, fruits and vegetables are the perfect choices for a snack, even for young children.
- Prefer seasonal, local products: knowing your local food not only enables you to buy the freshest and tastiest food, but is also key to sustainable agriculture and a sustainable economy, which enables savings.
- Use fresh ingredients, whenever possible: this helps reduce needless packaging, at home and when eating out.
- Reduce consumption of packaged food: these foods are especially rich in sugars, fats and salt, as indicated in the nutritional information labels, hence they are not considered sustainable foods for your health.

- Increase your intake of whole-wheat grains: whole-wheat rice, barley, oat, corn and rye have high nutritional benefits, they help prevent many diseases and they require less work, hence less energy and water to produce the same amount of food.
- Avoid sugary drinks: replacing water with sodas and fruit juices leads to weight gain in the long term, it is not therefore recommended for a sustainable diet.
- Increase your intake of pulses: a moderate consumption of pulses is a great way to adopt a sustainable diet, because it provides fibers and substitutes animal proteins with plant-based ones, benefiting the environment.
- Reduce consumption of red and processed meat: it is better to choose other sources of proteins, such as pulses. Rearing animals for meat is one of the farming businesses with the highest environmental impact.
- Buy fish from sustainable sellers: this helps protect marine fauna and flora, increasingly threatened by overfishing.
- Look for products that come from free-range farms and pastures: consumer choices also have an impact on the quality of life of the animals we use for food.

Box 7. Edible mushrooms.

Fungi have been grown and gathered by people as a source of food for many years, with more than 400 known edible types. In 2016, mushroom farmers in the United States grew over 946 million kilos of fresh mushrooms. The blossoming fungi rich in protein are a staple for the majority of people following a vegetarian and vegan lifestyle and they present ample space for culinary development and experimentation. But what specifically is required to grow such quantities of mushrooms?

Scientists have demonstrated that mushrooms are one of the top sustainable sources of protein available today. The Mushroom Sustainability Story: Water, Energy and Climate Environmental Metrics 2017, is a 2-year investigation highlighting the environmental impact of 21 home mushroom growers, representing a third of the overall fresh mushroom market.

The researchers reported that one pound of mushrooms needs just 1.8 gallons of water and 1.0 kilowatt hours of energy and generates just 0.7 pounds of CO2 emissions (Center for Sustainable Systems, University of Michigan. 2017.). Additionally, they reported that for each square foot of space for mushroom growth, an average of 7.1 pounds can be produced per year. This means that for each acre of mushroom production, up to 1 million pounds can be grown!

In comparison, average requirements for the production of a pound of beef or chicken include 1,799 and 468 gallons of water each (Harris, 2016). Additionally, beef and chicken produce 26 pounds and 5.2 pounds of CO_2 emissions, per pound, each (Center for Sustainable Systems, University of Michigan, 2017).

A main vital aspect regarding mushroom sustainability is the manner in which they are harvested. Mushroom farmers have created diverse techniques for the production of edible fungi, nevertheless, large-scale mushroom farmers which grow on a year-round cycle need a controlled and precise setting. The beginning of the mushroom cycle sets off with raw organic materials. These substrates, most often soil, straw, or sawdust, give nutrients for to the budding mushrooms. The mushroom spores are bought from a commercial laboratory and combined with the substrate, thenallotted to a bed/tray, often stacked by the hundreds.

Mushrooms are a sustainable source of protein, one particularly high in micronutrients and fiber. They maintain CO_2 emissions and energy utilization under control, help with soil conservation, maintain net high yield under suitable conditions, and can be dried for later use.

Livestock production has an enormous impact on climate change emissions, resource use, habitat loss, and the availability of staples for consumers in developing countries. Despite this, macro marketers have paid little attention to environmentally sustainable diets. Although researchers in health studies have identified the need for mainstream plant-based diets, they downplay the socio-cultural meanings associated with meat and vegetable consumption.

The field of nutrition will face numerous challenges in coming decades; these arise from global consumption patterns and lead to a the high use of resources. Actors Players in the catering sector face difficulties in promoting their solutions for a more sustainable situation in their field, one of them being the lack of acceptance from consumers. We must ask the question of how to influence consumer behavior and bring forth a transition towards more sustainable food consumption.

The practice of eating out is highly dependent on external factors. Busy lifestyles, mobility routines and a perceived lack of time prompt the decision to eat out. Consumers consciously do so to save time and effort and to streamline their schedules. Mobility seems to be an important driver for eating out. Participants try to limit the ways they undertake eating out yet often stop for a meal in-between appointments spontaneously. Research has shown that knowledge of nutrition and sustainable ways of thinking carry minimal effect on the food consumption decisions made when away from home.

Criteria for food intake sustainability is are categorized with agricultural technology, which reduces the utilization of soil-harming substances and promotes sustainable, renewable utilization of energy. These cover bio, biodynamic and integrated farming practices. Eco-toxic research related to freshwater has demonstrated that main wheat used for feed as well as other peas and cereals may have 18–91 times the negative external impact on the environment, while soybeans can reach up to 1159 times more compared to grass. For 1 kg of food produced, bread has twice, milk has three times, minced beef has 50 times, chicken filet has 138 times, and minced pork has 168 times greater outer values than the smallest effect of pea soup. Science demonstrates that the environmental effects of foods of plant origin are less than that of foods of animal origin. In addition, it seems that the same nutrient quantities originating from plants produce 26–48% fewer contaminants and have much lower environmental effects when compared to meat or dairy products. Therefore, when it comes to agricultural land utilization, this difference is eightfold, while it is nine-fold for acidification levels of food production zones, and fivefold for global warming. Yet, when it comes to crop production, the utilization of the appropriate technique is ideal. Among the vegetable and fruit-growing practices, the greenhouse has the strongest global warming potential (GWP), while there is almost no difference between the unheated greenhouse or the open field agriculture. Beans add mostly to the acidification of the soil, while leeks cause the lowest damage. Research in on this topic, however, demonstrate that tomatoes are grown with the biggest GWP, acidification and eutrophication, from the intensive employment of stimulants and pesticides.

It is an unfortunate point that because of the global food market, the resources employed for domestic products are used abroad. In the case, as an example, of the German market, the benefits of local freshwater employed both directly and indirectly for growing food is are mostly exported to Spain and Pakistan, and in the case of foods of animal origin, to France and Argentina. For land utilization, benefits mostly go to Argentina and Brazil, and through products of animal origin to the Netherlands and the Czech Republic. The freshwater likely to be available may be determined by the Water Allowance Coecient (WAC), which can be stated in financial terms following a monetary value adjustment, to create a more holistic complete and lighter comparison with natural results.

Nevertheless, Du et al. 2017 have reported that the water requirements behind food production displays a reducing trend because of the reduction in meat demand and an augmentation in fruit and vegetable intake. Eating in a sustainable manner is linked to varying social (quality of life) areas, so its fluctuation may have an effect on them. It is ideal to start to comprehend this process in agricultural practices, as this is the foundation of food production, and herein appear the strongest negative environmental outcomes on the production side (structural and qualitative changes of the soil as a result of the utilization of pesticides and stimulants, utilization of drinking water for irrigation, water contamination, gaseous emissions, impurities from storage). Health has its bases on this, since the nutritional value of food is reliant on agricultural processes and input factors (if something is missing or in surplus, diseases occur).Regarding health, having healthy food readily available is a pressing factor, which is highly reliant on socio-economic factors (employment, individual income, national welfare). This means that personal requirements and information are not sufficient to ensure suitable nutrition, and legal-policy decisions need to be backed up. However, the importance of flavor, the presence of cultural customs and the influence of religion, which as an end result create eating habits from generation to generation, must not be forgotten.

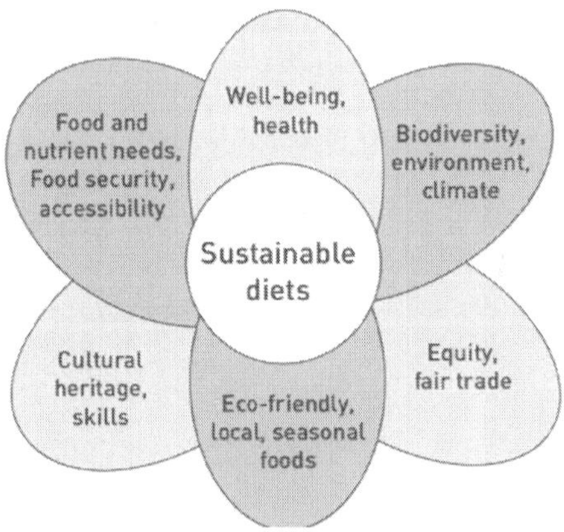

Figure 12. Key components of a sustainable diet.

Food production is a manufacturing process that, like all other production processes, implies the use of raw materials and resources (raw vegetables, arable land, water, energy, chemicals, animal products) and involves the emission of waste and pollutants (chemicals, manure, greenhouse gases) into the environment.

Animal food production involves a greater use of resources and production of pollution than plant food (Marlow et al., 2008; Springmann et al., 2016). A recent meta-analysis shows that animal products (namely meat, aquaculture, eggs, and dairy) use nearly 83% of the world's farmland and contribute from 56 to 58% of food's different emissions, but only represent 37% and 17% of protein and calorie global consumption (Poore &Nemecek, 2018). This is because livestock consumes more calories from plant-based feed, grown for this purpose, than they produce in the form of meat, milk or eggs. Most of the calories consumed by livestock is used for their vital functions and not tissue products for human consumption (Alsaffar, 2016). Each vegetable-to-animal transformation causes a loss of energy. Therefore, choosing nourishment directly from plant-based foods leads to a drastic reduction in resource consumption and pollutant emission (Poore &Nemecek, 2018).

The "protein conversion ratio" from plant-based feed to animal food varies for different species, ranging from a ratio of 20:1 to 4:1, with a calculated average value around 9:1 (Tilman & Clark, 2014). This means that on average an animal will convert 9 grams of feed proteins to 1 gram of edible animal protein. Worldwide, half of the cereal (77% in Europe and the USA the : 87%) and 90% of soybeans are grown to feed livestock and are not used for human consumption (Figure 11 below; FAO, 2001).

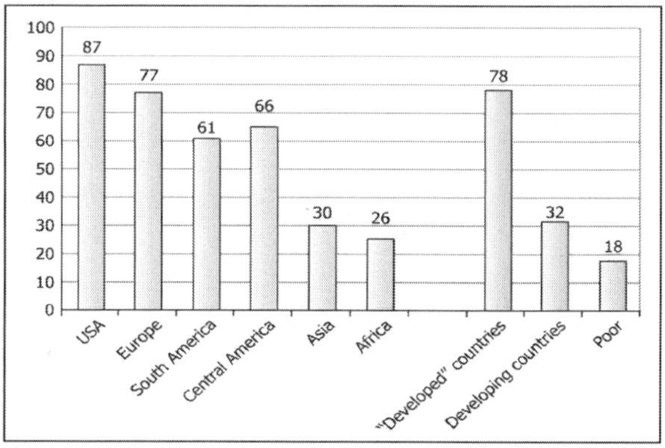

Figure 13. Percent production of cereals (blue) and soy (pink) around the world.

(FAO, 2001).

Goal 12: Ensure sustainable consumption and production patterns.

Consumption and production at a global scale— a determining force of the international economy — relies on the utilization of nature as well as on natural resources in such a way that keeps having a strong negative impact on Earth.

Economic and social development during the past several decades has been in tandem with environmental degradation that is putting at risk the very systems on which future development — and even survival — relies upon.

Some facts:

- Each year, about a third of all food produced – equal to approximately 1.3 billion tones worth around $1 trillion – decomposes in the bins of consumers and sellers or rotting because of deficient transportation and harvesting practices.
- If people all over the world changed to light bulbs that are energy-efficient, US$120 billion would be spared yearly.
- If the Earth's population reaches 9.6 billion by 2050, the equivalent of about three planets will be needed to have the natural resources required to maintain current ways of living.

Modern food production and intake practices must not be seen as sustainable as it leads to challenges with its wide scope regarding various factors. Additionally, in the face of demographic change and a growing global population, sustainability issues originating from food systems will in all likelihood turn more pressing in the future. To illustrate this point, outputs from agriculture must deal with the effects of climate change, ever more demanding land-utilization conflicts, and increasing health and social costs on both personal and community levels. The lack of sustainability of modern setups originates from the industrialization and internationalization of agricultural practices and food processing, the change in intake patterns demanding higher amounts of products of animal origin, the emergence of modern food styles that rely heavily on processed products, the worldwide increasing distance between rich and poor, and the paradoxical insufficient food security while experiencing an abundance of food. These components can be attributed to national and international rules and regulations, in addition to popular business methods and, specially, consumers' values and practices. The most likely ways for rich countries to lower the environmental effect of their eating practices isto lower the intake of meat and dairy products (especially beef), to prefer organic fruits and vegetables, and to limit goods that have been moved by air on both individual and institutional levels (e.g., public procurement, public catering).

The main raw materials to focus on when attempting environmental sustainability include water, energy and food.

Water

- Below 3 percent of the world's water is drinkable, from which 2.5 per cent percent is frozen in Antarctica, the Arctic and glaciers. People must hence depend on 0.5 per cent percent for all of man's ecosystems and freshwater requirements.
- People are contaminating water in rivers and lakes quicker than it is naturally possible to recycle and purify it.
- Over 1 billion individuals still lack access to freshwater.
- Over utilization of water adds to the global water stress.
- Water is free from nature, yet the infrastructure required to deliver it is costly.

Energy

- If individuals all over the World opted for more efficient appliances and electronics, the world would require US$120 billion less per year.
- Regardless of technological developments that have championed energy efficiency gains, energy utilization in OECD countries will keep growing an additional 35 per centpercent by 2020. Commercial and residential energy utilization is the second-fastest growing area of global energy utilization following transportation.
- In 2002, the car stock in OECD countries was 550 million vehicles (75 percent of which were for private use). A 32 per centpercent higher rates of car ownership occurred by 2020. Simultaneously, car kilometers are likely to go up by 40 per centpercent and global air travel is likely to triple.
- Homes use 29 per centpercent of overall energy and hence contribute to 21 percent of corresponding to CO2 emissions.
- The share of green energy in final energy utilization had peaked at 17.5% in 2015.

Food

- While significant environmental effects from food happen in the production step (agriculture, food processing), homes affect these impacts via food selection and eating practices. This in turn has an impact on the environment by way of food-related energy usage and waste production.

- Annually, about 1/3 of all produced food items – equivalent to 1.3 billion tons worth around $1 trillion – finishes going bad in the bins of commensals and sellers.
- Approximately 2 billion people worldwide are considered to be overweight or obese.
- The degradation of the land, lower soil fertility, unsustainable water utilization, fishing in excess and aquatic environment degradation are collectively reducing the possibility of securing a sufficient food supply from natural resources.
- Big Food is responsible for approximately 30 percent of the Global energy utilization and accounts for approximately 22 percent of total emissions of Greenhouse Gases.

The sustainability of food production and agriculture is connected to practically every side of human society. It affects the most basic global and local issues of the current time (LNV, 2009). In regard to making food production and consumption more sustainable, it is not simply about a way of making agriculture and food production less environmentally damaging. It also has to do with basic questions regarding humanity's connection to food, with nature and with each other. It has to do with questions regarding the definitions of what is consider as suitable food and suitable agriculture and how sustainability should be carried out, through augmented scale and technology, or a system built more around nature (Lang & Heasman, 2004). Daily eating habitsare often far from these points. Even though there might be an awareness of sustainability around food and agriculture, the true implications for eating habits at a personal level are not always so clear.

The energy invested into the promotion of sustainability in consumption patterns has gone up in the recent past (DEFRA, 2006; EC, 2004b; Garnett, 2008; PBL, 2008). For example, the Dutch government aims to develop a food and agriculture branch which that is more in line with values regarding animal rights, human health and the environment (LNV, 2009; WUR, 2008). Sustainability in food production and services are is seen as one of the quickest growing, stable markets in the food retail and services sector (EZ, 2012). Nevertheless, ample research has reported that regardless of the seemingly growing awareness of food-related sustainability issues, the attention given to sustainability in daily habits of food selection and services (for example organic food, Fair Trade products, eating less meat) is still minimal (Bartels et al., 2009; WUR, 2008). So as to improve this, investigations are targeted at a better comprehension of consumers' specific preferences, values and beliefs so as to adapt 'green' messages, products and services so as to be more attractive. Nevertheless, this is usually carried out with disregard to the contexts and settings consumers are part of and the setups of food provisioning. In this way, with the goal so strongly set on personal ways of thinking represents a risk on of missing out on the wider scope.

Consumers these days have the chance more than ever before to select food products and services which that are less damaging to the environment, which take into account animal and ecological welfare, as well as the wellbeing of farmers at home and abroad. A wide collection of technologies, agricultural systems, social movements and entrepreneurial practices related to agriculture add to the development of a more ecologically and socially sound international food production system. The sector for alternative food production, specifically organic/biodynamic agricultural practices and sales, has slowly yet regularly increased into a viable alternative food system.

There are currently three main trends which that may be employed to describe the degree of sustainability in food production sold and used in services in Western Europe.

Alternative Food Networks

In various European countries, including the Netherlands, the first alternative food networks (AFN's) (Renting et al., 2003; Roep&Wiskerke, 2012) were created by leading farmers and entrepreneurs during the early twentieth century. These groups of people were concerned with the unviable and unsustainable form of industrialized farming practices (Winkel, 2012). In accordance to with one definition 'AFN's ... [build] new producers-consumer alliances and [create] experimental spaces to develop novel practices of food provision that are more in tune with their values, norms, needs, and desires, that built on the reproduction and revaluation of local sources, and that results in the food of distinct and better appreciated qualities' (Roep&Wiskerke, 2012: p. 206). Attention tofactors including seasonality, crop diversification, the quality of produce and healthier and ecologically sound production/processing techniques is apparent from this definition. AFN's are focused on the re-localization of food chains and the development of ecologically and socially-sound agricultural practices linked to food systems in accordance to principles of ecologically sound cycling of resources in addition to the connection between soil and food quality. AFN has suggested a way for producers to gain more reliable incomes from farming and continuity in the face of food chains that become more and more globalized and social and ecological degradation of hyper-industrialized and intensive practices in the farm (Renting et al., 2003).

From the point of view of the consumers, the interest in AFN's is in the search for strongly trusted, higher-quality foods which that make more ecological and social sense. Many times, consumers are looking for a more authentic, more direct connection with food producers. Consumers search for options to Big Food which is now often associated with lesser quality, poorer taste and production that is not sustainable. AFN's are developed through initiatives such as farmers stores and markets, consumers buying directly from farmers, direct producer-retailer and producer-food service provider cooperation and networks, regional logistics (Hendriks et al., 2004) and agriculture backed up by the community (CSA, Pergola) initiatives which regularly cover box-schemes (Otters, 2008).

Ankey characteristic of various AFN's is that they are set up by food producers and consumers themselves. All over Europe producers of food and consumers 'find each other' in common requirements and wishes for improved food. Farmers depend less on the mass-scale delivery and economic systems, substituting this with a more direct one-to-one setup linking consumer and producer. Consumers help fund producers by way of box-schemes and community/consumer funding systems. Occasionally, consumers directly aid with financial provision to farmers which who are just setting up a farm. Hence, in various AFN's the interests of consumers and producers are the same, and represent an independent, community-based response to local/regional socio-economic challenges linked to food. It can be said that, in such instances, the AFN's go beyond what a food label may offer consumers. That is, where labels (such as the EU Eco label in Europe) remain abstract, AFN's give consumers more personal and tangible connection to their everyday food items, and to the farmers and the land that supply them.

Diversification in Food Retail and Services

Additionally, there is a growing preference for wider diversity in the food retail and services system, and a general professionalization or mainstreaming of the 'alternative' sector. At Biofach 2008, this was recognized as a main trends in the market for organic products. 'Large organic supermarkets, organic convenience stores in train stations or shopping centers, organic discounters, organic wine or tea shops, organic butchers and bakers, natural cosmetic and textile shops'. Specialized companies have entered the Dutch market with offers of organic and Fair Trade snacks located at train stations, organic catering services and numerous restaurants that currently serve seasonal, local and/ or organic food. Hollander (2005) highlights that after the 'price wars' of Dutch supermarkets in 2003 food sellers had to select between specialization strategies targeting quality, or those centering on price, a tendency also apparent in the organic food sector. Within the Netherlands and the United Kingdom, numerous store formulas have been put in place (e.g.Marqt, Rio de Bio, Estafette, Goodyfood, Lazuur, the People's Supermarket). These formula's components cover various sustainability aspects such as animal, environmental and trade welfare, with issues like the closer connection with natural processes, (re)localization, seasonality and rural welfare, in addition to culinary quality ('good food') and dietary benefits.

Agro-food industry, public procurement and sustainability

Furthermore, a desire for more transparency exists and the link to sustainability criteria within the agro-food industry and supermarket industry are expanding all over the World, with Europe in particular. This covers initiatives such as integrating sustainability guidelines into production methods and delivery systems, and greater product transparency through tracking and certification systems and labeling (e.g. MSC, Fair Trade) (Oosterveer, 2005). Corporate policies include those which have begun greening sections of their supply chain (e.g. Unilever with MSC), those which have made their entire business/ services more sustainable (e.g. Fishes, Peeze), wholesalers with their own certification schemes and non-governmental certification organizations connecting with companies setting up sustainable production and procurement guidelines.

As an example, from the government of the Netherlands, there are various initiatives including the Dutch covenants for market stimulation towards organic food products and the Platform Sustainable Development of Food, both set up by the former Ministry of Agriculture, in addition to the sustainable procurement programs also set up and championed by the Dutch government. The latter aims to encourage and facilitate procurement in a more environmentally sustainable way among the public sector of the Netherlands, in addition to the private sector. Guidelines on sustainable procurement is given on areas including realizing/building greener buildings, ways in which to save energy, cleaning, maintenance and catering. Practically, this translates into selecting suppliers in accordance with criteria for sustainability, in addition to demanding environmental and social standards from producers and suppliers. Any organization or business that procures goods and services may be seen as a consumer. The Dutch government and public sector have come to be explicit regarding responsibilities targeting sustainable procurement, demanding that it answers for its 'consuming behavior'. Additionally, it is the protector of public interests, with a well-established responsibility to be a good example regarding responsible consumerism.

Goal 13: Take urgent action to combat climate change and its impacts.

Changes in the world's climate will bring major shifts in food production (Rosenzweig, 1993). In some places, temperatures will rise and rainfall will increase; in others, rainfall will decrease. In addition., coastal flooding will reduce the amount of land available for agriculture (Schneider, 1989).

In general, food crops are sensitive to climate change. Such change, which affects soil temperature and moisture levels, also determines the vitality of both beneficial organisms and pests.

Due to the enormous uncertainties surrounding global climate change, estimates of cropland reductions vary widely--from 10 to 50 percent (Stevens, 1989). But this much is clear: global warming is likely to alter the production of rice, wheat, corn, soybeans, and potatoes--staples for billions of people and major food crops in both North America and Africa.

While climate change will have global impacts on agriculture, regional variations will be significant. Africa and North America exemplify the regional variations that may occur. These differences underscore the difficulty in proposing general strategies for adapting new agricultural technologies to deal with climate change.

By 2030, according to one scenario, atmospheric carbon dioxide concentrations will be double pre-industrial concentrations, other greenhouse gases will increase substantially, and temperatures in North America and Africa will rise approximately 2 degrees Centigrade.

If these changes occur, projected average rainfall in central North America will be 10 percent lower than now; in eastern and northern Africa, it may be 10 percent higher (Keepin, 1988). While more rain holds the promise of increasing African agricultural productivity, higher temperatures may offset this advantage by decreasing soil moisture (PMSSACC, 1990). As a result, dry agricultural regions may continue to suffer the effects of inadequate water supplies, even if levels of rainfall increase.

Agricultural production will be affected by the severity--and pace--of climate change. If change is gradual, there will be time for political and social institutions to adjust. As Slow change also may enable the natural biota to adapt. However, even a minor change (for example, one-tenth of a degree per decade) could spark significant changes in the frequency of climate extremes, including heat waves, floods, and droughts.

Rapid climate change could jeopardize agriculture, forestry, and biodiversity worldwide (Woodwell, 1989). Compounding this problem is the fact that some African societies lack the capacity to adapt to these changes on their own.

Goal 14: Conserve and sustainably use the oceans, seas and marine resources for sustainable development

The expansion of protected areas for marine biodiversity and existing policies and treaties that encourage responsible use of ocean resources are still insufficient to combat the adverse effects of overfishing, growing ocean acidification due to climate change and worsening coastal eutrophication. As billions of people depend on oceans for their livelihood and food source and on the transboundary nature of oceans, increased efforts and interventions are needed to conserve and sustainably use ocean resources at all levels.

Ocean acidification is caused by the uptake of atmospheric CO2 by the ocean, which changes the chemical composition of the seawater. Long-term observations of ocean acidification over the past 30 years have shown an average increase of acidity of 26 per centpercent since pre-industrial times, and at this rate, an increase of 100 to 150 percent is predicted by the end of the century, with serious consequences for marine life.

To achieve sustainable development of fisheries, fish stocks must be maintained at a biologically sustainable level. Analyses reveal that the fraction of world marine fish stocks that are within biologically sustainable levels declined from 90 per centpercent in 1974 to 66.9 per centpercent in 2015.

Table 1. Ecological footprint of different diets.

Type of Food	Area required
Vegetarian food	500 m^2
Dominant vegetarian food	700 m^2
Western diet	4 000 m^2
Mainly meat diet	7 000 m^2

Source: FAO

Illegal, unreported and unregulated fishing remains one of the greatest threats to sustainable fisheries, the livelihoods of those who depend upon them and marine ecosystems. A framework of international instruments has been developed that addresses different aspects of fisheries management. Most countries have taken measures to combat such fishing and have adopted an increasing number of fisheries management instruments in the past decade.

Small-scale fisheries are present in almost all countries, accounting for more than half of total production on average, in terms of both quantity and value. To promote small-scale fishers' access to productive resources, services and markets, most countries have developed targeted regulatory and institutional frameworks.

Goal 15: Protect, restore and promote sustainable use of terrestrial ecosystems, sustainably manage forests, combat ***desertification, and halt and reverse land degradation and halt biodiversity loss***

Protecting important sites for terrestrial and freshwater biodiversity is vital for ensuring long-term and sustainable use of terrestrial and freshwater natural resources. The global mean percentage of each key biodiversity area covered by protected areas increased from 33.1 per centpercent in 2000 to 46.1 per centpercent in 2018 for terrestrial areas, from 30.5 per centpercent in 2000 to 43.2 per centpercent in 2018 for freshwater areas, and from 32.9 per centpercent in 2000 to 44.7 per centpercent in 2018 for mountain areas.

There are some encouraging global trends in protecting terrestrial ecosystems and biodiversity. Forest loss is slowing down, more key biodiversity areas are protected and more financial assistance is flowing towards biodiversity protection. Yet, the 2020 targets of Sustainable

Development Goal 15 are unlikely to be met, land degradation continues, biodiversity loss is occurring at an alarming rate, and invasive species and the illicit poaching and trafficking of wildlife continue to thwart efforts to protect and restore vital ecosystems and species.

What are the modern methods of sustainable food production?

Sustainable food production is "a method of production using processes and systems that are non-polluting, conserve non-renewable energy and natural resources, are economically efficient, are safe for workers, communities and consumers, and do not compromise the needs of future generations" (Foresight, 2011).

A sustainable approach to food production includes the promotion of novel techniques that can be thought of as pro-environment. Promoters of sustainable food production stick to specific methods that impact, in a positive manner, the environment and thus the management of lands. Such practices may include respecting minimum stocking densities, exclusive use of organic fertilizers, maintaining traditional landscapes, ploughing plowing of organic matter and so on. The facts that organic products tend to sell for higher prices, and that consumers are willing to meet that difference, reflects the acknowledgement of additional costs accrued from environmentally-friendly production. Additionally, the price difference reflects the possible loss of potential income foregone by those producers in their resistance to intensification or competition. Market initiatives to highlight these differences in production methods might make use of labels or certifications that explicitly and deliberately connotes `environmental superiority' over other products (Erickson and Kramer-LeBlanc, 1996).

Table 2. The grid of sustainable food systems.

	Environment	Nutrition	Economic	Socio-cultural
Agriculture	Follow sustainable agricultural practices Enhance resilience of production systems Deploy and maintain diversity	Promote diverse food Produce nutritionally dense product	Deploy affordable cultivation practices Promote self reliance through local produce	Maintain traditional agriculture practices and promote local varieties
Food Production	Reduce impact of production, processing, commercialization	Preserve nutrients throughout the food chain	Strengthen local food systems Produce affordable food	Produce culturally acceptable foood
Consumption	Reduce the environmental impact of feeding practices	Promote dietary diversity, food balance and seasonality	Promote access to dietary diversity	Safeguard food traditions and culture Meet local preference & taste

Protected Designation of Origin

Food items that highlight the region of origin are an additional effort to support methods of sustainable food production. More common in Europe than in other Western countries, this approach aims to connect the creation of a demand for a specific product with the appreciation of specific territories and their particular qualities. This approach protects and enhances local identity, hence highlighting the visibility of a specific region including its environment and culture. Numerous local product marketing initiatives in Europe, especially those located within designated landscape areas, such as national parks, are an example of this. Additionally, they contribute significantly to the region's tourism profile.

In their analysis of the European PDO (Protected Designation of Origin) and PGI labels, Parrott et al (2002) highlight the distinction between `northern' and `southern' European food culture. Their study proposes Southern European food culture as being particularly suitable to the emergence of quality food supply chains with a basis on territorial and cultural specificity.Nevertheless, many of the food production chains within both Europe and North America are tightly connected to the promotion of tourism. Supporters of PDO practices regularly assume that consumers are in effect buying directly into a collective of positive developmental practices, including stronger environmental quality and territorial development. Not only is it by no means certain that environmental sustainability and/or rural development rather than consumer health is the key driver for consumer purchase (Lockie and Collie, 2002) but the connection of tourism to gastronomic experience introduces a very different set of relationships between consumers and producers and the territory they are likely to share (Enteleca, 2001). Notwithstanding, food producers within PDO practices have often been clever in connecting consumer interest in their quality products with the wider public goods to be derived from particular production methods and their location within particular places. This might be seen as a particularly effective way of translating consumer concerns into land-management actions.

Box 8. Ultra-processed foods and the NOVA system

Some foods are highly processed or ultra-processed. They most likely have many added ingredients such as sugar, salt, fat, and artificial colors or preservatives. Ultra-processed foods are made mostly from substances extracted from foods, such as fats, starches, added sugars, and hydrogenated fats. They may also contain additives like artificial colors and flavors or stabilizers. Examples of these foods are frozen meals, soft drinks, hot dogs and cold cuts, fast food, packaged cookies, cakes, and salty snacks.

Ultra-processed foods, also called highly processed foods, can be cheap, convenient and tasty. But they may have lots of refined carbohydrates, saturated fats and salt. Although the NOVA system authors assert certain additives may be unsafe, any additives used in food must pass safety tests by the Food and Drug Administration. They also tend to pack a lot of calories into each bite. That means you're likely to eat a lot before you feel full.

Ultra-processed products are made to be hyper-palatable and attractive, with a long shelf-life, and able to be consumed anywhere, any time. Their formulation, presentation and marketing often promote overconsumption. Studies based on NOVA show that ultra-processed products now dominate the food supplies of various high-income countries and are increasingly pervasive in lower-middle- and upper-middle-income countries. The evidence so far shows that displacement of minimally processed foods and freshly prepared dishes and meals by ultra-processed products is associated with unhealthy dietary nutrient profiles and several diet-related non-communicable diseases. Ultra-processed products are also troublesome from social, cultural, economic, political and environmental points of view.

Genetically Modified Foods

Around the World, the land area planted with Genetically Modified (GM) crops saw an increase from 1.7 million hectares (ha) in 1996 to 148 million ha in 2010, with a higher proportion among developing countries. In 2010, there were 29 "biotechnology countries" made up of 19 developing countries and 10 developed countries, with 17 from the 29 growing crops on 50,000 ha or more (James, 2010). This phenomenon goes against the expressed preferences of most consumers, at least within the European Union, who do not approve of GM products (Gaskell et al. 2010). In Europe, differently from the United States, Canada, or South America, public concern over safety has been strongly voiced and has in effect stopped the commercial development of GM foods (Millstone & Lang, 2008). The growth of these foods has also given place to global discussions, focusing primarily on the consequences of releasing GM material into the environment, the environmental impacts of the increasing use of pesticides, possible market monopolies, and public angst of the unknown risks of consuming GM foods (Pechan& de Vries, 2005; Oosterveer& Sonnenfeld, 2012).

However, in general, the European Union tolerates modified seeds and allows member countries to set their own processes for keeping traditional and modified crops separate. In a small (yet growing) number of European countries (such as Spain, Portugal, and Germany), a few GM varieties are permitted. Apart from Denmark, the Netherlands, and the Czech Republic, all EU member states have installed "GMO-free zones" (Consmüller et al. 2012), and in the EU the labeling of GM food is compulsory for all products made from or containing GMOs, as well as all GM additives and GM flavorings. Foodstuffs originating from animals fed with GM feed, however, do not fall under this legislation. Therefore, Germany and Austria have introduced "free from GMO" labels that are applicable to foodstuffs to which neither GM additives nor GM feed have been introduced.

Genetically modified organisms (GMOs) may be defined as organisms (including plants, animals or microorganisms) whose genetic material (DNA) has been changed in a manner that does not happen in nature either by mating and/or natural recombination. The technology is often referred to as "modern biotechnology" or "gene technology", occasionally also "recombinant DNA technology" or "genetic engineering". It permitsspecific individual genes to be moved from one organism to another, also acrossnon-related species. Food developed from or using GMOs is often called GM food.

GM foods are created – and marketed – since there is some possible advantage for either the producer or consumer of said items. This is supposed to turn into a food with a reduced price, larger benefit (in terms of shelf life or nutritional composition) or both. Initially, GM seed developers desired their products to be wanted by producers and have targeted innovations that provide direct benefit to farmers (and Big Food overall).

One of the goals for creating plants from GM seeds is to increase the protection of crops. The GM crops available on the market today are mostly targeted at a larger level of crop protection by way of resistance to plant diseases from insects or viruses or from better toleranceto herbicides.

Resistance to insects is managed by adding the gene for toxin production from the bacterium Bacillus thuringiensis (Bt) into a food. This toxin is being used as a common insecticide in agricultural practices and is safe for people to eat. GM crops that naturally produce this toxin have been identified as needingless quantities of insecticides under certain situations, for example where pest pressure is strong. It is possible to achieve resistance to a virus by introducing a gene from specific viruses which cause plant diseases. Virus resistance allows plantsto be less vulnerable to diseases caused by such viruses, resulting in greater crop yields.

Tolerance to herbicides is managed through the addition of a gene from a bacterium carrying resistance to certain herbicides. In situations where weed pressure is elevated, the use of such crops has translated into a reduction in the amount of the herbicides required.

Overall, consumers believe that traditional foods (that have an established record of safe consumption over time) are safer. Any time a novel version of organisms for food use are is created using traditional breeding techniques that had been around prior to the introduction of gene technology, some of the characteristics of organisms may be modified, either in a positive or a negative form. National food authorities may be asked to examine the safety of these conventional foods developed from novel varieties of organisms, but this is not always so.

Contrastingly, the majority of national authorities believe that specific evaluations are required for GM foods. Specific systems have been developed for the detailed evaluation of GM organisms and GM foods in relation to both human health and environmental impacts. Similar evaluations are usually not carried out for conventional foods. Therefore, there is currently a strong difference in the assessment process before marketing for these two food categories.

The WHO Department of Food Safety and Zoonoses has the goal of helping national authorities in the identification of foods that ought to be subject to risk assessment and to provide guidelines suitable for safety assessment. The WHO suggests the use of Codex Alimentarius guidelines when national authorities decide to conduct safety assessments of GM organisms.

The assessment of safety of GM foods usually targets:

- direct health implications or possible toxicity
- potential allergen city
- specific components likely to provide nutritional or toxic effects
- inserted gene stability
- nutritional outcomes linked to genetic modification
- any unintentional outcomes which may result from the gene insertion

While theoretical debates have overseen a wide number of aspects, the three key issues discussed are the likelihood to provoke allergen city, gene transfer and out crossing.

Allergen city

As a guiding principle, the movement of genes from commonly allergenic organisms to non-allergic organisms is not encouraged unless it is possible to demonstrate that the protein product of the transferred gene will not cause allergies. While foods created employing traditional methods are usually not tested for allergenicity, protocols for the testing of GM foods have been assessed by the Food and Agriculture Organization of the United Nations (FAO) and WHO. No allergen city has been discovered linked to GM foods currently being traded.

Gene transfer

The transfer of genes from GM foods to cells of the body or to bacteria in the gastrointestinal tract may cause concern if the transferred genetic material has a negative effect on human health. This is especially relevant with antibiotic resistance genes, used as markers when developing GMOs, were to be worked with. Even though the likelihood of transfer is low, the utilization of gene transfer technology not involving antibiotic resistance genes is preferred.

Out crossing

The migration of genes from GM plants into conventional crops or connected species in nature (referred to as "out crossing"), in addition to the mixing of crops originating from conventional seeds with GM crops, can present an indirect effect on the safety and security of the food supply. Cases have been known where GM crops approved for the use as feed for animals or industrial utilization were detected at minimal levels in the products developed for human consumption. Various nations have taken up strategies to minimize mixing, such as a clear separation of the fields within which GM crops and conventional crops are farmed.

Risk assessment of the environment covers both the GMO concerned and the possible receiving environment. The process for assessment includes evaluating the characteristics of the GMO and its environmental effect and stability, linked with ecological properties of the environment in which the introduction will happen. The assessment also covers unintended effects which could occur from the insertion of the desired gene.

Genetically modified foods available on the international market today have undergone safety assessments and are not likely to be a risk for the health of the consumer. Additionally, no human health impact has been identified resulting from the intake of such foods by the general population in the nations where they have been allowed. Regular safety assessments following the Codex Alimentations principles and, when applicable, suitable post-market monitoring, should be the basis for assuring the safety of GM foods.

Food production and nanotechnology

Nanotechnology is one of the key tools in modern agriculture, with agri-food nanotechnology likely to become a leading economic force in the upcoming years. Agri-food themes around sustainable development and protection of foods from agricultural practices, including crops for human intake and animal feed. Nanotechnology brings new agrochemical components and new delivery routes to better crop production, with the promise of reducing pesticide utilization. Nanotechnology can increase agricultural production, and its applications can cover:

- nano formulations of agrochemicals for the application of pesticides and fertilizers for the improvement of crops
- the application of nano sensors/ nano biosensors for the protection of crops and identification of diseases and residues of agrochemicals
- nano devices for the genetic modification of plants
- diagnostics of plant disease
- animal health, animal breeding, poultry production;
- postharvest management.

Techniques for precision farming may be used to further improve crop production but not harm soil and water, lower nitrogen loss from leaching and emissions, in addition to enhancing nutrients long-term incorporation thanks to soil microorganisms. Nanotechnology applications include nano particle-mediated gene or DNA modification in plants for the creation of insect-resistant varieties, food processing and storage, nano feed additives, and prolonged product shelf life. Nanotechnology is a possible way to speed up the development of biomass-to-fuels production technologies. Scientists believe that the possible benefits of nanotechnology for agriculture, food, fisheries, and aquaculture require a balance between concerns for the soil, water, and environment and the occupational health of workers. Increasing awareness of nanotechnology in the area of agricultural food production, covering feed and food ingredients, smart packaging and quick-detection systems, is one of the main ways to have an influence acceptance from consumers. Based on just a handful of toxicological research, worries exist in regards to the safety of nano materials, and scientists and companies will be required to prove that such nanotechnologies do not have higher negative environmental impacts.

The branch of agriculture referred to as "farming" is the process of growing food, feed, fiber, and several other wanted items by the cultivation of specific plants and the rearing of livestock. Agriculture is the base of most countries under development, and it is a source of food for humans, directly and indirectly. The world's demographics will grow to an estimated 8 billion people by 2025 and 9 billion by 2050, and it is widely accepted that international production from agriculture must augment to feed a steeply growing global population. The agricultural production of food is of key importance, as it is one of the main shapers of the economy. Additionally, it can provide ways to develop value-added yields. Agriculture is often in on the public attention radar since climate change, energy and resource restrictions, and a fast-growing world population are is placing pressure as never before on food and water resources. The Food and Agriculture Organization of the United Nations estimates that yearly meat production of 200 million tons will be needed by 2050 to answer to the food requirements presented by a growing international population, and this estimated higher demand for products of animal originplace further pressure on agricultural soil since farmers must produce yields to secure animal feed. Space required for food yields also must answer to increasing competition from the requirement for crops with other purposes – including the production of befouls and pharmaceuticals. Hence, food production capability is faced with several challenges, such as a falling ratio of arable land to people. Agricultural practices as a way to produce food is are turning evermore pressing in a world of less resources and an ever-growing world population. From this increasing world population, the use of modern technologies is required including nanotechnology and nano biotechnology in agricultural and food sciences. Nanotechnology has a huge potential to modernize agriculture and connected disciplines, including aquaculture and fisheries. Nano agriculture these days centers on selected farming that includes the use of nano particles with particular properties to strengthen crop and livestock productivity.

Nanotechnology in agricultural food production is a multidisciplinary field. Its applications to the agricultural and food sectors are fairly new compared to its implementation in the field of pharmaceuticals. Nanotechnology has the possibility to protect plants, track and measure plant growth, detect plant and animal diseases, augment international food production, improve food quality, and minimize waste for "sustainable intensification". Food and agricultural production are two of the most impactful fields for the application of nanotechnology.

Nano scale is the name given to size dimensions usually between approximately 1–100 nm (or more appropriately, 0.2–100.0 nm) since it is at this scale that the characteristics of materials are different regarding their physical, chemical, and biological properties from those at a bigger scale. Just one nanometer (nm) is 1 billionth of a meter. Nanotechnology applies to the comprehension and manipulation of matter at nanoscale, where a particular phenomenon allows for new applications. Nevertheless, maintaining a limit on the size in nanotechnology to the 1–100 nm range rules out many materials and equipment, specifically in the pharmaceutical and agricultural spheres, and some scientists warn against a strict definition based on a sub-100 nm size. Any type of a material that has one or more dimensions in the nanoscale is referred to as nanomaterial. According to a different definition, "nanomaterial" translates into natural, incidental, or developed material made up of particles in an unbound form or as an aggregate or as an agglomerate and where, for 50% or more of the particles in the number size distribution, one or more external dimension is in the range 1–100 nm. Materials that have a single dimension in the nanoscale (and are extended in the other two dimensions) are layers, for example, graphene, thin films, or surface coatings. Materials that are nanoscale in two dimensions (and extended in one dimension) are known as nanowire and nanotube. Materials that are nanoscale in three dimensions are particles, such as precipitates, dendrimers, fullerenes, colloids, and tiny particles of semiconductor materials (quantum dots). Nanomaterial-specific qualities derive mostly from their higher relative surface area and quantum properties. Any material that is purposely developed in the nanoscale to have certain properties or made up in a specific way can be called a manufactured/ engineered nanomaterial. These types of engineered nanomaterials carry different characteristics when in comparison to their conventional options. A nanoparticle is a discrete entity that has all three dimensions in the nanoscale.

Traditional Food Production Methods

Traditional Agriculture can be defined as a primitive style of farming that involves the intensive use of indigenous knowledge, traditional tools, natural resources, organic fertilizer and cultural beliefs of the farmers. It is noteworthy that it is still used by about 50% of the world population.

Characteristics of traditional agriculture:

1. Extensive farming with indigenous knowledge and tools
2. Indigenous tools like axe, hoe, and stick
3. Method: Slash & Burn, and Shifting Cultivation
4. Cattle raisin helps to create fallow land
5. Absence of accountability and responsibility to the Environment
6. Lacked by surplus production

The primitive style of framing like slash and burn decreases the organic matter from the soil and within a short period of time the nutrient content of the soil taken up by the crops. This makes the farmers move to another place for farming. It is the process of the removal of a forest or stand of trees where the land for the conversion of forestland to farms, ranches, or urban use. The most concentrated deforestation occurs in tropical rainforests. The slash & burn, and shifting cultivation required massive cutting down of the forest which leads to the situation of deforestation. It is a process of the removal of topsoil by the natural physical forces of water and wind or through forces associated with farming activities such as tillage. The roots of the plant and trees firmly hold the soil, but the deforestation exposed the soil to get eroded by the weathering forces like rain, wind and storms which causes the loss of top fertile soil.

Hence, we can say, it is our duty to deal with the most mundane problems of life where each individual matter, like dealing with safe and clean drinking water, hygienic living conditions, clean and fresh air, fertile land, healthy food and sustainable development.

Modern agriculture, the most practised form of agriculture around the world, became commonplace following the two world wars, as it was during that era that knowledge about chemistry greatly increased. Modern agriculture is based on treating the soil and plants with products that are more likely than not noxious, and more likely than not synthetically produced in a laboratory. These products are used to prevent disease or pests from blighting the plant.

The result is that these products – and the same applies to products used in organic agriculture – find themselves in our food. It has been proven that these products accumulate in our fatty tissues, and when the level is high enough, the chance of developing an illness, like cancer, is higher.

One of the biggest problems with modern agriculture is that it kills off life in the topsoil and subsoil. In order to be worth anything, soil needs microflora (bacteria, fungi and actinobacteria) and microfauna (protozoa, nematodes and arthropods). Use The use of powerful chemical products that destroy or inhibit harmful fungi or fungal spores (fungicides), that kill or inhibit harmful insects and other pests (insecticides) and that control unwanted vegetation (herbicides) has ultimately contributed to the reduction in microbial life in the soil, to the point that, in order to yield sufficient crops, it is necessary to use very large amounts of fertilizsers. This all, in turn, results in near-barren land unable to generate its own organic matter.

If we consider the diversity of a planet made up of 195 countries, the global diet is strangely non-diversified. Approximately 75% of food destined for human consumption originates from just 12 plants and animal species. In addition, approximately 60% of the global food energy intake originates from just 3 plants: rice, maize and wheat (Food Navigator, 2019).

Instead of placing their product on the local markets, farmers in current times are more likely to target large, complex supply chains of which they are usually just a minimal component. As an outcome, just one-fourth of the retail food price reaches the farmers, in comparison to about 50% a half-century ago (Tischner&Kjaernes, 2007). The integration of local food markets into larger industrial food systems also translates into additional "food miles," referring to the transportation required from the site of food production (farms) to the point of sale (food industry) to the consumers. This global food system includes not only environmental impacts from production but also covers cultural and environmental costs (Blay-Palmer, 2008).

An initial step to environmental management within food production covers the protection, maintenance, and encouragement of current forms and methods of food production that are often `traditional' (low density, grass-based, extensive) and hence likely to be more environmentally friendly than what would replace them. Said traditional food production practices aim to differentiate themselves in the market from products that are produced en mass, at far greater intensities, and with lower regard to the methods of production. For the majority of these schemes, it is the intrinsic environmental qualities of the production territory that add both to the quality of the product and to the environmentally beneficial nature of the production process.

Urban Agriculture

The idea of an urban ecological footprint may be used as an example of how surrounding rural and natural areas are being impacted by cities. Ecological footprint analysis takes for granted that every type of energy and material utilization and waste discharge needs the productive or absorptive capacity of a limited area of land or water (Wackernagel& Rees, 1996). The totality of all soil and water needed to meet material utilization and waste discharge of a specific population is that populations' ecological footprint on the planet. This must not necessarily match (and often does not) with the populations' home area. Ecological footprint research demonstrates the growing competing requirements on natural capital, and it also highlights the issues both of equity and the long-term sustainable production. By setting the ecological footprint of different lifestyles, infrastructure, consumption habits and certain densities separately, it is likely that strategies to reduce environmental effects and the wipeout of natural resources can be developed. Some cities are now required to identify the possible activities to lower the ecological footprint, while simultaneously augmenting the life quality for their population. Food supplies to cities are a key component of urban footprints.

Cities need wide areas of land for their sustenance and have becomedependent on huge quantities of food being provided from outside the land area they populate. London, as an example, has a surface area of about 160,000 ha. With just 12% of Britain's population, London needs the equivalent of 40% of Britain's wholeworkable land for its food. In actuality, these land surfaces, stretch to far-flung locations including wheat prairies of Kansas and Iowa, the soybean fields of Mato Grosso, the orchards of France and Spain, and the tea gardens of Assam or Mount Kenya. But this international dependence of Londoners has historically not beenan issue. Food is there to be bought and enjoyed – the environmental effect of food production, including the energy needed for the production of food, processing and transport, is not often talked about.

Nevertheless, today's sales and food logistics systems, depending on motorizedforms of transportation and, more and more, airfreight exact a strong environmental effect in terms of fossil-fuel utilization, air contamination and harm to wildlife habitats through road building (SAFE Alliance, 1994). The biggest land surfaces needed for providing food to cities in developed countries are for growing grains, and animal feed including maize and soybeans to cover the need for meat. As countries with a large population, such as China and India, urbanize, global demand for land to feed cities will keep increasing. Sooner or later, cities that have come to require large imports of food for granted might requirea consideration of redesigning agricultural production in cities or the urban fringe to lower the demand for land surfaces somewhere else.

In a world increasingly dominated by cities, the international community is starting to address the issue of sustainability in cities. The process started in Rio with Agenda 21 and stretched to the 1996 UN City Summit in Istanbul. The 100-page Habitat Agenda, signed in Istanbul by 180 countries stated: "Human settlements shall be planned, developed and improved in a manner that takes full account of sustainable development principles and all their components, as set out in Agenda 21".

It is generally agreed that cities these days over employ natural resources and createexcessive amounts of waste. The ecological footprints of cities are eliminating the habitat of many species. The city's impact goes far beyond its physical boundaries. In addition, urban areas are confronted with a growing number of people and, hence, an increasing amount of people to feed. Along with other initiatives and activities, agricultural practices in cities ,therefore, have a key role in contributing to the future sustainable development of urban areas. The economic explosion of the last years has made way for the assumption that urban citizens will purchase food, not produce it themselves. But at a moment when work sharing is extensively seen as basic for ensuring a dignified existence for a significant number of citizens, extra opportunities for people to develop livelihoods for themselves are important. Growing food in cities is certainly one of the alternatives.

Urban populations that have undergone an industrial decline, provision of derelict land for food growing is for sure a planning policy alternative. In cities such as Detroit and New York in the United States, thousands of acres of land have been turned over to people out of workfor the production of food. In Britain, city-farm projects have been set on areas of derelict land in approximately 20 cities. In Germany, land in previously coal-mining areas in locations such as Essen is being set apart for urban agricultural development.

There are worries regarding the suitability of polluted urban land for the growth of food, and it has been pointed out as a possibility that it is wise not to grow crops less than ten meters from main roads, especifcally in nations where lead fuel remains in use. Overall, land contaminated by heavy metals, for example, cadmium and lead, needs specific guidelines. Nevertheless, investigations in the USA and the UK hasdemonstrated that these challenges can be addressed in various ways: firstly, maintaining a high pH with extra quantities of lime, and elevated organic matter levels through additions of compost or manure aids with the fixation of heavy metals in the soil.

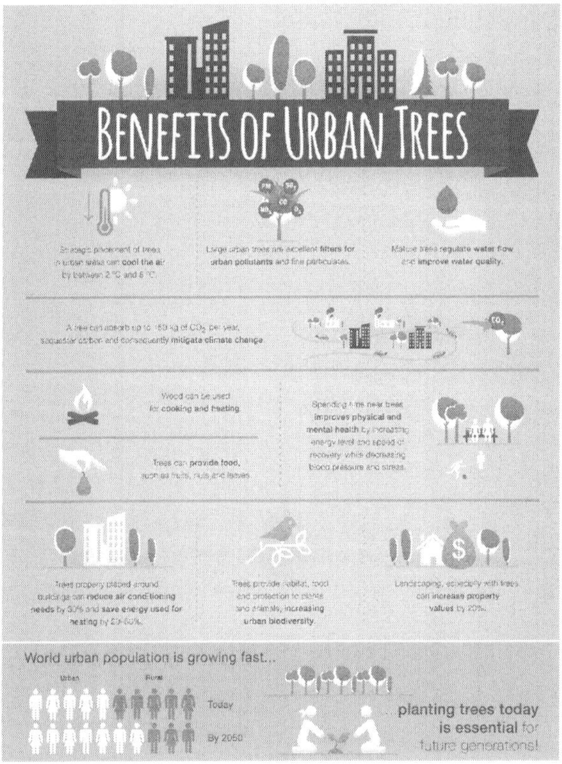

Figure 14. Benefits of urban trees.

How is food sustainability quantified?

As of the writing of this book, no fixed framework exists on the quantification of sustainable food production. The degree to which specific foods or diets are sustainably produced remains to be measured. Nevertheless, indicators may include:

Closed-Loop Systems

Any system that provides for its own energy needs is inherently sustainable. This concept can be extended beyond things like biofuels and solar power to what permaculturists call "inputs," like food and fertilizer. For example, rather than importing fertilizer to a farm or garden, the system could be designed to provide for its own fertility needs – perhaps from livestock manure or cover crops. And if you're raising livestock, you should certainly aspire to provide all the food for your animals from on-site, whether raising grain, forage crops, or recycling kitchen waste as animal feed. Any permaculturist worth their salt would remind you that a successfullyclosed loop system "turns waste into resources" and "problems into solutions." "You don't have a snail problem, you have a duck deficiency," Mollison was fond of saying, which makes perfect sense if you've ever seen how gleefully ducks wolf down snails.

Perennial Crops

Permies aren't the only ones to recognize that tilling the ground once or twice a year isn't particularly good for the soil. Which This is why they advocate using perennial crops that are planted just once, rather than annual crops which require constant tillage. Agroforestry, the cultivation of edible tree crops and associated understory plants, is emphasized – think shade-grown coffee or cacao plantations in South America. The only problem is that few crops that most of us eat are perennials; but there is no doubt that if we could replace all the monocultures of corn, soy, and wheat in the world with agroforestry systems (while still feeding the world), agriculture which be is much more sustainable.

Multiple Functions

One of the more original ideas of permaculture is that every component of a structure or a landscape should fulfill more than one function. The idea is to create an integrated, self-sufficient system through the strategic design and placement of its components. For example, if you need a fence to contain animals, you might design it so that it also functions as a windbreak, a trellis, and a reflective surface to direct extra heat and light to nearby plants. A rain barrel might be used to raise aquatic food plants and edible fish, in addition to providing water for irrigation. Permies call this "stacking functions."

Eco-Earthworks

Water conservation is a major focus on permaculture farms and gardens, where the earth is often carefully sculpted to direct every last drop of rain toward some useful purpose. This may take the form of terraces on steep land; swales on moderately sloped land(which are broad, shallow ditches intended to capture runoff and cause it to soak into the ground around plantings); or a system of canals and planting berms on low swampy ground. The latter is modeled on the chinampas of the ancient Aztecs, an approach to growing food, fish, and other crops in an integrated system, often heralded by permaculturists as the most productive and sustainable form of agriculture ever devised.

Let Nature Do the Work for You

The permaculture creed is perhaps best captured in the Mollisonian mantras of "working with, rather than against, nature" and of engaging in "protracted and thoughtful observation, rather than protracted and thoughtless labor." On a practical basis, these ideas are carried out with things like chicken tractors, where the natural scratching and bug-hunting behavior of hens is are harnessed to clear an area of pests and weeds in preparation for planting – or simply planting mashuaunder your locust trees. Locust trees are known for adding nitrogen to the soil, while mashua, a vining, shade-tolerant root crop from the Andes, needs a support structure to grow on. Thus, the natural attributes of the locust eliminate the need to bother with fertilizer or building a trellis, while providing shade, serving as a nectar source for bees and looking pretty. By letting nature do the work of farming and gardening for you, one achieves another of Mollison's famous maxims: "maximizing hammock time."

Developing a sustainable food system should start with an assessment aimed at understanding the current state of the local food system. An assessment will help in identifying issues and challenges faced by citizens, provide appropriate information to decision-makers to facilitate goal setting and policy development to improve food security, and establish baseline data and indicators for monitoring systems. Assessments have the potential to increase community involvement, develop broader awareness and understanding of food-related issues, improve collaboration across diverse stakeholder groups, and better integrate, scale-up, or scale-out existing programs and initiatives which directly or indirectly touch upon urban food systems.

It can be complicated, costly, and lengthy to perform a comprehensive analysis of the food system at the city level, however, a full assessment is not always necessary and a rapid assessment of only key aspects may be sufficient to inform an initial sustainable food system. Methods may include an overview of previous research, document analysis, interviews, stakeholder consultations, evaluation panels, etc. Whether an assessment is comprehensive or rapid, it may consult a broad range of stakeholders, look at a diversity of food system issues, and be methodologically rigorous.

There are a number of excellent guides and toolkits which can provide some advice on the details of planning, designing and implementing an assessment (see the end of the section for more details). However, the analysis should have a holistic approach to the food system, considering vertical (stages of the food system) and horizontal (action fields) dimensions of the food chain. Some elements that you may want to consider in your own assessment include:

Assessing the vertical dimension of the food system: stages

- Food production (what food is produced locally, by whom and under what working conditions, and using which production techniques)
- Processing (what processing companies operate in the city-region, how their input and output related to the local economy and society)
- Distribution and storage (how food distribution is organized in the city-region; where and how people acquire food; the retail, state, and civic food distribution structures; the role and importance of short food supply chains within the existing food system)
- Consumption (who is consuming what kinds of food, in what context and in what amounts; affordability of food for all socioeconomic classes, which groups are already at risk of food inse- curity, and the impact of food consumption habits on health-related issues, such as obesity)
- Waste (source and volume of waste, the lifecycle of food waste at all steps in the food system, GHG emissions of current food system).

Assessing the horizontal dimension of the food system: areas of concern and themes

- Assessment in this dimension is related to the objectives and context of an UFS and changes in human wellbeing that a strategy is expected to bring about. If the focus is on public health the assessment can look at food safety regulating bodies and laws, labeling practices, the presence or lack of promotion and support of healthy lifestyles.
- Many cities put a high priority on environmental objectives and their food assessment looks specifically at food miles, GHG emissions related to food production and transportation, short supply chains, distribution, and waste management practices.
- Economic assessment deals with the impact on the regional economy and local livelihoods implicated in all stages of the food system, and the emergence of new business models in the area of local food economies.
- Food production and consumption are loaded with social and cultural meanings, therefore assessment can look at the diversity of foods and cuisines consumed in the city-region, needs of immigrants, valorisation valorization of traditional foods and practices including local breeds, varieties and farming systems.
- Social justice – fair and just practices along with the entire food system – is an important aspect to consider if cities see food as a key element for responsible businesses and inclusive communities. Food security for all – food poverty and assistance measures for people in need are critical in the assessment.
- Assessment can also look at knowledge, learning and empowerment opportunities and practices that might be valorized and developed further (e.g. best practices, identification ofgood food ambassadors, pioneers and innovators, presence of education and awareness activities promoting sustainable and healthy food consumption).

Furthermore, it is paramount to map, get to know and analyze the existing food policies, regulations and institutions in force in your respective city. Including:

- Food policies: Policies ,directly and indirectly, related to food; processes of embedding food policy in the broader policy agenda;

integration with other policies; implications of national, regional, or EU food-related frameworks.

- Institutions: Visions, norms and values driving food policies and institutions; laws and regulations; community and civic values related to food system functioning and management; relevant bodies implicated in food system policy and management.
- Instruments and measurements: Programs ,which support or undermine the functioning of various aspects of the food system; tools and processes used to monitor and track efficiency and effectiveness of food-related policy or program interventions.
- Participation structures: Approaches and norms that encourage or limit stakeholder participa- tion; existing and potential opportunities for civil society to participate in defining, planning, and implementing food policies and interventions; existing levels of participation by various stake- holders; measures taken to ensure the involvement of various stakeholders.

Chapter 2 Findings

FOOD SECURITY

Food security exists when all people, at all times, have physical, social and economic access to sufficient, safe and nutritious food which meets their dietary needs and food preferences for active and healthy life (FAO, 1996).

This widely accepted definition points to the following dimensions of food security:

Food availability: The availability of sufficient quantities of food of appropriate quality, supplied through domestic production or imports (including food aid).

Food access: Access by individuals to adequate resources (entitlements) for acquiring appropriate foods for a nutritious diet. Entitlements are defined as the set of all commodity bundles over which a person can establish command given the legal, political, economic and social arrangements of the community in which they live (including traditional rights such as access to common resources).

Utilization: Utilization of food through adequate diet, clean water, sanitation and health care to reach a state of nutritional well-being where all physiological needs are met. This brings out the importance of non-food inputs in food security.

Stability: To be food secure, a population, household or individual must have access to adequate food at all times. They should not risk losing access to food as a consequence of sudden shocks (e.g. an economic or climatic crisis) or cyclical events (e.g. seasonal food insecurity). The concept of stability can therefore refer to both the availability and access dimensions of food security.

Over the years, much progress has been made to improve food security, with global undernourishment halved between 1992 and 2017 from 23% to 11% of the world population. But improvement has been uneven across countries and regions, and significant challenges remain. According to estimates by the UN Food and Agriculture Organization, over 800 million people worldwide remain food insecure today.

Challenges to achieving food security will be compounded by a growing world population with an increasing appetite for meat and fish, alongside demands from competing agricultural products such as cotton and biofuels. The impact of climate change and the rise in extreme weather conditions will further challenge producers, as crops are destroyed and production has to shift to new regions, creating short-term fluctuations in food availability.

Climate change, growing populations, increases in food costs, and environmental stressors will have powerful yet undefinable impacts on food security. Thus, strategies and international policies to address these factors are urgently required, including:

- Options for handling water allocation
- Optimized land use patterns
- Improved food trade
- Low environmental impact food processing practices
- Regulation of food prices and safety

Work on ensuring food security therefore must cover analysis of cash transfers, promotion of sustainable agricultural technologies, building resilience to unexpected phenomena, and managing trade-offs in food security, including reaching an equilibrium between the nutritional benefits of specific foods against the ecological costs of production.

Improvements in farm productivity and environmental sustainability will occur mainly through innovation and technical change, ongoing structural change and more sustainable management of natural resources. Farms in different regions and sectors face specific natural and structural conditions, different market and policy incentives, and hence may use different technologies and practices. As a result, farm productivity and environmental sustainability performance vary widely across time and space.

The world has never produced or consumed so much food. And yet it is one of the most troubling moments in the history of food. Gains in productivity have come at an enormous environmental cost. Each year, more than 10 million hectares of agricultural land are lost to degradation, much of it due to industrial farming. Agro-chemicals have polluted rivers and aquifers. Agriculture and land-use change account for around one-third of all greenhouse gas emissions. In the last century alone, we've lost three-quarters of the world's agricultural biodiversity. If that wasn't bad enough, roughly one-third of all food produced goes to waste.

At the same time, food consumption patterns are changing. The rising middle class is demanding more meat and processed foods are becoming more popular. Many parts of the world are experiencing a "triple-burden": the co-existence of chronic hunger, malnutrition and over nutrition. In the world's rapidly growing urban areas, these conditions often exist side by side.

Sustainable food systems are those food systems that aim at achieving food and nutrition security and healthy diets while limiting negative environmental impacts and improving socio-economic welfare. Sustainable food systems are therefore protective and respectful of biodiversity and ecosystems, as well as human well-being and social equity. As such they provide culturally acceptable, economically fair, affordable, nutritionally adequate, safe and healthy foods in a way that balances agro-ecosystem integrity and social welfare.

With this definition we recognize that:

- Delivering affordable, nutritionally adequate, safe and healthy (and even culturally or religiously acceptable) food is a necessary but not sufficient condition for a food system to be sustainable;
- To be sustainable a food system also needs to aim at reducing food waste and food losses and at minimizing its present and future impacts on the environment and society;
- In that regard, we see the balance and the trade-offs between agro-ecosystems integrity and social well-being as being at the core of sustainable food systems;
- By definition, the sustainability of a food system is locally (and possibly timely) determined. There is no such thing as a global sustainable food system.

HOW DO MODERN METHODS OF FOOD PRODUCTION COMPARE?

According to the United Nations, there are five key principles to consider when aiming for social, economic and environmental sustainability:

- improving efficiency in the use of resources
- conserving, protecting and enhancing natural ecosystems
- protecting and improving rural livelihoods and social well-being
- enhancing the resilience of people, communities and ecosystems
- promoting good governance of both natural and human systems.

It is recommended that these five principles provide a basis for developing national policies, strategies, programs, regulations and incentives that will guide the transition to food production practices that are sufficiently productive, economically viable, environmentally friendly, and which are based on the principles of social equality.

Food systems can be thought of in terms of production units, which differ along with multiple characteristics: production structure, environmental impact and environmental sustainability, innovation behavior, commercialization focus, openness towards cooperation, input intensity and capital endowment, diversity of production, individual characteristics such as age or education, as well as locational conditions. Multi-dimensional indices consisting of different variables that measure underlying farm characteristics relevant for the dimension of the specific index to approximate are defined to approximate these farm characteristics. They are then estimated statistically, and incorporated as elements of an identification vector.

These individual index components can be equally weighted with regard to their importance for the overall index score. The principal components analysis (PCA) is applied as a statistically well-defined and empirically tested multivariate method to estimate significant and robust weights for the indices' components. The PCA is a method to conduct a conceptual factor analysis that will then create statistically robust indices based on different variables

The multi-dimensional indices and their components are used in the analysis to identify the farm characteristics driving productivity performance. Table X provides a list of the variables potentially used in the estimations. Thus, the comparison of productivity, variables and estimated indices allows the characterization of each food system. It also sheds light on the potential linkages between performance and other characteristics, and across characteristics Finally, it helps identify the characteristics of the most sustainable food system.

Interpretation needs to consider the composition of the indices, which reflects data availability and may differ by country or system. However, the core components are the same for each index. This composition of the multiple indices can be summarized as follow:

- The farm structure index reflects the farm's physical size in terms of number of hectares or animals, and the reliance on family labor. Classes with a negative value for the farm structure index include larger than average farms with lower reliance on family labor (i.e. more hired labor than the average of all farms). Conversely, a higher than average (positive) index is found for smaller-scale farms that are relying on family labor to a greater extent than the average of all farms.
- The environmental sustainability index is a local measure, which reflects the low intensity in chemical, fuel use and stocking density, and the use of environmentally sustainable practices, as measured by the probability to have organic production and the value of payments from voluntary participation in agri-environmental schemes, which is linked to the implementation of more environmentally sustainable practices. When interpreting the index, it should also be kept in mind that it may not reflect all the dimensions of environmental sustainability such as the impact on the climate. In addition, the pressure of farm practices on the environment depends on the state of natural resources at the local level. For example, low stocking density can be environmentally unsustainable in fragile areas.
- The innovation-commercialization index reflects investments, expected to purchase new technologies, investment in land, new activities (agritourism, biofuel, contract farming) and sometimes the use of practices requiring specific technology.
- The technology index groups various indicators of capital, labor and material intensity per hectare, per cow, or per worker as relevant.
- The diversity index reflects the diversity of production using the Herfindahl index, which measures the degree of specialization based on output shares, and in some countries the presence of

other (e.g. forestry) activities on the farm. A higher index is found for less diversified farms.

- The human capital index reflects the gender, age, education and experience of the farm manager.
- The location index indicates whether the farm is located in a favorable or more constraining environment, e.g. in terms of altitude, distance from urban centers, natural handicaps or specific environmental constraints.
- The household index reflects the importance of off-farm income and the relative participation of women in the labor force, as well as other household characteristics if relevant.
- The financial index reflects the financial health of the farm operation, including the size of assets, low debt level and the value of subsidies.

Table 3. Proposed components for comparison of food system sustainability.

Component	Farm Structure Index	Environmental Sustainability Index	Innovation/Commer-cialization Index	Technology Index	Diversity Index	Human Capital Index	Location Index	Household Index	Financial Index
Agricultural area	X								
Age of operator						X			
Agritourism			X						
Altitude							X		

Biofuel income			X						
Chemical use per ha		X							
Contract farming			X						
Education						X			
Environmental subsidies		X							
Female/male labor share								X	
Forestry production					X				
Fuel per land		X							
Herd size	X								
Land irrigation			X						
Land rental			X						
Nitrate degradation		X							
Off-farm income								X	

Organic production		X							
Ownership	X								
Part-time farming								X	
Production diversity					X				
Profit monitoring program			X						
Rural/urban classification							X		
Soil classification							X		
Tillage area		X							
Water charges			X						

SUSTAINABLE FOOD SYSTEMS

Food systems have the potential to nurture human health and support environmental sustainability; however, they are currently threatening both. Providing a growing global population with healthy diets from sustainable food systems is an immediate challenge. Although global food production of calories has kept pace with population growth, more than 820 million people have insufficient food and many more consume low-quality diets that cause micronutrient deficiencies and contribute to a substantial rise in the incidence of diet-related obesity and diet-related non-communicable diseases, including coronary heart disease, stroke, and diabetes. Unhealthy diets pose a greater risk to morbidity and mortality than do unsafe sex, and alcohol, drug, and tobacco use combined. Because much of the world's population is inadequately nourished and many environmental systems and processes are pushed beyond safe boundaries by food production, a global transformation of the food system is urgently needed.

Table 4. Climate smart agriculture.

CSA technology	Description	Crop	Potential effects on yields and GHG emissions
No tillage	Minimum or no soil disturbance, often in combination with residue retention, crop rotation, and use of cover crops	Maize, wheat	• Positive or neutral effects on yields • Uncertain effect on GHG emissions
Integrated soil fertility management	Combination of chemical fertilizers, crop residues, and manure/compost	Maize, wheat	• Positive effects on yields • Variable effects on GHG emissions
Alternate wetting and drying	Repeated interruptions of flooding during the season, causing the water to decline as the upper soil layer dries out before subsequent re-flooding	Rice	• Lower to no significant changes in yields. • High confidence in lower GHG emissions due to reduction of methane emissions
Nitrogen use Efficiency	Practices and technologies to enhance the uptake of inorganic soil nitrogen by crops	Rice	8 Positive results on yields • Reduction of GHG emissions

One of the ways in which a food system can strive to become more sustainable is by moving production as close to consumption as possible. In doing that food waste is reduced, as is energy employed in transportation, storage and distribution of goods. This move, however, is not always feasible, as the reintroduction of food production into areas for local consumption often requires hefty investments.

Livestock, the largest land use sector on Earth, is an important part of this puzzle. Many solutions to the challenges of feeding the world sustainably lie in how we manage this sector. The demand for livestock products is projected to grow substantially in the coming decades (Alexandratos, 2012). This growth will be driven by increasing populations, economic growth, and rapid urbanization in many parts of the developing world. The main conclusion from such projections is that a shift to diets with more animal products and fats is likely to happen, mostly in the developing world, as a result of increased incomes and urbanization (IAASTD, 2009). Although the consumption per capita of cereals is likely to stabilize, population growth will increase the total quantities of both meat (almost doubling) and cereals (50%) needed to feed the world in 2050.

The supply response of the global agriculture and livestock sectors, if current trends continue, is likely to be able to accommodate these demand increases (Alexandratos, 2012). The most recent projections have important common features:

- Local production under current yield trends in many parts of the world, like Sub-Saharan Africa (SSA) and parts of Asia, will not be able to meet local food demand. Hence, increases in food trade are projected to increase in the future in some parts of the world.

This is a key aspect of balancing the food supply and demand equation.

- Although increases in the yields of crops and livestock have occurred in most regions of the world (apart from SSA), projections show a variable increase in cropland and grassland expansion to meet demand (Smith, 2010).
- Animal numbers will increase. However, monogastric production (pork and poultry) will grow at faster rates than ruminants (especially, for meat and less so for milk).
- These factors lead to net increases in greenhouse gas emissions (GHGs) from the agricultural and livestock sectors but a diminishing trend in the emissions intensities across commodities (GHGs per unit of product).
- Projections of water use show increased pressure on total fresh water resources, notably on blue water (irrigation), and moderate increases in the efficiency of green water use (CA, 2007). Other studies have also demonstrated large quantities of reactive nitrogen used and potential disruption of phosphorus cycles in the future (Bowman, 2011).

Food production can be attained under current productivity and demand trends but not necessarily in ways that make progress in achieving environmental goals or social goals.

Much has been written about Climate Smart Agriculture (CSA) and its potential benefits but most of the existing analyses are based on local experiences and no study has so far attempted to quantify these benefits on a global scale. Our results show that widespread adoption of CSA practices can increase production and lower world prices of wheat, maize, and rice under future unfavorable climatic conditions. The reduction in prices is projected to make food products more accessible to millions of people thereby lowering the number of people at risk of hunger and that of undernourished children. These gains can be obtained while improving soil fertility and with a reduction in GHG emissions. Taken all together, results suggest that CSA practice can deliver benefits across its three foundational pillars on a planetary scale.

However, what clearly transpires from our results is that to make a significant impact, the principles of CSA must be applied widely across production systems and for this to occur significant investments must be made. Ideally, as others have suggested, the same or similar principles should be applied across the whole food system (i.e. trade, stocks, nutrition and social policies). It is also clear that the wide-ranging and multidimensional effects, sometimes unintended or unforeseen, must be understood and managed. CSA with its multi-objective approach may provide a useful framework for decision-making ranging from the farm to the policy level.

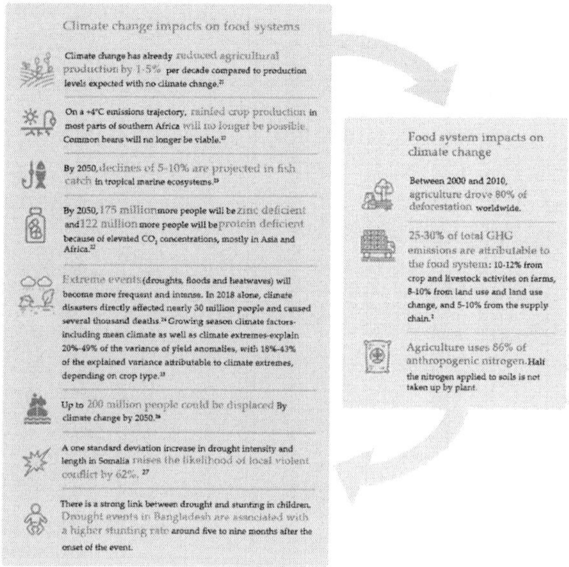

Figure 15. Climate change and food systems by the numbers.

Growing Food in a City Setting

Populations around the world are growing and becoming predominantly urban, fueling the need to re-examine how urban spaces are developed and urban inhabitants are fed. One remedy that is increasingly being considered as a solution to inadequate food access in cities, is urban agriculture. As a practice, urban agriculture is beneficial in both post-industrial and developing cities because it touches on the three pillars of sustainability: economics, society, and the environment. Historically, as well as currently, economic and food security are two of the most common reasons for participation in urban agriculture. Urban agriculture not only provides a source of healthful sustenance that might otherwise be lacking, it can also contribute to a household's income, offset food expenditures, and create jobs. Social facets are another reason for populations to engage in urban agriculture. A garden or rooftop farm is a place where people come together for mutual benefit, often enhancing the common social and cultural identity for city residents.

Larger urban farms also participate in community enrichment through job training and other educational programs, many of which benefit underserved populations. Finally, urban agriculture can play an important role in the environmental sustainability of a city. As a form of green infrastructure, urban farms and community food gardens help reduce urban heat island effects, mitigate urban stormwater impacts and lower the energy embodied in food transportation

Box 9. Traditional foods.

Traditional foods are foods and dishes that are passed through generationsor which have been consumed for many generations. Traditional foods and dishes are traditional in nature, and may have a historic precedent in a national dish, regional cuisine or local cuisine. Traditional foods and beverages may be produced as homemade, by restaurants and small manufacturers, and by large food processing plant facilities.

Some traditional foods have geographical indications and traditional specialties in the European Union designations per European Union schemes of geographical indications and traditional specialties: Protected designation of origin (PDO), Protected geographical indication (PGI) and Traditional specialties guaranteed (TSG). These standards serve to promote and protect names of quality agricultural products and foodstuffs.

Traditional foods have played a major role in the traditions of different cultures and regions for thousands of years. They include foods that have been consumed locally and regionally for an extended time period. Preparation methods of traditional foods are part of the folklore of a country or a region. Unfortunately, throughout Europe, some traditional foods are at risk of disappearing due to altered lifestyles. Therefore, it is important to study and document traditional foods to sustain important elements of European cultures.

Most people can probably name at least one traditional food of the region they come from. Searching the internet for 'traditional foods' shows that numerous collections of traditional food recipes are available from countries worldwide. However, defining traditional foods is not as easy as it might be presumed. There are very few definitions available, and most of them have been developed relatively recently.

Agriculture and Sustainable Practices

Apart from meeting humanity's basic requirements for food, feed, fiber and fuel, agriculture provides employment for over one in three of the world's working force. It also provides a source of livelihood for rural households totaling 2.5 billion people (FAO, 2013). Agriculture contributes to social unity in rural locations, and upholds cultural traditions and heritage (Van Huylenbroecket al., 2007). In addition, agriculture contributes with important, but largely unrecognized, benefits to landscape and wildlife management, the protection of wildlife habitats, water management and quality, flood control and climate change mitigation. Nevertheless, current agricultural practices are far from being ideal, and historic agricultural output is not a guarantee of future production. The patterns of growth in agricultural production and productivity followed to date are unsustainable. Food production on land and in water systems already dominates much of the global terrestrial surface, and has major negative impacts on the Earth's ecosystems. At the same time, rural areas are still home to the majority of the world's poor and vulnerable populations, who rely heavily on "natural capital" for their livelihoods, and lack secure access to these resources. Weak or absent governance for the tenure of natural resources results in their degradation, perpetuates inequalities, and exacerbates conflicts.

Agricultural production systems, and the policies and institutions that underpin global food security, are increasingly inadequate. The world's food systems are heading towards an unprecedented confluence of pressures over the next 40 years (Foresight UK, 2011) which, if the current trajectory is maintained, will seriously compromise our long term global capacity to produce both food and the economic benefits needed for food security.

Box 10. Appellation d'Origine Contrôlée.

Protected designation of origin") is the French certification granted to certain French-geographical indications for wines, cheeses, kinds of butter, and other agricultural products, all under the auspices of the government bureau Institut national des appellations d'origine, now called Institut national de l'origine et de la qualité (INAO). It is based on the concept of terroir.

Many other countries have based their controlled place name systems on the French AOC classification. Italy's Denominazione di OrigineControllata and Denominazione di OrigineControllata e Garantita followed the model set by the French AOC, and the EU standard for Quality Wines Produced in Specified Regions (QWpsr) also corresponds closely.

While Spain's denominación de origen is very similar, the classification of Rioja in 1925 and Sherry in 1933 preceded the French AOC system by a few years and show that Spain's DdO system developed parallel to France's AOC system to some extent. Similarly, Germany's Qualitätswein bestimmterAnbaugebiete is a wine classification system based on geographic region, but it differs from the AOC in important ways. Qualitätswein bestimmterAnbaugebiete wines are commonly seen as less prestigious than Qualitätswein mitPrädikat, making it more similar to the Vin de Pays or Vin Délimité de Qualité Supérieure systems.

Portugal's Denominação de OrigemControlada, Austria's Districtus Austria Controllatus, South Africa's Wine of Origin, and Switzerland's AOC-IGP are all similar to the French AOC system as well.

It appears also that AOC influenced the development of the European Union's protected designation of origin (PDO) system.

Regenerative Agriculture

Regenerative agriculture (RA) is the term given to farming and grazing practices that help reverse climate change by rebuilding the organic matter of soil as well as helping restore degraded biodiversity of soils. These practices result in carbon drawdown and an improved water cycle (Regenerative Agriculture Initiative, 2017).

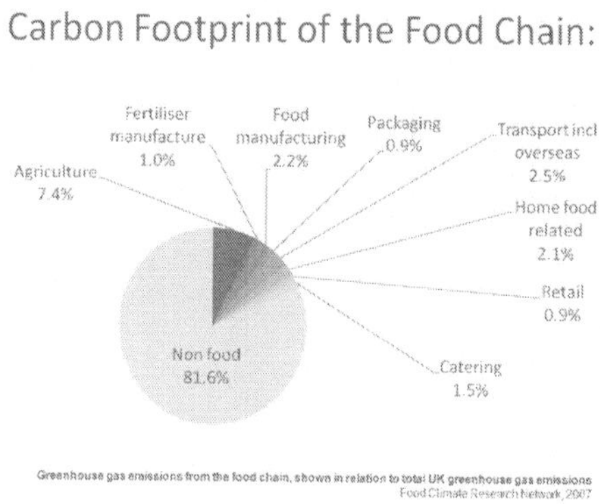

Figure 16. Carbon footprint of the food chain.

Source: https://kindling.org.uk/sites/kindling.org.uk/files/SustainableUrban-FoodPresentation.jpg

RA improves the health degree of soil, mostly via increasing organic matter. This not only helps to increase soil microbial diversity, it also increases biodiversity both above and below the soil surface. This is done in tandem to increasing both the holding capacity of water and sequestering carbon at even greater depths. In this way, CO2 levels in the atmosphere are reduced, and soil structure is improved. Scientists continue to discover the harmful effects on soil from tillage, agricultural chemicals usage and carbon mining. RA aims to reverse this paradigm to build for the future.

RA practices must:

(i) contribute to developing soils and soil fertility and health

(ii) augment water percolation, water retention, and the runoff of clean and safe water

(iii) protect and promote biodiversity and ecosystem health and resiliency

(iv) invert the carbon emissions of our current agriculture to one of remarkably significant carbon sequestration

Thus, RA practices can include (but are not limited to):

- No-till/minimum tilling. Tillage pulverizes soil and fungal communities while adding excess oxygen to the soil for increased respiration and emissions of CO2. Tilling can be one of the most degrading agricultural practices, strongly augmenting soil erosion and loss of carbon. A side effect is the capping of soil in addition to slaking, which can plug soil spaces for percolation leading to increased water runoff and loss of soil. Conversely, no-till/minimum tilling, in tandem with other regenerative practices, increases soil aggregation, water infiltration and retention, and carbon sequestration. Nevertheless, certain soils may gain from occasional ripping to break apart, allowing increased root zones and yields and thus improving the health of soils.
- The fertility level of the soil is augmented in regenerative agricultural practices through the use of cover crops, crop rotations, compost, and animal manures. These help in the restoration of the plant/soil microbiome and in promoting the liberation, transfer, and cycling of key soil nutrients. The use of synthetic fertilizers has led to imbalances in the structure and function of soil microbiomes, skipping the natural biological uptake of nutrients for the plants, creating a dependent system and weaker, less resilient plants.

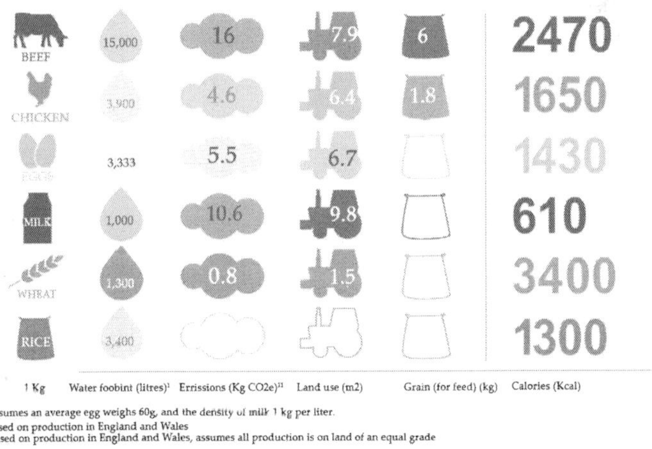

Figure 17. Ecological footprint of food production.

- Scientists have discovered that excessive use of synthetic and artificial fertilizers add strongly to climate change by:

(i) increasing the energy costs of production and transportation of such fertilizers

(ii) their migration into water resources and the atmosphere

(iii) distorting of soil microbial communities

(iv) accelerating decomposition of soil matter

- Creating ecosystems that are biologically diverse starts with inoculation of soils via composts or compost extracts for the restoration of soil microbial communities, the restoration of structure and functionality of soils by implementing full-time planting of multiple crop inter- crop plantings, multispecies cover crops, and borders planted for bee habitat and other beneficial insects.
- Well-managed grazing practices stimulate improved plant growth, increased soil carbon deposits, and overall pasture and grazing land productivity while greatly increasing soil fertility, insect and plant biodiversity, and soil carbon sequestration. These practices not only improve ecological health, but also the health of the animal and human consumer through improved micronutrients availability and better dietary omega balances.

Soil Management

Global demand for food is increasing in terms of the quantity, quality and reliability of supplies. Currently, over 90 % of our food is grown on (or in) a virtually irreplaceable, non-renewable natural resource – soil. Soil management is an integral part of land management and may focus on differences in soil types and soil characteristics to define specific interventions that are aimed to enhance the soil quality for the land use selected. Specific soil management practices are needed to protect and conserve the soil resources.

Reversing the degradation of soil, water and biological resources and enhancing crop and livestock production through appropriate land use and management practices are essential components in achieving food and livelihood security. Symptoms of soil degradation are numerous and include:

- decline of soil fertility
- development of acidity

- salinization
- alkalization
- deterioration of soil structure
- accelerated wind and water erosion
- loss of organic matter and biodiversity

As a result, farm labor productivity and revenues from agriculture are falling, migration to urban areas is increasing, rural poverty is exacerbated. Efforts to restore the productivity of degraded soils must be coupled with other measures that affect the land use practices in particular conservation agriculture, good agricultural practices and irrigation management and integrated plant nutrient management. Some soil management practices have been used to mask the effects of soil degradation on food production (e.g., additions of chemical fertilizers), but comprehensive soil conservation practices are required to respond to the multiple problems of soil degradation if the world is to be able to feed more than 9 billion people by 2050.

Soil degradation affects human nutrition and health through its adverse impacts on the quantity and quality of food production. A decline in crops' yields and agronomic production exacerbate food-insecurity that currently affects 854 million people globally, and low concentration of protein and micronutrients (e.g., Zn, Fe, Se, B, I) aggravate malnutrition and hidden hunger that affects 3.7 billion people, especially children. Soil degradation reduces crop yields by increasing susceptibility to drought stress and elemental imbalance. Strategies include:

- improving water productivity
- enhancing soil fertility and micronutrient availability
- adopting no-till farming
- promoting conservation agriculture
- adapting to climate change.

There are also new innovations such as using remote sensing of plant nutritional stresses for targeted interventions, applying zeolites and nanoenhanced fertilizers and delivery systems, improving biological nitrogen fixation and mycorrhizal inoculation, conserving and recycling (e.g., wastewater) water using drip/sub-drip irrigation ,etc. Judiciously managed and properly restored, world soils have the capacity to grow adequate and nutritious food for present and future populations.

Permaculture

Permaculture, originally 'Permanent Agriculture', is often viewed as a set of gardening techniques, but it has in fact developed into a whole design philosophy and for some people a philosophy for life. Its central theme is the creation of human systems which provide for human needs, but using many natural elements and drawing inspiration from natural ecosystems. Its goals and priorities coincide with what many people see as the core requirements for sustainability. In other words, permaculture is a holistic, living-in-harmony-with-nature worldview, as well as a technical approach for how to do so.

Permaculture tackles how to grow food, build houses and create communities, and minimize environmental impact at the same time. Its principles are being constantly developed and refined by people throughout the world in very different climates and cultural circumstances.

By thinking carefully about the way we use our resources - food, energy, shelter and other material and non-material needs - it is possible to get much more out of life by using less. We can be more productive for less effort, reaping benefits for our environment and ourselves, for now, and for generations to come.

This is the essence of permaculture - the design of an ecologically sound way of living - in our households, gardens, communities and businesses. It is created by cooperating with nature and caring for the earth and its people.

Permaculture is not exclusive - its principles and practice can be used by anyone, anywhere:

- City flats, yards and window boxes
- Suburban and country houses/garden
- Allotments and smallholdings
- Community spaces
- Farms and estates
- Countryside and conservation areas
- Commercial and industrial premises
- Educational establishments
- Waste ground

Permaculture encourages us to be resourceful and self-reliant. It is not a dogma or a religion but an ecological design system that helps us find solutions to the many problems facing us - both locally and globally.

The 12 permaculture design principles are thinking tools that, when used together, allow us to creatively re-design our environment and our behavior in a world of less energy and resources. These principles are seen as universal, although the methods used to express them will vary greatly according to the place and situation. They can be applied to our personal, economic, social and political reorganization and the ethical foundation of permaculture guides the use of these design tools, ensuring that they are used in appropriate ways.

Each principle can be thought of as a door that opens into a whole system of thinking, providing a different perspective that can be understood at varying levels of depth and application.

- Observe and interact

This element of stillness and observation forms the key to permaculture design. In a world of instant makeovers, of 'fast' every-thing, having the capacity to observe the seasons, watch the changing microclimates on a patch of land, understand how the patterns of wind, weather and slope affect the frost pockets and plant growth, is an opportunity to begin to learn the deeper aspects of Earth Care. It also makes us more capable of making wise decisions about how we design or eco-renovate our houses and plan our gardens and farms.

- Catch and store energy

Intimately connected to observation is the art of capturing energy in a design,so that we minimize the need to seek resources from the outside. In a garden, this is about avoiding planting tender seedlings in frost pockets in spring or maximizing solar gain by siting a greenhouse/conservatory on the south side of a building so that we can both extend the season and heat a house with passive solar gain. We are attempting to capture water, sunlight, heat, soil, biomass and fertility whenever we can in order to become more self-resilient.

- Obtain a yield

Food can account for as much as one-third of our ecological footprint so it makes sense to grow as much as we can, even if this is limited to tasty sprouted grains on the windowsill of a flat. So a permaculture garden is by default an edible landscape with good floral companions to attract beneficial insects, and a building is a potential heat store and structure for solar panels. But the concept of 'yields' is not merely about renewable energy or veggies;

a yield can be about social capital. At PM, to see people changing their lives for the better, building community links and reducing their carbon after reading our books or magazines is the ultimate positive yield for a publisher.

- Apply self-regulation and accept feedback

When we burn fossil fuels we release CO2 into the atmosphere, trapping heat and increasing temperatures. This causes ice to melt which leads to loss of reflective surfaces, leading to more absorption of sunlight and even higher temperatures. We must accept responsibility for our actions.

- Use and value renewable resources and services

Whenever possible, permaculture seeks to use resources that can be renewed. This naturally applies to energy but also to ecological building, coppicing, soil conservation, and the planting of perennial food crops, as well as annuals with seed saving. The dangers of relying on non-renewables, technological fixes and speculative money are becoming ever more evident.

- Produce no waste

In the UK, we throw away the equivalent of 24 bags of sugar per household per week: 14.1 kg. That's 29 million tonnes (55% of that is household) per year. I have a favorite saying that the landfill of today will be the 'mine' of tomorrow. At PM we have no waste collection and our business is designed on permaculture principles. We reuse first and recycle all possible materials: paper, cardboard, textiles, glass and compost all organic materials, from kitchen waste to shredded paper. The subsequent compost feeds the edible container garden outside our office and provides a medium for growing plants for other projects at the Sustainability Centre.

- Design from patterns to details

When Tim Harland and I designed our house and garden, we read up on permaculture design, forest gardening, renewable energy, eco-architecture and eco-renovation as much as we could. We spent a year observing the land before we started planting and planned how best to make our house a happy, energy-efficient place to live in. We observed the seasons, the climatic variations, the weather, the soil patterns, the slope and our own human activities on the site as a family.

We also considered the 'edge' between house and garden and how we might make this both aesthetic and productive in terms of food crops and energy harvesting. In other words, we started off looking at the bigger picture, the pattern of what sustainable living might be, with examples from other places, and then we refined our exploration into the detail appropriate for our particular site. We didn't make a 'shopping list' of individual items or projects and try to mesh them together in a hotchpotch of what might be regarded as 'green'.

- Integrate rather than segregate

We have a cultural tendency to separate veggie gardens from flower gardens and use hard edges to design our spaces. Companion gardeners will know however that the more integrated the orchard is with the wildflower meadow, or the vegetables are with flowers frequented by beneficial insects, lesser pests will prevail. The same is true for people. Cultural diversity yields a robust and fertile culture, whereas a rigid monoculture of politics and religion can bring sterility, even social and political repression.

- Use small and slow solutions

Our society currently depends on vast inputs of fossil fuels, whilst our biosphere is over-loaded by their outputs. The more accessible and fixable our technology and chains of supply are, the more robust the system. This principle speaks of hand tools, of appropriate technology that can easily be fixed, and of relocalization.

Currently, we have a three-day 'just in time' supply chain of supermarkets. If the fuel supply is interrupted, the supermarket shelves will empty at an alarming rate. Better to build resilience into our systems by relocalizing our essential needs as much as possible and having technological alternatives that we can fix.

- Use and value diversity

Biodiversity creates healthy ecosystems. Diversity in terms of crops, energy sources, and employment, makes for greater sustainability. Valuing diversity amongst people makes for a more peaceful, equitable society. Conflict and wars are the biggest slayers of sustainable development.

- Use edges and value the marginal

Examples of 'edge' in nature are: where canopy meets clearing in the woodland, inviting in air and sunshine and a profusion of flowers; where sea and river meet land in the fertile interface of estuaries, full of invertebrates, fish and bird life; where the banks of streams meet the water's edge and fertility is built with deposited mud and sand in flood time, giving life to a riot of plant life; where plains and water meet, flooding and capturing alluvial soils.

Edge in nature is all about increasing diversity by the increase of inter-relationship between the elements: earth, air, fire (sun), and water. This phenomenon increases the opportunity for life in all of its marvelous fertility of forms. In human society, the edge is where we have cultural diversity. It is the place where free thinkers and so-called 'alternative' people thrive. where new ideas are allowed to develop and ageless wisdom is given its rightful respect. Edge is suppressed in non-democratic states and countries that demand theological allegiance to one religion.

- Creatively use and respond to change

In nature, there is a process of succession. Bare soil is colonized by weeds that are in turn superseded by brambles. Then pioneers follow; like silver birch, alder and gorse which stabilize the soil. The latter two even fix nitrogen to create an environment that can host slow-growing temperate climate species like oak, beech and yew. But nature is dynamic and succession can be interrupted by browsing animals, storms that fell trees and create clearings or a changing climate that is less hospitable for certain climax giants like oak and beech.

The challenge of a permaculture designer is to understand how all these factors interact with each other in a landscape or on a particular plot of land, and design accordingly. It is no good restoring coppice without fencing out deer, or planting trees if they will shade out the solar panel in a decades' time. Equally well, we need to appreciate how climate change will affect our agriculture, with higher summer temperatures, greater volumes of rain in winter and springtime, and more violent storms with higher wind speeds. Hotter summers may allow more vineyards on the gentle southern slopes of the chalk downland. They may also make English oaks less viable in the south. What then do we plant and how do we design in resilience to our settlements?

With permaculture design, we create the potential for a powerful beneficial relationship with the Earth. We can become stewards for our world whilst still maintaining an openness and humility to accept nature as perhaps our most powerful and wisest of teachers. What a culture we could build if these two perspectives were the bedrock of our civilization. I believe that as we awaken as human beings and our awareness grows, we turn away from designing our own private Eden and engage more fully with the rest of humanity and the biosphere. We cannot build ecological arks on a failing planet. We are part of an inter-dependent ecological system. There can be no 'them' and 'us' in ecology. Permaculture is about low carbon, eco-friendly, even abundant living. It is also an ethically based design system for people who want to not only transform their lives and the lives of the people around them but also to play their part in bringing an ecologically balanced, equitable and kinder world into existence. That is our challenge.

Water

We often consider the carbon footprint of our food, but most of us don't consider the water footprint. Water scarcity is increasing; in a climate-changed world, water stress is becoming more widespread. Rainfall and water availability are likely to become more uncertain (WWF, 2013), with significant consequences for food production.

The world is facing a complex challenge. Population growth, urbanization and rapidly developing economies are driving consumer demand for food. An expanding middle class leads to more people choosing western-style diets. These diets are high in protein, sugar and fat, all of which are expensive in terms of water for food production.

Without more effective management of water usage in food and drink production worldwide, there may be major repercussions; rising food prices, food shortages, pollution, famine, social unrest, and geopolitical instability. It has even been suggested that this could lead to a 'world water war' (Goldenburg, 2014).

Population growth will require 60% more food by 2050 and thus a 19% increase in agricultural water use2. The water consumed in the production of an agricultural or industrial product is termed 'virtual water' (Renault, 2002). Every day a person drinks 2-4 L of water, but they will also consume 2,000-5,000 L of virtual water embedded in their daily food. There is a hidden cost of water in the food we eat.

Dietary choice has a significant impact on water consumption. Calculations of the water consumed in meat production in the US indicate that beef requires 11 times more irrigated water than pork or poultry rearing (Eshel, 2014).

Agriculture is the single biggest user of freshwater, accounting for at least 70% of current water use by humans. However, water scarcity is not the only production issue for food; available new arable land is also limited.

Globally, less than 30% of the water used for irrigation is actually taken up by the crop for transpiration and growth (Wallace, 2000), and in water-scarce areas, this can be as low as 5%. Improving the efficiency of irrigation has huge potential for improving water use, especially in areas where water is scarce.

In the UK, some food and drink companies are already making significant improvements in water consumption, showing that reductions of 20–50% can be achieved through good management and adoption of the best practise (UK Government, 2006).

In the UK, the top five approaches (UK Government, 2013) to water use reduction in food manufacture processes have been identified as:

1. Reuse of cooling water (25%)
2. Fixing water flow and leaks (12%) 3. Automatic shut-off (6%)
4. Control of overflows (6%)
5. Optimising supply pressure (5%)

Box 11. Water and food production.
European sugar beet processing is one of the most water-efficient methods of food production (NFU, 2011).
The industry has made considerable progress to reduce water usage. Sugar beet can withstand drier conditions than many other crops without significantly impacting yields e.g. 95% of sugar beet crops in Europe are rain fed.
Typically 75% of sugar beet is water and this water content is used in sugar production (CIBE, 2003). In the UK over 60% of all the water used in production processes comes from the sugar beet itself22. Water used in sugar production from sugar beet is then treated on-site and either reused for agriculture or discharged into local water sources. Anaerobic digestion of grey water also produces biogas, which can then be used as a fuel for thermal processes (CIBE, 2003). This is a good example of an integrated process developed and implemented through the application of chemical engineering principles.
According to GRACE Communications Foundation, the food we eat makes up two-thirds of our total water consumption. If we really want to preserve clean service water for our future generations, we should not only save water, but also change our eating habits. But how can we eat more water than we drink? We must consider the indirect water usage, i.e. the "virtual water" necessary for the production of specific foods.

The Water-Energy-Food nexus

Water, energy and food are essential for human well-being, poverty reduction and sustainable development. Global projections indicate that demand for freshwater, energy and food will increase significantly over the next decades under the pressure of population growth and mobility, economic development, international trade, urbanization, diversifying diets, cultural and technological changes, and climate change (Hoff, 2011). Agriculture accounts for 70 percent of total global freshwater withdrawals, making it the largest user of water. Water is used for agricultural production, forestry and fishery, along the entire agri-food supply chain, and it is used to produce or transport energy in different forms (FAO, 2011a). At the same time, the food production and supply chain consumes about 30 percent of total energy consumed globally (FAO, 2011b). Energy is required to produce, transport and distribute food as well as to extract, pump, lift, collect, transport and treat water. Cities, industry and other users, too, claim increasingly more water, energy and land resources, and at the same time, face problems of environmental degradation and in some cases, resource scarcity.

The Water-Energy-Food Nexus has emerged as a useful concept to describe and address the complex and interrelated nature of our global resource systems, on which we depend to achieve different social, economic and environmental goals. In practical terms, it presents a conceptual approach to better understand and systematically analyze the interactions between the natural environment and human activities, and to work towards a more coordinated management and use of natural resources across sectors and scales. This can help us to identify and manage trade-offs and to build synergies through our responses, allowing for more integrated and cost-effective planning, decision-making, implementation, monitoring and evaluation.

The water-food-energy nexus is central to sustainable development. Demand for all three is increasing, driven by a rising global population, rapid urbanization, changing diets and economic growth. Agriculture is the largest consumer of the world's freshwater resources, and more than one-quarter of the energy used globally is expended on food production and supply.

Optimal chemical engineering solutions for water use reduction in food processing must also give full consideration to a third component, energy. The water challenge cannot be solved in isolation. An understanding of the water-energy-food nexus (Martin-Nagel, 2012) is essential if we are to address food and water security effectively. Energy is required for food production and also to produce the process water upon which food production depends. Some routes to food-grade water are particularly energy-intensive, eg desalination. Water is also consumed in all forms of power generation.

Agriculture looks set to remain the biggest user of water into the middle of this century. While the shift to biofuels is generally welcomed, their production could demand as much water as fossil fuels. In terms of food, the volume of demand is growing with population expansion, and we are seeing a significant global move away from a mainly starch-based diet to an increasing demand for more water-intensive meat and dairy as incomes grow in many countries.

Efficiency measures along the entire agrifood chain can help save water and energy, such as precision irrigation based on information supplied by water providers, which can motivate farmers to invest in their systems to ensure the best returns from their water investment.

Most of the world's rapidly growing cities are in low-income countries where authorities and utilities can have limited capacity to plan for and control urban expansion and its impacts on water and energy demand.

Consumption can be reduced, and supplies made more reliable, by such practices as using multiple water sources, including rainwater harvesting and wastewater reuse, and only treating water to be ready for its intended use, rather than treating all water to a safe drinking standard. Removing biosolids from wastewater and using them for cooking or heating, for example, can help replace fossil fuels and reduce the amount of processing at the wastewater treatment plant.

Globally, there is sufficient water to produce food for everyone, but food and nutritional insecurity remain widespread. Furthermore, where people have limited or no access to safe water or sanitation, the prevalence of diarrhoeal diseases is a major factor in high child mortality rates, malnourishment and loss of productivity.

In water-scarce regions, there needs to be robust strategies to protect water availability to maintain agricultural production and avoid food price volatility. Advances in genetics and technologies that allow the sustainable intensification of crops, livestock and fish production can help meet demand as efficiently as possible.

Hydroponics

Hydroponicsis a type of horticulture and a subset of hydroculture, which is a method of growing plants, usually crops, without soil, by using mineralnutrientsolutions in an aqueoussolvent. Terrestrial plants may be grown with only their roots exposed to the nutritious liquid, or, in addition, the roots may be physically supported by an inert medium such as perlite, gravel, or other substrates.Despite inert media, roots can cause changes of the rhizospherepH and root exudates can affect the rhizosphere biology.

The nutrients used in hydroponic systems can come from many different sources, including (but not limited to) fish excrement, duckmanure, purchased chemical fertilizers, or artificial nutrient solutions..

Plants commonly grown hydroponically, on inert media, include tomatoes, peppers, cucumbers, strawberries, lettuces, marijuana, and model plants like Arabidopsis thaliana..

Hydroponics offers many advantages, one of them being a decrease in water usage for agriculture. To grow 1 kilogram of tomatoes using intensive farming methods requires 400 liters of water;using hydroponics, 70 liters; and only 20 liters using aeroponics.Since it takes much less water to grow produce, it could be possible in the future for providers in harsh environments with little accessible water to grow their own food.

Although the benefits of hydroponics have sometimes been questioned, there seem to be many advantages in growing without soil. Some hydroponic growers have found they get yields many times greater when they switch from conventional methods. Because hydroponically grown plants dip their roots directly into nutrient-rich solutions, they get what they need much more easily than plants growing in soil, so they need much smaller root systems and can divert more energy into leaf and stem growth. With smaller roots, you can grow more plants in the same area and get more yield from the same amount of ground (which is particularly good news if you're growing in a limited area like a greenhouse or on a balcony or window-ledge inside). Hydroponic plants also grow faster. Many pests are carried in soil, so doing without it generally gives you a more hygienic growing system with fewer problems of disease. Since hydroponics is ideal for indoor growing, you can use it to grow plants all year round. Automated systems controlled by timers and computers make the whole thing a breeze.

It's not all good news; inevitably there are a few drawbacks. One is the cost of all the equipment you need—containers, pumps, lights, nutrients, and so on. Another drawback is the ponic part of hydroponics: there's a certain amount of toil involved. With conventional growing, you can sometimes be quite cavalier about how you treat plants and, if weather and other conditions are on your side, your plants will still thrive. But hydroponics is more scientific and the plants are much more under your control. You need to check them constantly to make sure they're growing in exactly the conditions they need (though automated systems, such as lighting timers, make things quite a bit easier). Another difference (arguably less of a drawback) is that, because hydroponic plants have much smaller root systems, they can't always support themselves very well. Heavy fruiting plants may need quite elaborate forms of support.

Seafood and Sustainability

Increasing attention by consumers to the social and environmental dimensions of the food they eat has generated many different responses, including certification programs, watch lists and local/slow food movements. This article examines the more recent entry of seafood into these consumer social movements. Although a concern with the family farm—as well as the tendency to equate national security with food security—has long connected terrestrial food production with other cultural concerns, fisheries have tended to be regarded more as natural resources. Considering seafood as part of the "food system" would enhance the management of fisheries, while the long engagement in fisheries with co- and adaptive management and the politics of knowledge would enrich the debate in the agri-foods literature.

Making responsible seafood choices is one of the most important ways that you can contribute to healthier oceans. Thankfully, there is growing consumer demand for seafood that is both ethical and sustainable. An increasing number of people want to ensure they are making responsible decisions when it comes to their seafood choices, and more than 80% of global seafood consumers believe it is important for seafood to be protected for future generations. The challenge is that the path to making sustainable seafood choices is not a clear one.

There are many problems associated with the fishing industry, including overfishing, habitat destruction, bycatch, fish fraud, and even slavery. But most importantly, seafood species are being extracted from the oceans faster than wild populations can replenish. Currently, 93% of wild fish populations are considered fully-fished or overfished. Some fishing methods, like trawling, can also cause enormous collateral damage and irreversible harm to ocean habitats. Bycatch, or catching wildlife that is not the target species, is another serious concern. Bycatch, which is commonly discarded, can include other vast amounts of non-commercial fish species, including sea turtles, sharks, seabirds, and marine mammals like dolphins and seals. Fish fraud is another concern facing seafood consumers. In one study, 21% of seafood that was sampled in U.S. stores and restaurants was mislabeled. For example, an item labeled as sea bass, snapper, or caviar might be something entirely different! Finally, parts of the fishing industry are susceptible to slavery and forced labor. While these impacts are daunting to consider, they underscore the importance of making educated choices when it comes to seafood.

Sustainable seafood is seafood that is caught or farmed (also called aquaculture) with minimal environmental and social impacts. When done correctly, sustainable seafood sourcing prevents overfishing, minimizes incidental impacts to other ocean wildlife and habitats, identifies and protects essential fish habitats, and takes into account the social and economic impacts on the communities from which the seafood is sourced.

When considering sustainability, it is important to consider the carbon footprint of seafood. The seafood industry in general has a substantial carbon footprint. Transportation on boats, planes, and delivery trucks, processing and packaging, and refrigeration all contribute to seafood's carbon footprint. When you buy local seafood caught with sustainable methods at markets, the carbon footprint can be greatly reduced. Local seafood has the added benefit of supporting local businesses, and in some places, you can buy the seafood directly from the fishermen who caught it.

Another way to reduce the impact of your seafood choices is to choose seafood species that are lower on the food chain, like oysters and mussels, which tend to be better options for a variety of reasons. One reason is that these animals are a primary food source for other animals, and so they reproduce faster than predatory species like tuna. Other options that are low on the food chain like domestic tilapia and catfish, clams, and sea urchins tend to hit most of the boxes on the sustainability checklist.

Current Sustainable Food Production Frameworks

Food is essential to life. It also forms an important part of our cultural identity, and plays an important role in the economy. People are aware that the food they eat is an important factor affecting their health, but what is less well known is the impact producing and consuming food has on the world's resources. Alongside the cars we drive and the energy we use to heat our houses, the food we produce and consume has a significant impact on the environment through, for example, greenhouse gas emissions, the use of land and water resources, pollution, depletion of phosphorus, and the impact of chemical products such as herbicides and pesticides.

Globally, and in many regions including Europe, food production is exceeding environmental limits or is close to doing so. Nitrogen synthesis exceeds the planetary boundary by a factor of four and phosphorus use has reached the planetary boundary. Land use change and land degradation, and the dependence on fossil energy contribute to about one- fourth of Greenhouse Gas emissions. Agriculture, including fisheries, is the single largest driver of biodiversity loss. Regionally, water extracted by irrigation exceeds the replenishment of the resource.

There are many different views as to what constitutes a 'sustainable' food system, and what falls within the scope of the term 'sustainability'. Strictly speaking, sustainability implies the use of resources at rates that do not exceed the capacity of the Earth to replace them. For food, a sustainable system might be seen as encompassing a range of issues such as security of the supply of food, health, safety, affordability, quality, strong food industry in terms of jobs and growth and, at the same time, environmental sustainability, in terms of issues such as climate change, biodiversity, water and soil quality.

1. Ecosystem Approach to Fisheries and Aquaculture

This publication provides guidance on how to implement the FAO Code of Conduct for Responsible Fisheries (CCRF) using an ecosystem approach to fisheries and aquaculture. The CCRF is a voluntary code covering all aspects of the management and development of fisheries and is designed to ensure that they are developed sustainably without adversely affecting the livelihoods of local communities that share the same resources as the fisheries.

The authors outline the basic principles of the CCRF, describe concrete steps to be taken to use the ecosystem approach effectively, and recommend certain institutional changes and reforms that will be necessary for the Asia-Pacific region if the potential of the ecosystem approach is to be realized.

The most significant reform that is needed to achieve the potential of the ecosystem approach to fisheries and aquaculture is a paradigm shift in policy from one that is production oriented to one that is benefits oriented (social and economic). There is evidence that this is already happening in the region with efforts being made to limit access, reduce the number of fishing vessels and introduce community-based rights systems. Stakeholder participation is essential and existing legal instruments and practices that interact with or impact fisheries may also need to be reconsidered, and adjustments made where necessary. In the future, it may even be necessary to regulate the inter-sectoral interactions and impacts through primary legislation, e.g. laws controlling coastal development.

To promote broader adoption and implementation of the ecosystem approach by member countries, a wide range of regional activities is suggested by the authors and includes a media campaign, the building of fishery alliances among countries and capacity building in fishery agencies.

Ensuring the sustainable development of fisheries is crucial if food security and economic well-being are to be achieved throughout the APFIC region. Hopefully, the ideas included in this publication will help shape the future of fisheries in the region (Staples and Funge-Smith, 2009).

2. "Save and Grow"-the framework program for sustainable crop production intensification

Save and Grow addresses the crop production dimension of sustainable food management. In essence, it calls for "greening" the Green Revolution through an ecosystem approach that draws on nature's contributions to crop growth, such as soil organic matter, water flow regulation, pollination and bio-control of insect pests and diseases. It offers a rich toolkit of relevant, adoptable and adaptable ecosystem-based practices that can help the world's 500 million smallholder farm families to achieve higher productivity, profitability and resource use efficiency, while enhancing natural capital.

This eco-friendly farming often combines traditional knowledge with modern technologies that are adapted to the needs of small-scale producers. It also encourages the use of conservation agriculture, which boosts yields while restoring soil health. It controls insect pests by protecting their natural enemies rather than by spraying crops indiscriminately with pesticides. Through judicious use of mineral fertilizer, it avoids "collateral damage" to water quality. It uses precision irrigation to deliver the right amount of water when and where it is needed (FAO, 2011).

3. Global Agenda for Sustainable Livestock

The Global Agenda for Sustainable Livestock is a multi-stakeholder partnership (MSP) with the vision to enhance the contribution of the livestock sector to sustainable development. It has more than 100 institutional partners constituted in seven stakeholder clusters and nine technical action networks. The Global Agenda engages in policy dialogue, produces tools, shares experiences, makes evidence available and agrees on joint action. It provides an important global platform to demonstrate solutions and best practices in the livestock sector and contributes to the achievement of the sustainable development goals of the UN Agenda 2030.

GASL consists of seven stakeholder clusters: i) public sector, ii) social movements, iii) private sector, iv) donors, v) academia, vi) NGOs, and vii) inter-governmental and multi-lateral organizations. The Clusters assure inclusive participation of society in a manner that is open and voluntary, inclusive and oriented towards consensual change, while being knowledge-based and showing respect for a diversity of views. Each Cluster is represented in a Guiding Group (GG), consisting of 35 members and observers, that provides overall direction to GASL. An Agenda Support Team (AST), which is hosted at FAO headquarters in Rome, and an elected Chair support it. The Chair leads the Guiding Group and MSP and facilitates the provision of overall strategic direction and guidance. The Chair also leads resource mobilization in GASL. Rules and Procedures approved by the Guiding Group form the institutional reference frame. In addition, GASL has nine Action Networks that are thematic technical expert groups, creating evidence, designing available tools and guidelines and enhancing practice change. Action networks focus on different regional and thematic issues regarding sustainability (SDG, 2019):

i) resource use efficiency
ii) grasslands restoration
iii) waste to worth (bio-economy)
iv) silvo-pastoral systems
v) environmental performance (LEAP)
vi) dairy in Asia
vii) antimicrobial resistance
viii) livestock for social development
ix) animal welfare

4. Sustainable Forest Management

Managing forests' sustainably means optimizing their benefits, including timber and contributions to food security, to meet society's needs in a way that conserves and maintains forest ecosystems for the benefit of present and future generations.

Despite the significant progress made towards SFM at the global level, its implementation is highly variable, particularly in the tropics where the capacity to utilize or enforce SFM policies, laws and regulations remains uneven. Furthermore, other land uses such as agriculture are often financially more attractive in the short term compared to forest management, motivating deforestation and land-use changes.

The Food and Agriculture Organization of the United Nations (FAO) helps countries overcome these challenges by providing policy advice, technical support and capacity building through field projects, workshops, and hands-on training. The Organization also helps countries in assessing their forest resources, defining the elements of SFM and monitoring their progress towards it. The FAO helps identify, test and promote innovative, multipurpose forest management approaches and techniques that respond to the need for mitigating and adapting to a changing climate, increased demand for wood and non-wood forest products and services, and threats from fires, pests and natural disasters.

The FAO promotes SFM by working at the international level and through collaborative partnerships to address and help solve regional and global forest-related issues.

5. Global Soil Partnership

The Global Soil Partnership (GSP) is a globally recognized mechanism established in 2012. Their mission is to position soils in the Global Agenda through collective action. Their key objectives are to promote Sustainable Soil Management (SSM) and improve soil governance to guarantee healthy and productive soils, and support the provision of essential ecosystem services towards food security and improved nutrition, climate change adaptation and mitigation, and sustainable development. The GSP is an open, interactive, responsive and voluntary partnership that includes FAO Member countries and GSP partners - Governmental Organizations, Universities, Civil institutions, Research centers, Soil science societies, UN agencies, NGOs, Private companies, Farmer associations, Donors.

6. Climate-Smart Agriculture

Climate-smart agriculture (CSA) is an approach that helps to guide actions needed to transform and reorient agricultural systems to effectively support the development and ensure food security in a changing climate. CSA aims to tackle three main objectives: sustainably increasing agricultural productivity and incomes; adapting and building resilience to climate change; and reducing and/or removing greenhouse gas emissions, where possible.

CSA is an approach for developing agricultural strategies to secure sustainable food security under climate change. CSA provides the means to help stakeholders from local to national and international levels identify agricultural strategies suitable to their local conditions. CSA is one of the 11 Corporate Areas for Resource Mobilization under the FAO's Strategic Objectives. It is in line with FAO's vision for Sustainable Food and Agriculture and supports FAO's goal to make agriculture, forestry and fisheries more productive and more sustainable".

CSA is not a set of practices that can be universally applied, but rather an approach that involves different elements embedded in local contexts. CSA relates to actions both on-farm and beyond the farm, and incorporates technologies, policies, institutions and investment.

Different elements of climate-smart agricultural systems include:

- Management of farms, crops, livestock, aquaculture and capture fisheries to balance near-term food security and livelihoods needs with priorities for adaptation and mitigation.
- Ecosystem and landscape management to conserve ecosystem services that are important for food security, agricultural development, adaptation and mitigation.
- Services for farmers and land managers to enable better management of climate risks/impacts and mitigation actions.
- Changes in the wider food system including demand-side measures and value chain interventions that enhance the benefits of CSA.

7. Coping with Water Scarcity

The report aims to provide a conceptual framework to address food security under conditions of water scarcity in agriculture. It has been prepared by a team of FAO staff and consultants in the framework of the project "Coping with water scarcity – the role of agriculture", and has been discussed at an Expert Consultation meeting organized in FAO, Rome, during the period 14–16 December 2009 on the same subject. It was subsequently edited and revised, taking account of discussions in the Expert Consultation and materials presented to the meeting.

The purpose of the Expert Consultation was to assist FAO to better design its water scarcity program. In particular, the experts were requested to provide recommendations on the range of technical and policy options and associated principles that FAO should promote as part of an agricultural response to water scarcity in member countries.

The document offers views on the conceptual framework on which FAO's water scarcity program should be based, proposes a set of definitions associated with the concept of water scarcity, and indicates the main principles on which FAO should base its action in support to its member countries

Feeding a Hungry Planet

An estimated 820 million people did not have enough to eat in 2018, up from 811 million in the previous year, which is the third year of increase in a row. This underscores the immense challenge of achieving the Sustainable Development Goal of Zero Hunger by 2030.

The pace of progress in halving the number of children who are stunted and in reducing the number of babies born with low birth weight is too slow, which also puts the SDG 2 nutrition targets further out of reach, according to the report.

At the same time, adding to these challenges, overweight and obesity continue to increase in all regions, particularly among school-age children and adults.

The chances of being food insecure are higher for women than men in every continent, with the largest gap in Latin America. Hunger is increasing in many countries where economic growth is lagging, particularly in middle-income countries and those that rely heavily on international primary commodity trade. The annual UN report also found that income inequality is rising in many of the countries where hunger is on the rise, making it even more difficult for the poor, vulnerable or marginalized to cope with economic slowdowns and downturns.

The situation is most alarming in Africa, as the region has the highest rates of hunger in the world that are continuing to slowly but steadily rise in almost all subregions. In Eastern Africa in particular, close to a third of the population (30.8 percent) is undernourished. In addition to climate and conflict, economic slowdowns and downturns are driving the rise. Since 2011, almost half the countries where rising hunger occurred due to economic slowdowns or stagnation were in Africa.

The largest numbers of undernourished people (more than 500 million) live in Asia, mostly in southern Asian countries. Together, Africa and Asia bear the greatest share of all forms of malnutrition, accounting for more than nine out of ten of all stunted children and over nine out of ten of all wasted children worldwide. In southern Asia and sub-Saharan Africa, one child in three is stunted.

In addition to the challenges of stunting and wasting, Asia and Africa are also home to nearly three-quarters of all overweight children worldwide, largely driven by consumption of unhealthy diets.

Conserving water, recycling waste, creating a transparent supply chain, and partnering with environmental groups and each other are just a few of the measures food companies are taking in an effort to promote sustainability while feeding the world.

An increasingly important element of corporate social responsibility (CSR), sustainability has evolved from an expected part of good corporate citizenship to a driver of business strategy and a key decision-making consideration for consumers.

According to research conducted by the International Food Information Council Foundation (IFIC), 59% of consumers surveyed in 2018 said it was important that the foods they purchased and consumed be produced in a sustainable way, up from 50% in 2017 (IFIC, 2018).

After spending five years studying why people crave meat, then analyzing meat sources at the molecular level and working to recreate the texture, taste, and aromas using plant-based ingredients, he debuted the Impossible Burger in 2016. The product quickly gained a following, and Brown scaled up his company, inaugurating a factory in Oakland to produce more than 1 million pounds of plant-based meat per month. Today, the Impossible Burger is available in more than 1,800 restaurants across the United States.

Despite the rapid growth of Impossible Foods, its focus on ecological and conservation concerns continues to take center stage. The company's first sustainability report, released in 2017, noted that the Impossible Burger uses about 75% less water, generates about 87% fewer greenhouse gases, and requires around 95% less land than conventional ground beef from cows. It's produced without hormones, antibiotics, cholesterol, or artificial flavors. The report goes on to state that "widespread adoption of plant-based meats will make it 100% possible to feed the population, provide nourishment and enjoyment, and help preserve the planet for future generations."

There's no question that the popularity of plant-based foods is on the rise. But conscious consumerism doesn't necessarily mean vegan. Finding inventive ways to conserve, reduce, and recycle often requires the melding of different perspectives and areas of expertise. Collaborations between environmental groups and food and ingredient manufacturers are becoming one of the most successful ways to tackle the challenges that accompany a commitment to sustainable food production.

It's clear that older, narrower definitions of sustainability are being overthrown in favor of more all-encompassing approaches that challenge companies to be proactive about finding new opportunities to extend their environmental stewardship and CSR initiatives. But what qualifies as a sustainable food or beverage? It varies. For less engaged consumers, healthy food is seen as inherently more sustainable: fresh, less processed foods—especially organic—are seen as 'better for me, better for the world.' For more engaged consumers, standards are higher. The most sustainable foods are those one has grown oneself, and beyond that, whole foods—preferably domestically produced—that one processes and cooks oneself. For food and ingredient companies, sustainably produced products start with practices that are good for both the company and the consumer.

Box 12. Cacao production.

One of the most visible examples of the importance of focusing on fair trade practices is in cocoa production. Cultivated by millions of small farms in Africa, Asia, and Latin America, cocoa has a far-reaching economic and environmental impact. Ensuring a transparent and ethical supply chain is a central concern to food companies and ingredient suppliers who use and produce it.

Theobroma cacao is, by biological design, an under-story tree in humid tropical forests. Its' aboriginal home consisted of multi-layered forest systems with a diverse arboreal canopy providing shelter from intense sun and rain as well as providing nutritious leaf litter. A multi-layered forest system continues to be the optimum environment for its cultivation as well as, we would like to suggest, for its sustainable and commercial cultivation. Cocoa grown in this type of system holds enormous potential for environmental and cultural conservation in regions under intense pressure from logging, development and conventional, monocrop agriculture.

These cultivation conditions for what we can call "sustainable cocoa" include a multi-tiered, vertically diverse forest canopy with 40 - 70% shade density. This may not be primary growth rainforest but these conditions encourage and support organism diversity to move toward the restoration of a mature forest system. The benefits of this type of system include the attraction of beneficial insects for pest control, breeding opportunities for natural pollinators, and varieties of habitat for diverse populations of flora and fauna. The inputs required for organic cacao cultivation are minimal compared to conventional methods, reducing the expense and risk of using chemicals for the growers.

Because of low revenues, farmers cannot invest in the maintenance of existing trees or in planting new trees on their plantations. Instead of replacing old and diseased cocoa trees, they often use new farmland for cocoa - at the expense of sustainable, ecological and diversified farming. By intensive farming they wear out the soil and are then forced to put even more land under cocoa, sometimes clearing rainforest lands, as well. This has implications not only for the environment, but also for farmers′ income. Up to 40% of the cocoa crop is lost every year due to incorrect maintenance. The use of pesticides and chemical fertilizers is promoted in cocoa cultivation, but a lack of knowledge leads to misuse or overuse of the chemicals. These practices worsen the quality of local water resources and lead to soil contamination. Furthermore, when areas of rainforests are cleared to extend cocoa production biodiversity is further threatened.

In conclusion, instead of increasing farmers′ revenues, current cocoa farming practices can cause lower yields and harm the environment. Such practices are therefore unsustainable.

Overall, cocoa farmers lack training and guidance on sustainable and diversified agriculture to improve productivity, to increase the quality of their cocoa beans and practice agriculture in ways that are not harmful to the environment.

Current Food Production and Distribution Systems are Failing to Feed the World

According to the UN Hunger Report, hunger is the term used to define periods when populations are experiencing severe food insecurity—meaning that they go for entire days without eating due to lack of money, lack of access to food, or other resources.

Here are some widely accepted definitions of key terms:

- Hunger is the distress associated with a lack of food. The threshold for food deprivation, or undernourishment, is fewer than 1,800 calories per day.
- Under nutrition goes beyond calories to signify deficiencies in energy, protein, and/or essential vitamins and minerals.
- Malnutrition refers more broadly to both under nutrition and over nutrition (problems with unbalanced diets).
- Food security relates to food availability, access, and utilization. When a person always has adequate availability and access to enough safe and nutritious food to maintain an active and healthy life, they are considered food secure.

Hunger is strongly interconnected with poverty, and it involves interactions among an array of social, political, demographic, and societal factors. People living in poverty frequently face household food insecurity, use inappropriate care practices, and live in unsafe environments that have low access to quality water, sanitation, and hygiene, and inadequate access or availability to health services and education—all of which contribute to hunger.

Conflict is also a key driver of severe food crises, including famine—a fact officially recognized by the UN Security Council in May 2018 Hunger and under nutrition are much worse when conflicts are prolonged and institutions are weak. The number of conflicts is on the rise, some worsened by climate-related shocks. People and organizations working to combat hunger must take conflict-sensitive approaches, much more so than in the past.

Weather-related events, in part associated with climate change, have also impacted food availability in many countries and thus contributed to the rise of food insecurity. Economic downturns in countries dependent on oil and other primary-commodity export revenues have also affected food availability and decreased people's ability to access food.

The latest available estimates indicate that about 821 million people in the world were undernourished in 2018. One in nine people do not get enough food to be healthy and lead an active life. Hunger and malnutrition are the biggest risks to health worldwide — greater than AIDS, malaria and tuberculosis combined. Considering all people in the world affected by moderate levels of food insecurity together with those who suffer from hunger, it is estimated that over 2 billion people do not have regular access to safe, nutritious and sufficient food, including 8 percent of the population in North America and Europe.

Africa is the region with the highest prevalence of undernourishment, at almost 20 percent. Hunger is also slowly rising in Latin America and the Caribbean, although its prevalence is still below 7 percent. In Asia, Western Asia shows a continuous increase since 2010, with more than 12 percent of its population undernourished.

If there is enough food to feed the entire world, why don't we use it to end world hunger? Many believe the answer to ending world hunger is producing more food, but this misconception derives from the belief that there is a global "food shortage" that results in 12 percent of the global population — more than 800 million people — suffering from malnutrition.

The truth is that there is too much food in too few places; impoverished communities on a local, national and global level simply do not have the access to a consistent food supply. Consider this: a third of food produced in the world is either lost or wasted, and this number equates to more than 1.3 billion tons of food each year. To put this in perspective, food waste in the United States and Europe alone could feed the entire world three times over.

In recent years, initiatives have been made to harness the power of conservation to end world hunger and have led to an increase in governmental participation. For example, just last year France unanimously passed legislation that requires supermarkets to donate unsold food of good quality to charity. Following France's lead, Italy passed similar legislation, and the United Kingdom, Finland, Canada and Chile are also considering implementing such a policy.

Rescuing Leftover Cuisine

To encourage businesses to participate in this growing movement, the Rescuing Leftover Cuisine (RLC) has worked with American businesses to achieve "zero hunger." Founded by Robert Lee, the organization has worked to transport food quickly and efficiently by lowering transportation costs through a strong and active volunteer base.

Since 2015, RLC has grown rapidly and works with large chains like Starbucks and Panera as well as local restaurants. Lee's model, though quite simple, combines youth activism, increased technology and willingness from businesses to participate in his efforts.

Though Lee's campaign is in only eleven cities in the U.S., his model can be used as an example to end world hunger. Lee believes this and has said, "We're eliminating hunger community by community," he says. "Wherever there's food waste, I want people to know there's an alternative to throwing it out."

Sustainable Food Systems

Eliminating food waste is the start of eliminating world hunger. National campaigns like those in France and Italy as well as local efforts like the RLC are making significant impacts in increasing access to food. Similar approaches like the creation of sustainable food systems that lower agricultural and manufacturable food wastes are also part of the effort. On a more individual level, raising awareness on the issue can help families be more conscious of how much food they're wasting each day.

The combination of effective legislation, grassroots campaigns and scientific research is proving effective. Still, there are questions regarding the efficacy of this solution on a global scale. In short, how has decreased food waste helped resolve hunger in developing nations where 98% of undernourished people live?

Box 13. Food Waste campaigns in France and Italy.

France

Five years ago, the French government started showing a strong commitment to tackling the issue of food waste. In 2012, they launched a new law to reduce the amount of organic waste sent to landfills.

Since then, the French Ministry of Ecology, Energy and Sustainable Development has required the private sector to recycle their organic waste if they produce more than 120 tons of it per year. However, this amount has been lowered gradually to include not just supermarkets and agrifood firms, but also companies in the hospitality and food service sector. Failure to comply with the legislation could result in fines of up to €75,0000.

Now, recycling is mandatory for all businesses, including those in the hospitality and foodservice industry, that produce at least 10 tonnes of organic waste per year. It represents roughly 33 kilos per day, which for a restaurant serving 150 meals a day is the equivalent of 50% of all their eateries.

Last year, France became the first country in the world to ban supermarkets from throwing away or destroying unsold food. Instead, it forces them to donate surplus food to charities and food banks. According to the French regulation, large supermarkets are no longer allowed to throw away good quality food approaching its "best-before" date.

France's ban on surplus food being thrown away by supermarkets requires any store larger than 4,305 square feet to sign donation contracts with not-for-profit organizations. Failure to do so could result in fines of up to €75,000, or two years of imprisonment. It makes it easier and faster for the retail industry to give their surplus produce directly to charities and food banks.

Furthermore, all French supermarkets are also banned from destroying food as a way to prevent so-called "dumpster divers" or "freegans" from foraging in garbage bins.

The food waste law, which was adopted unanimously at the French senate, is the result of strong campaigns led by municipal councilor, ArashDerambarsh. He has been designated as the person in charge of persuading French MPs to adopt the regulation after a petition collected more than 200,000 signatures in just four months.

Italy

In 2013, the Environment Ministry launched a National Plan for Food Waste Prevention, and three years later, the government passed a law introducing a series of measures to cut food waste by at least 1 million tons annually, and making it easier to donate unsold food.

According to the survey carried out by Waste Watcher Observatory, among 400 families, Italian households currently throw an average of 84.9 kg of food every year, while the individual wastage would amount to 36.9 kg. Overall, the food waste in the country was estimated as 2.2 tons in 2018.

France became the first country in the world to ban supermarkets from disposing of unsold foods and require them to instead donate the products to charities and food banks. The Italian Parliament has become the second to introduce food waste reform. In contrast to its French counterparts, however, Italy's bill rewards supermarkets for helping reduce food waste instead of punishing them for not doing their part.

Current law requires stores to declare each donation five days in advance, preventing supermarkets from giving away excess. Once the new bill becomes law, markets will only need to submit a document detailing what was given at the end of the month. The donations will go to public authorities and non-profit organizations.

The new legislation also allows markets to donate mislabeled food products if the expiration date and allergy information are properly indicated. A food education program for schools, a national awareness campaign and a take-out system for restaurants will follow within the next three years.

Food Waste

Food waste is a global problem, and the United Nations estimates that around 40 percent of food produced is wasted in developing countries. The problem of food wastage can be attributed to a lack of advanced technology that leads to extreme losses of water and energy every year. To end world hunger, small farmers from poor countries must be supplied with adequate technology, and this empowerment can significantly increase crop yields.

Thankfully, efforts are already being made to accomplish just that. In India, for example, the Promethean Power Systems uses solar power during production to decrease energy waste. In Uganda, biogas is being used as a cooling system, and initiatives from the United States and other industrialized nations are already being implemented in developing countries. The CoolBot, for instance, has transformed post-harvest care, and unified efforts across the world are bringing technology where it is needed the most — thus making a huge difference.

The effort to reduce food waste has been promising, and world hunger has sharply declined in the past decade as a result. This has inspired efforts to not only lower world hunger, but to also eliminate the issue completely. By eliminating food waste, zero hunger is achievable.

Becoming an Agent of Sustainable Change

In most cases, sustainability requires engaging people in profound change, an inner shift in people's values, aspirations and behaviors guided by their mental models as well as an outer shift in processes, strategies and practices. Research by Baan, Long and Pearlman shows that successful sustainability leaders embody nine personal capacities:

1) Being Present
2) Suspension and Letting Go
3) Intention Aligned with Higher Purpose
4) Holding Paradoxes/Ambiguities and Multiple Worldviews
5) Compassion
6) Personal Power
7) Whole System Awareness
8) Whole Self Awareness
9) a Sense of Humour

Today's economy is experiencing serious economic and social problems affecting all citizens of the world, both rich and poor. The earth seems to become insufficient to meet the standards of living that the developed societies expect. The classic marketing approach is seen as the cause of many such problems. It contributed to the emergence of behaviors that should be changed. With its indisputable impact on market development, marketing has a strong influence on degradation, but it can also build positive behaviors of consumers, enterprises, organizations, and entire societies. Understood as a philosophy of action, a way of thinking and doing business, sustainable marketing, which I am interested in, promotes credibility and responsibility, leading to better consumption, better relationships, and more responsible business, thus influencing the creation of a better world.

Sustainable marketing is not just about producing better and cheaper, and refrain from cutting down trees. This is a genuine practical value of doing business, which influences efficiency, inspires creativity, promotes and preserves cooperation. Thanks to balancing the needs of people, the global environment and economic development in the long run, sustainable marketing provides businesses and organizations with faith and strength to create "more" while using less funds and resources. On an operational level, sustainable marketing aims to influence customer behavior and utilize consumer social evolution in order to create positive social change and thus to achieve a new long-term profit. It is also meant to influence what the customer receives - create brands that are part of the commercial and social future. Finally, it is supposed to provide goods and services, through managing in a responsible manner, being open to fair cooperation in marketing communication. As we are at a critical point in history where growing, financial, environmental and security instabilities suggest a need for reorientation of marketing activities and marketing strategies in order to take into account the concept of sustainability as a new strategic imperative. This phenomenon has not yet been comprehensively examined in the context of Marketing Management Science, nor is it sufficiently exposed in the existing literature. The purpose of the paper is to highlight the vital role that marketing plays in achieving behavioral change among customers as well as emphasize the changes in marketing practice that are required to help businesses adopt more sustainable practices.

The author would like to introduce concepts and approaches applied in the field of sustainable consumption and production with an emphasis on preventive strategies to reduce their environmental footprint. The new value represented in some studies is located in introducing a discussion on sustainable marketing and its fundamental importance in the development of contemporary marketing theory. To become thoroughly sustainable in our business activities and in lifestyles, marketing will have much to contribute to during the coming decade. As marketing aims to allow a business to work as efficiently as possible, so sustainable marketing will be well placed to facilitate the transition to more sustainable development and negotiate change between all stakeholders involved in the economic, social and environmental arena.

Sustainable Food Consumption

Contemporary food production and consumption cannot be regarded as sustainable and raises problems with its wide scope involving diverse actors. Moreover, in the face of demographic change and a growing global population, sustainability problems arising from food systems will likely become more serious in the future. For example, agricultural production must deal with the impacts of climate change, increasingly challenging land-use conflicts, and rising health and social costs on both individual and societal levels. The unsustainability of current arrangements arises from the industrialization and globalization of agriculture and food processing, the shift of consumption patterns toward more dietary animal protein, the emergence of modern food styles that entail heavily processed products, the growing gap on a global scale between rich and poor, and the paradoxical lack of food security amid an abundance of food. These factors are attributable to national and international policies and regulations, as well as to prevalent business practices and, in particular, consumers' values and habits. The most effective ways for affluent societies to reduce the environmental impact of their diets are to reduce consumption of meat and dairy products (especially beef), to favor organic fruits and vegetables, and to avoid goods that have been transported by air on both individual and institutional levels (e.g., public procurement, public catering).

Despite considerable progress in the development of sustainability targets and indi- cators worldwide, there is as yet no commonly agreed-upon definition of sustainable food consumption. Perhaps the most encompassing attempt is that introduced by the UK Sustainable Development Commission (2005; 2009), defining "sustainable food and drink" as that which is safe, healthy, and nutritious for consumers in shops, restaurants, schools, hospitals, and so forth; can meet the needs of the less well off at a global scale; provides a viable livelihood for farmers, processors, and retailers whose employees enjoy a safe and hygienic working environment; respects biophysical and environmental limits in its production and processing while reducing energy consumption and improving the wider environment; respects the highest standards of animal health and welfare compatible with the production of affordable food for all sectors of society; and supports rural economies and the diversity of rural culture, in particular by emphasizing local products that minimize food miles. Other researchers have also pointed out that sustainable food styles must fit into people's everyday lifestyles (i.e., must be "feasible," available, affordable, and accessible) and should allow for sociocultural diversity (Eberle et al. 2006). Policies for sustainable food consumption, therefore, should learn from and build on evidence from effective consumer policies (Reisch, 2004).

Food Loss and Food Waste

Food loss and waste reduction should be seen as a means toward achieving other objectives, including improving food security and nutrition, reducing greenhouse gas emissions, lowering pressure on water and land resources and can increase productivity and economic growth. Food loss is the decrease in the quantity or quality of food resulting from decisions and actions by food suppliers in the chain, excluding retailers, food service providers and consumers (SOFA, 2019). Food waste refers to the decrease in the quantity or quality of food resulting from decisions and actions by retailers, food service providers and consumers (SOFA, 2019).

Food waste has become a dangerous habit: buying more than we need at supermarkets, letting fruits and vegetables spoil at home or ordering more than we can eat at restaurants.

Each year, about 1/3 of the food we produce globally is lost or wasted. In developing countries, a large part of this food (40%) is lost at the harvest or processing stage. This is called food loss. In developed countries, this same percentage (40%) is lost at the consumer or retail stage, throwing away food that is not bought at stores or food that is not eaten at home, restaurants and cafeterias. This is called food waste. There is a lot of room for improvement worldwide in relation to food loss and waste. We have formed habits that hurt our world and put extra strain on our natural resources. When we waste food, we waste the labor, money and precious resources (like seeds, water, feed, etc.) that go into making the food, not to mention the resources that go into transporting it. In short, wasting food increases greenhouse gas emissions and contributes to climate change.

But habits can change. Here are some easy things you can do to make not wasting a way of life:

- Start small – Take smaller portions at home or share large dishes at restaurants.
- Leave nothing behind – Keep your leftovers for another meal or use them in a different dish.
- Buy only what you need – Be smart with your shopping. Make a list of what you need and stick to it. Don’t buy more than you can use.
- Don’t be prejudiced - Buy “ugly” or irregularly shaped fruits and vegetables that are just as good but look a little different.
- Check your fridge – Store food between 1 and 5 degrees Celsius for maximum freshness and shelf-life.
- First in, first out – Try using produce that you had bought previously and, when you stack up your fridge and cupboards, move older products to the front and place newer ones in the back.

- Understand dates - "Use by" indicates a date by which the food is safe to be eaten, while "best before" means the food's quality is best prior to that date, but it is still safe for consumption after it. Another date mark that you can find on food packages is the "Sell by" date, which is helpful for stock rotation by manufacturers and retailers.
- Compost – Some food waste might be unavoidable, so why not set up a compost bin!
- Donate the surplus – Sharing is caring.

In a vast world of 7 billion people where all you hear about are our differences, there are some important things that connect us, and one of these is food. Food connects us all. We all need it, depend on it, survive because of it and derive happiness from it.

In fact, food is part of who we are. It's part of our habits and cultures. Hundreds of TV shows, movies and podcasts revolve around the topic of food, and cookbooks always sit among the bestsellers. Food is even part of how we interact with others. Foodies promptly and amply share recipes and dining experiences. And who hasn't posted a photo of their favorite dish on their social media channels? The talk of food is all around us.

So if we love food so much, why do we let so much of it go rotten in our fridges, get left behind at our parties, get thrown out in our stores or dumped off of our plates? One-third of all food produced globally is lost or wasted. We love food, but we don't take care of it. We don't respect it. We all want the respect that Aretha Franklin sang about and to get it we should give it.

Box 14. Ugly Veggies.

It is often said that beauty is in the eye of the beholder. But when it comes to fruit and vegetables, one-third of them never even make it to our grocery store shelves because they are rejected on their way from the farm to the store. While supermarkets have a part to play in this, we must also examine our own consciences. Would we choose the oval-shaped, matte-colored apple or the perfectly rounded shiny one? One of these would definitely make a nicer Instagram photo than the other, but in the end, both would taste equally as good and would satisfy your hunger.

More than 820 million people go hungry every day, while the world as a whole wastes or loses 1/3 of what is produced. In the case of fruits and vegetables, almost half (45%) is wasted. In our world of increasing extreme weather events and changes in climate, saving ugly fruit isn't only an issue of ethics, it is a question of resources. Valuable natural resources go into producing the food we throw away. It takes 13 liters of water to grow 1 tomato and 50 liters of water to produce one orange. It also takes seeds, soil, labor of farmers and even the fuel that goes into transporting the food. All of these resources are lost when the fruit (pun intended) of these labors is lost.

Waste can happen in many ways and at many different parts of the value chain. Let's hear the stories of a carrot, banana and potato.

The carrot's story

A carrot often faces many obstacles before even getting to a supermarket. It must pass the rigid requirements that supermarkets have for their fruits and vegetables. Sometimes, carrots must go through photographic sensor machines that analyze them for aesthetic defects. If they are slightly bent, not bright orange, have a blemish or are broken, they are moved into the pile intended for livestock feed even though they are still fit for human consumption. In total, about 25-30% of carrots, don't make it to the grocery store because of physical or aesthetic defects. At farmers' markets or farm shops, sales of carrots can bypass some of the strict aesthetic standards that supermarkets have, but would you buy an untraditional-looking carrot?

The banana's story

Bananas are a particularly fragile fruit. Even if they make it to the grocery stores or markets, the way they are stacked or the way they have been packaged can damage these softies. Handling bananas roughly can negatively impact their appearance and can cause the fruit to spoil more quickly. Consumers are then not normally keen to buy produce that is over-ripe, soft, discolored or damaged. So, here's a tip for you: If you intend to eat the fruit the same day, buy the ones that are already ripe. If no one chooses them, they will end up in the garbage instead of someone's stomach.

The potato's story

Some food, like potatoes, are lost or wasted when they are processed into other types of food. For example, potatoes destined to be French fries can be wasted on the stage where they are cut into strips. These strips break easily during the processing and packaging stages. The broken pieces are then often thrown out because it is usually cheaper to dispose of them than to reuse them. Other potatoes that get damaged during the loading or transport phase get excluded before even making it to the packaging factory. Developing markets for "sub-standard" produce and products, like broken potatoes, which are still safe for consumption, nutritious and taste good, would be one way to reduce food waste or losses caused by errors in processing, packaging or transporting.

Most of this waste is preventable. Choosing ugly produce, storing fruits and vegetables properly and eating what you already have in the refrigerator before what is newly purchased are just some things that each of us can do in our daily lives to create a zero hunger world and combat climate change. Make room in your heart for ugly fruits so that they fill stomachs and not landfills.

All over the world, holidays mean the return of certain specialties: Olivier salad for New Year's in Russia, Red bean porridge for solstice in Korea, Haleem for Ramadan in India and the Middle East, Mince pies for Christmas in England, Pogača bread for Orthodox Easter, Banana cakes for

Lunar New Year in Vietnam. Whatever the holiday is and wherever in the world it is celebrated, there is usually a type of special food that goes along with it.

The holidays are a great time to celebrate food and to appreciate it. Yet, in some parts of the world, holidays have become synonymous with over-eating and food waste. In general, 1/3 of all the food produced in the world is either lost or wasted. That amounts to 1.3 billion tons per year. And food isn't the only thing that is wasted when it goes uneaten: all of the resources (like seeds, water, feed, etc.), money and labour that go into making it are also lost. While we celebrate the people and ideas that we value, let us make saving food one of them.

Here are six tips on how to avoid and reduce food waste:

- Be realistic – Plan in advance and don't prepare food for 50 people if only 5 are coming to dinner.
- Freeze leftovers or give them to guests – If you do cook too much food, encourage guests to take some home with them. Whatever is left, put it promptly in the freezer for another day. In general, food should not be left at room temperature for longer than two hours.
- Turn the leftover food into the next day's lunch or dinner – There are many creative recipes on the internet for using leftovers. In fact, several dishes like casseroles, goulash, fattoush and panzanella started from the desire not to waste fruits, vegetables or even excess bread. Make sure that you store any leftovers in the refrigerator and use it as soon as possible.
- Finish leftovers before making something new – The instinct to make something different for every meal is quite common, but before cooking a new dish, see if you have anything already prepared and still safe to eat to finish first. Alternatively, turn your old leftovers into a new dish. Just remember to avoid re-heating food and then putting it back into the refrigerator later.
- Allow guests to serve themselves so they can choose as much or as little as they want – As nice as it is to serve people, a host might not accurately gauge how much or how little someone wants to eat, and usually errs on the side of too much. Allowing guests to serve themselves means that they can choose the amount that they would like to eat. (As a food waste tip for guests: when a meal is self-serve, don't take more than you can eat!)

- Donate what you don't use – If you buy extra cans, dried goods or other non-perishable food that can be donated, there are many local charities that happily accept these foods. Check the internet for places near you that accept donations.

At holidays, remember that having enough food is a privilege. Don't waste it!

Interventions Towards Food Sustainability

The agriculture, food, and nutrition security interventions that facilitate sustainable food production and have a positive impact on health or risk factors for health outcomes include: bio-fortification of maize; agriculture interventions that aim to increase household food production; organic farming and diet; reduction in meat production and consumption; and agriculture policies. For genetically modified foods, there was insufficient evidence to determine whether their effect on human health is positive or negative. The impact of the interventions on health inequalities is also unknown, with the exception of taxes and subsidies—food pricing strategies have the potential to reduce health inequalities. Regarding cost-effectiveness, there is evidence to suggest that biofortification of rice and wheat and aflatoxin control strategies in maize and groundnuts are very cost-effective interventions; while taxes and subsidies are also potentially cost-saving; and strategies to combat acidification and ozone have net benefits.

By their very nature, sustainable food production interventions can have positive impacts on more than one dimension of the integrated framework for sustainable development. As well as impacting health (inclusive social development), most interventions had the potential to impact on inclusive economic development and/or environmental sustainability, though these effects were rarely assessed.

In regards to taxes and subsidies, strategy design and implementation must ensure that there is no compensatory purchasing that results in negative impacts on health. This may be achieved by balancing taxes on unhealthy foods with subsidies on healthy foods (Eyles et al., 2012), and by taxing certain food groups (e.g., cakes, cookies, candy, soft drinks) or more processed foods rather than single nutrients (Thow et al., 2010).

For genetically modified foods, further research is needed to determine whether these foods have beneficial or harmful effects on human health. Care needs to be taken to ensure that they are free of conflicts of interest (Diels et al., 2010). Moreover, all studies must be made available to the general public—whether positive or negative— so that a fair impact assessment can be made.

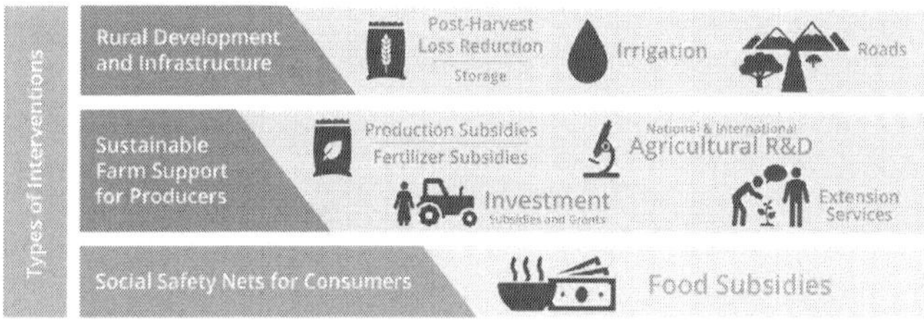

Figure 18. Interventions towards food sustainability.

(https://ceres2030.org/estimating-the-cost/)

What is needed now is the careful implementation of interventions whose impacts are likely to be positive, along with rigorous evaluation. Collaboration across sectors will likely result in greater benefits for all involved. The possible impact on health inequalities needs to be considered and measured in future primary studies (and systematic reviews), as does the impact of interventions and combinations of interventions on all dimensions of sustainable development, and potential adverse impacts. For genetically modified foods, further research is needed to determine whether these foods have beneficial or harmful effects on human health.

Chapter 3 Implications of Sustainable Food Systems

The demand for food will greatly increase due to rising incomes and an additional two or three billion people to feed. Agriculture needs to change to meet that demand. Investing in agriculture is also one of the most effective strategies for achieving critical post-2015 development goals related to poverty and hunger, nutrition and health, education, economic and social growth, peace and security, and preserving the world's environment.

Agriculture is the world's largest use of land, occupying about 38% of the Earth's terrestrial surface (Foley et al., 2011). The agricultural community has had tremendous successes in massively increasing world food production over the past five decades and making food more affordable for the majority of the world's population, despite a doubling in population. Global production of main grains has roughly tripled since 1960, with corresponding decreases in price in most markets (Godfrey et al. 2010). The Green Revolution was a spectacular success credited with saving millions of lives and millions of hectares of natural ecosystems.

The transformation of agriculture over the past 50 years to what we now know as "modern" agriculture took advantage of inexpensive fossil fuels to raise agricultural productivity in many world regions. Technological innovations, investments in infrastructure and supporting policies including subsidies were effective in some regions but others have been left behind, particularly in Sub-Saharan Africa (Fuglie et al., 2012). Yield trends in the past 50 years and current yield gaps vary widely among and within countries (Mueller et al., 2012; Ray et al., 2012).

Contemporary food systems have also exerted undesirable pressure on terrestrial and aquatic ecosystems and they are failing to provide adequate nutrition to billions of people. An estimated 870 million people still lack sufficient caloric intake, while a billion or more suffer from micronutrient deficiencies. Another 1.4 billion suffer from overweight or obesity. Progress in reducing poverty and hunger has slowed down in recent years (FAO, 2012).

ENVIRONMENTAL IMPLICATIONS OF SUSTAINABLE FOOD SYSTEMS

Current methods of food production worldwide must be modified in order to reduce their environmental impact and to support the world's capacity for future food production. Similar to other modern-day activities, the production of food adds to climate change, water scarcity, soil degradation and the destruction of biodiversity. (Foresight, 2011).

It has been estimated that approximately 25% of the total global greenhouse gas emissions are directly caused by crop and animal production and forestry (FAO, 2014). The crop and livestock sectors use about 70% of freshwater resources and, in addition to forestry, take up approximately 60% of the Earth's land surface (FAO, 2013).

The degree of environmental impact caused by food production is linked to where and how food is produced as well as to the local availability of natural resources, including water and soil. Often, there are environmental trade-offs with different methods of food production. Currently a set of principles to determine if one food product is more environmentally sustainable than another is lacking.

Food systems can have major environmental impacts. Food production may, for example, have impacts on land degradation, deforestation, loss of habitats and biodiversity, depletion of natural resources, and contamination of air, soil and waters (IPBES, 2018; Whitmee et al. 2015). For example, food systems account for about one-fourth of anthropogenic greenhouse gas (GHG) emissions, and agricultural production for 70% of global freshwater withdrawals (FAO et al. 2017; Vermeulen et al. 2012). The use of synthetic fertilizers and pesticides in agriculture and the use of hormones in animal husbandry cause chemical pollution of marine and terrestrial ecosystems with contamination of food products and ecosystems that in turn may lead to severe health consequences (Corsolini et al. 2005; Landrigan et al. 2017; UN Water 2016). Preventive antibiotic use in animal husbandry contributes to antibiotic resistance (Tang et al. 2017; WHO 2017). These practices will, in combination with the growing competition for land, water and energy affect the capacity for future sustainable healthy food production (Garnett,2014; Godfray et al, 2010; Whitmee et al, 2015).

Despite the substantial contribution that the promotion of healthy diets can have for enhancing sustainability, so far, it has seldom been examined within the field of sustainability science, as health is often a peripheral topic (Kajikawa et al. 2014). This article discusses some of the key interlinkages between healthy diets and sustainable food systems, and covers both opportunities for and challenges to a shift towards healthy sustainable diets. The article touches on issues closely aligned to sustainable food systems such as food waste reduction, and interactions between food and industrial crop systems, and discusses dietary transitions and emerging innovations in an interlinked health and sustainability perspective.

HEALTH IMPLICATIONS OF SUSTAINABLE FOOD SYSTEMS

Food has the potential to nurture human health and support environmental sustainability. Instead, our food is threatening both. The challenge before us is to provide a growing global population with healthy diets from sustainable food systems. While global food production of calories has generally kept pace with population growth, approximately 800 million people still lack sufficient food, and many more consume low- quality diets that result in micronutrient deficiencies and contribute to an alarming rise in obesity and diet-related non-communicable diseases (NCDs).

With much of the world's population inadequately nourished and many of the environmental systems that regulate the state of the planet pushed beyond safe boundaries by food production, the need for a global transformation of the food system is urgent.

Diets provide an inextricable link between human health and environmental sustainability. The scientific targets for healthy diets and sustainable food systems are integrated into a common framework (i.e. safe operating space for food systems) so that "win-win" diets (both healthy and environmentally sustainable) can be identified. The proposed framework is as follows:

Table 5. Healthy Reference Diet, with possible ranges, for an intake of 2500 Kcal/day.

Food Group	Food subgroup, examples	Reference diet (g/day)	Kcal/ Day[1]	Possible ranges (g/day)	Comments
Whole Grains[2]	Rice, wheat, corn, other	232	811	Total gains 0 to 60% of energy	Mix and amount of grains can vary to maintain isocaloric intake
Tubers/Starchy Vegetables	Potatoes, cassava	50	39	0 to 100	
Vegetables	All vegetables	300		200 to 600	
	Dark green vegetables	100	23		
	Red & orange vegetable	100	30		
	Other vegetables	100	25		
Fruits	All fruit	200	126	100 to 300	
Dairy Foods	Whole milk or derivative equivalents (cheese, etc.)	250	153	0 to 500	
Protein Sources	Beef, lamb	7	15	0 to 14	Exchangeable with Pork
	Pork	7	15	0 to 14	Exchangeable with Beef/lamb
	Chicken, other poultry	29	62	0 to 58	Exchangeable with eggs, fish, or plant protein sources
	Eggs	13	19	0 to 25	
	Fish	28	40	0 to 100	
	Legumes[2]				Legumes, peanuts, tree nuts, seeds, and soy are interchangeable
	Dry beans, lentils & peas	50	172	0 to 100	
	Soy foods	25	112	0 to 50	
	Nuts - Peanuts - Tree nuts	 25 25	 142 149	0 to 75	
Added fats	Plant oils - Palm - Unsaturated oils[3] - Dairy fats (included in milk) - Lard/tallow	 6.8 40 0 5	 60 354 0 36	 0-6.8 20-80 0-5	Some lard or tallow optional where pigs or cattle are consumed
Added sugars	All sweeteners	31	120	0 to 31	

[1] For an individual, an optimal energy intake to maintain a healthy weight will depend on body size and level of physical activity. The processing of foods such as partial hydrogenation of oils, refining of grains, and addition of salt and preservatives can strongly influence their effects on health but is not addressed in this table.
[2] Wheat, rice, dry beans and lentils are dry, raw
[3] Unsaturated oils are 20% each of olive, soybean, rapeseed, sunflower, and peanut oil

Source: Willet et al., 2019

Malnutrition in all forms, ranging from undernourishment to obesity and associated diet-related diseases, is one of the leading causes of death worldwide, while food systems often have major environmental impacts. Rapid global population growth and increases in demands for food and changes in dietary habits create challenges to provide universal access to healthy food without creating negative environmental, economic, and social impacts. This article discusses opportunities for and challenges to sustainable food systems from a human health perspective by making the case for avoiding the transition to unhealthy less sustainable diets (using India as an exemplar), reducing food waste by changing consumer behavior (with examples from Japan), and using innovations and new technologies to reduce the environmental impact of healthy food production.

Nearly, one-third of the global population is currently suffering from some form of malnutrition; ranging from undernourishment (i.e., the main hunger indicator), stunting (short-for-age), micronutrient deficiencies, to overweight and obesity with an associated risk of non-communicable diseases (NCDs), e.g., diabetes, cardiovascular diseases, and cancer. The prevalence of obesity is increasing and currently affects about 13% of the adult global population (FAO et al. 2017). The double burden of malnutrition refers to the coexistence of obesity and undernutrition as a consequence of high energy diets with poor nutritional content, and is a condition of increasing concern in areas with rapid nutrition transitions.

Between 2001 and 2011, the global middle class (depending on how the middle class is defined in different countries) doubled to at least 13% of the global population with most of the growth occurring in Asia and the South Pacific, where now half of the world's middle class is living (Pew , 2017). A global dietary study of 187 countries found that a dietary shift towards unhealthy food items (i.e., red meat, processed meat, and diets high in saturated fat, trans fat, free sugar, and sodium) also occurred in large parts of Asia between 1990 and 2010 (Imamura et al. 2015). This indicates that the transitions from low-income predominantly rural populations, towards middle-income and urban populations, particularly in emerging economies, areoften associated with changing dietary patterns (Satterthwaite et al. 2010). The transitions from traditional diets towards diets that include more unhealthy food items will increase the risk of diet-related NCDs (Iso, 2008).

Dietary choices—the types and amounts of foods that individuals consume—are a major determinant of human health and environmental sustainability. Nine of the top 15 risk factors for global morbidity result from poor dietary quality, while diseases associated with poor dietary quality, including coronary heart disease (CHD), type II diabetes, stroke, and colorectal cancers, account for nearly 40% of global mortality (GBD, 2013; IHME, 2018). Furthermore, agricultural food production emits □30% of global greenhouse gasses (GHGs) (Folay et al., 2011; IPCC, 2014); occupies

~40% of Earth's land (FAO, 2019); causes nutrient pollution that profoundly alters ecosystems and water quality (Vitousek et al., 1997); and accounts for ~70% of Earth's freshwater withdrawals from rivers, reservoirs, and groundwater (Molden, 2007), among other negative environmental effects (Ceballo et al., 2015; Lelieveld, 2015).

As to individual food groups, nuts, minimally processed whole grains, fruits, vegetables, legumes, olive oil, and fish are associated with significantly ($P< 0.05$) reduced mortality and/or reduced risk for one or more diseases. Consuming an additional serving per day of these 7 foods is associated with a significant reduction in risk for 20 of the 34 health endpoints for these foods (7 foods by 5 health outcomes; dose–response data for the association between olive oil and colorectal cancer was not available) and no significant change in disease risk for 14 of 34 health outcomes. We note, however, that because the health benefit of increasing consumption of these 7 foods is often nonlinear, the health benefit of consuming a second additional serving per day is often smaller than the health benefit of consuming the first additional serving per day. While data from the dose–response cohort metaanalysis were available for olive oil but not for other vegetable oils that are similarly high in unsaturated fatty acids and low in saturated fats, other types of health analyses suggest that other such vegetable oils might have health benefits similar to those of olive oil (Jacobsen et al., 2009).

Daily consumption of an additional serving of dairy, egg, and chicken is not significantly associated with disease incidence. However, the inability to fully control for potential dietary confounders (e.g., reduced consumption of red meat when chicken consumption increases) likely influences the observed associations between consumption of chicken and disease risk in particular, and between food consumption and health outcomes more generally (Shi et al., 2015). Similarly, consuming an additional 30 g of refined grain cereals was also not associated with a significant change in disease incidence, although consuming larger amounts of refined grain cereals has been associated with increased risk of diabetes. Substituting whole grain cereals for refined grain cereals has been associated with reductions in disease incidence (Sun et al., 2010; Liu et al., 2000).

Consumption of sugar-sweetened beverages, unprocessed red meat, and processed red meat is consistently associated with increased disease risk. Sugar-sweetened beverage consumption is associated with a significant increase in CHD, type II diabetes, and stroke, but not total mortality or colorectal cancer. Consumption of unprocessed and processed red meat is associated with significant increases in disease risk for all 5 health outcomes examined here. Of all of the foods examined, a daily serving of processed red meat is associated with the largest mean increase in the risk of mortality and incidences of CHD, type II diabetes, and stroke.

SOCIAL IMPLICATIONS OF SUSTAINABLE FOOD SYSTEMS

A movement toward greater equity and sustainability in the food system has generally required advocacy and involvement from civil society. In recent years there has been a new awareness regarding the lack of sustainability of current practices of production, distribution, and consumption of food and a new wave of social activism and citizens' involvement in food politics.

Many observers of the world economy have documented the social and policy changes coinciding with the intensification of global economic ties in recent decades—most of which were relevant, directly or indirectly, to the sustainability of food systems. In the post–World War II era, neo-liberal practices were characterized by the free movement of goods and services across borders, the shrinking role of the state in the economy, the dismantling of social programs, and changes in conditions of work, production, and consumption. From the 1950s to the 1970s, many governments made changes to public policies, programs, and institutions that tried to regulate markets at national levels; these included minimum wage laws, trade unions, environmental protection acts, unemployment insurance, public medicine, marketing boards, supply management, and cooperative structures.

In recent years, organically-grown produce for local markets has become more popular with consumers, and re-localising food chains have been put forward as a strategy for sustainable consumption due to the apparent benefits to local economies, communities, and environments. Notions of 'sustainable consumption' are contested, however, and can represent competing ideologies and perspectives about the environment and society.

The long-term health of a community's food system is an important indicator of its vitality and sustainability. A logical and appropriate way to revitalize a community is by the development of a local food economy. People throughout the World are designing and implementing sustainable, local food systems that are rooted in particular places, aim to be economically viable for farmers and consumers, use ecologically sound production and distribution practices, and enhance social equity and democracy for all members of the community.

In recent years a growing engagement of local public institutions in the promotion of sustainable food production, consumption and distribution systems can be witnessed. On the one hand, the procurement of sustainable (local, organic, fair, etc.) food to institutional marketing channels such as schools, hospitals and company canteens has strongly gained importance. On the other hand, several cities and metropolitan regions have started addressing sustainable food as an integral policy issue, as is expressed in 'urban food strategies' and 'food charters' of cities like London, Amsterdam, Malmö, Rennes, Vancouver or New York. The emergence of urban food policies represents an important rupture with the past, when the governance of agro-food systems was principally seen as a matter of private market forces, in which local public institutions outside the agricultural and rural sector and civic movements had little role to play. Put in this perspective, these developments raise important questions on how to conceptually address and assess the relevance and (potential) impact of new urban and regional strategies in enhancing the transition to sustainable agro-food systems. Also, important questions arise as to what are the most appropriate roles of state agencies, markets and civil society in the governance of sustainable agro-food systems at local and territorial levels.

In recent years important changes have occurred in approaches to the development of food systems, both in terms of the models and paradigms considered appropriate to guide their transition towards social, economic and environmental sustainability and of concrete practices of food system development associated with these. Roughly speaking two different agri-food paradigms and associated food geographies can be distinguished (Wiskerke, 2010):

1) the agro-industrial paradigm
2) the integrated territorial paradigm

The first paradigm is characterized by unfolding agri-food practices building on the principles of the agricultural modernization project which has guided the development of European agro-food systems in the last 30-40 years (Marsden, 2003; Van der Ploeg, 2004), contributing to the realization of a hypermodern food geography The agri-food modernization project, and the prevailing dynamics in food production and consumption patterns it has generated in the past decades, was characterized by three mutually reinforcing processes:

1. the modernization and industrialization of food provisioning systems (production, processing, distribution, sales)
2. the standardization of food production and processing practices and procedures
3. the globalization of food markets (Murdoch et al., 2000).

These processes were strongly supported by the EU's Common Agricultural Policy (CAP) and the World Trade Organization's Agreement on Agriculture (Kirwan et al., forthcoming; Van der Ploeg, 2004).

The agro-industrial paradigm for sustainable food systems, which is currently appearing, envisages an acceleration of the agri-food modernization process of past decades. Advocates share a firm belief in technological solutions for the problems of contemporary food systems, and claim that these may also contribute to an 'ecological modernization' of food production processes. Examples include:

a) upscaling primary production through labour-saving technologies to reduce cost prices
b) food production in agro-industrial parks, e.g. meat production in zero-emission livestock housing systems, aquaculture and fruit & vegetable production in energy-delivering greenhouses (Veldkamp et al., 2009)
c) the creation of healthy (defined as low-fat, low-calorie, vitamin-enriched, etc.) food stuff (i.e. functional food) by processing industries (Scrinis, 2007).

The hypermodern food geography is characterized by the ongoing industrialization and globalization of food production chains and standardization of food production and processing through globally applied regulations and quality assurance schemes (Marsden, 2003). Concomitant the hypermodern food geography is increasingly becoming footloose or placeless (Holl, 2004).

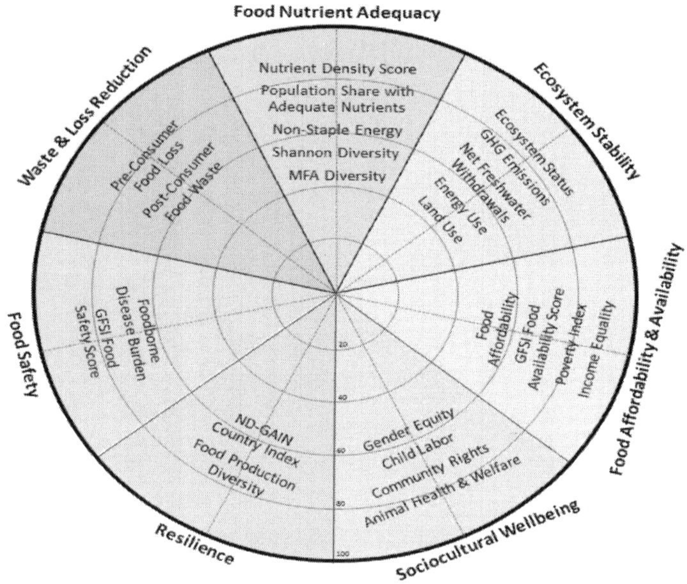

Figure 19. Pillars of Sustainable Food Systems.

Source: Gistafson et al., 2016. Available from: https://www.mdpi.com/2071-1050/8/3/196

The integrated territorial paradigm, which is emerging in recent years, supposes a rupture with the principles and policies of the modernization project. While the modernization project envisaged the reordering and standardization of agri-food systems into a generalized model with universally claimed validity (Renting et al., 2008), the integrated territorial paradigm aims to reinforce the capacity of food systems to valorize specific territorial resources and social relations of proximity. In many respects, territorial embeddedness is a common denominator for the emerging practices of the alternative, local food geography (Watts et al., 2005), i.e. agri-food systems are increasingly embedded in and based upon the distinctive features of the territory, and integrated with other activities such as nature & landscape conservation, tourism, care and education (Renting et al., 2008; Wiskerke et al., forthcoming). In line with this, the integrated, territorial paradigm is built around highly differentiated food quality definitions - reflecting differences in farming systems, networks, cultural traditions, consumer preferences, etc. – this in contrast with the standardized and 'placeless' quality characteristic for the agro-industrial approach (Renting et al., 2003: 394; Sonnino& Marsden, 2006: 186).

Moreover, shorter distances between production and consumption, the closing of regional nutrient cycles and the use of varieties and breeds adapted to local conditions are considered strategic for improving environmental sustainability (Nosi&Zanni, 2004). Basing food production on local physical conditions as well as socio-cultural traditions is also seen as a means to improve consumer trust, by using mechanisms of (geographical or cultural) proximity and reinforced social embeddedness (Renting et al., 2003). Finally, this paradigm differs in its approach to food-related health problems by rather advocating changes in diet composition (fresh and less processed food, reduced meat consumption, etc.) combined with more physical activity (Trichopoulou&Vasilopoulou, 2000).

The two outlined paradigms and associated food geographies resemble oppositional Weberian ideal types, i.e. "one-sided accentuations of one or more points of view according to which concrete individual phenomena ... are arranged into a unified analytical construct" (Slee& Kirwan, forthcoming). Although expressions of both paradigms can be found in practice, a significant part of contemporary food systems is best understood as a hybrid food geography, combining elements of both paradigms and part of ongoing, incomplete transition processes (Slee& Kirwan, forthcoming; Sonnino& Marsden, 2006). Or, to phrase Storper (1997: 255), today's food economy can "be conceived as a complex organisational puzzle, consisting of multiple and partially overlapping worlds in which reflexive collective action unfolds". Nevertheless, based on insights from comparative EU- wide research projects (IMPACT, SUS-CHAIN, COFAMI) in which sustainability performances and potentials of different sustainable food supply chain strategies were assessed, we believe that the integrated, territorial approach holds the most promising answers for the current challenges of European agri-food systems.

What would be Needed for Better Comparison?

Today, food is eaten and appropriated on a daily basis in various different places and contexts, from the caterer at work, the sandwich bar at the train station or the petrol station, to the Chinese take-away, etc. Food consumption thus involves a whole pallet of different home and out-of-home food consumption practices, each with its own dynamics of food provisioning, modes of access and use, and social interactions. Thus, especially in (sub) urban areas a major characteristic of food consumption is differentiation (Cheng et al., 2007) and 'flexibility' in terms of access to various food services and the use of convenient 'food solutions' to fit busy lifestyles, tight budgets, etc. and/or possibly a lack of cooking time and skills. Thus, although our food habits have become more individualistic, fitting our individual ideas, preferences and schedules, those with a big hand in shaping food values, preferences and tastes are likely to be food providers in the catering and food retail industry.

Practice perspectives hold that consumption patterns or behaviors, consumer attitudes and opinions on food are shaped by and within these everyday food practices (Warde, 2005). They indicate how different sets of considerations and priorities may play a role in different contexts, how people engage in food consumption for building and maintaining their lives (Jackson, 2007) and practices may be seen as ways to manage food needs in a manner which is personally convenient (Clarke et al., 2006; Connors et al., 2001). These (everyday) meaningful practices can show a certain pattern of choice, which can be seen to be 'rigid' and routinized to different degrees, but never without agency or the possibility for change.

Taking a more contextual perspective on sustainable development of food consumption is also important because aside from unsustainable food practices, unhealthy food consumption is a major problem in society today. In the Netherlands, obesity is a growing problem among adults and children and less healthy diets are seen especially within the lower socio-economic classes (Jansen et al., 2002; Kreijl, 2004). Here the lack of fresh vegetables and fruit intake and the excess intake of high-energy foods are two major causes of dietary deficiency (Kreijl, 2004; WHO, 2002).8 Studies have indicated that our 'obsogenic' environment promotes unhealthy eating patterns (Dagevos&Munnichs, 2007; Gezondheidsraad, 2003) and that the availability and accessibility of healthy foods is paramount in promoting healthier eating patterns (Brug&Lenthe, 2005; Kamphuis et al., 2006).

Indeed, the great demand for convenient-to-use food products and meal-components both within households and in the food services and catering industry (Bava et al., 2008; Carrigan et al., 2006; Lang, 2004; Regmi et al., 2005), means less food is made with fresh ingredients and often contains too high levels of added salt and sugar (FNLI, 2008; Gezondheidsraad, 2006). Issues of food sustainability and dietary health are connected, although they are not often approached as such. By employing a perspective that takes context into consideration the two are more likely to meet and opportunities might arise to tackle the two together.

Contexts of food consumption bring forth certain consumption patterns and are 'sites' of meaning creation related to food. Thus, people's associations on food sustainability, safety and quality, and definitions of 'good food' are reproduced and/or generated by participation in food practices. A practice perspective offers the inclusion of context in studying consumption and context is seen as both constraining and enabling. It matters not just because of its negative influencing power on our food habits (e.g. 'obsogenic environments'), but also because of its positive influencing power and the possibilities which it opens up for influencing food habit through culinary appreciation and enjoyment.

Suggestions for Modern Sustainable Food Systems

Actions to make food production more sustainable, as identified by the European Commission (European Commission, 2011), include:

1. Efficient use of natural resources
   - Reduction of fossil fuel use and optimization of water for food production
   - Optimization of land utilization and reduction of land conversion for agricultural practices
   - Setup of energy and water efficient food manufacturing facilities
2. Protect the quality of natural resources
   - Limit fertilizers and pesticides to prevent pollution of soils and waters
   - Diminish greenhouse gas emissions
   - Restore organic matter in soils
   - Prioritize biodiversity
3. Protect marine resources
   - Setup sustainable fishing practices
   - Reduce pollution of coastal areas
4. Employ sustainable ingredients for food production
   - Fish products certified by the Marine Stewardship Council (MSC).
   - Palm oil products certified by the Roundtable on Sustainable Palm Oil (RSPO) and similar programs.

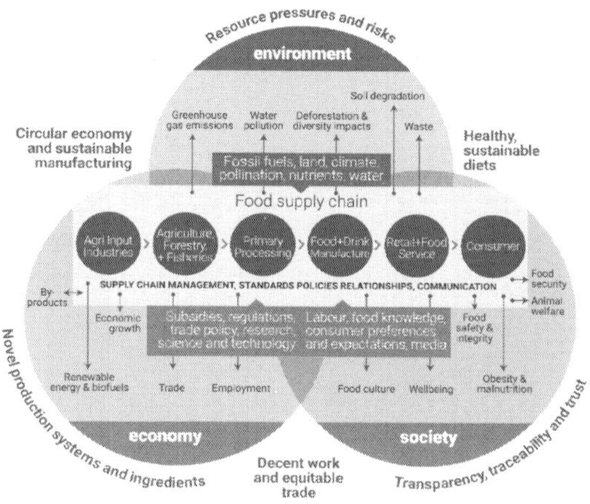

Figure 20. Modern Sustainable Food Systems.

5. Use environmentally efficient food packaging
- Optimize packaging use
- Use materials that have a lower environmental impact
- Recycle materials whenever possible

6. Avoid food waste
- Product reformulation to extend shelf life
- Use of functional packaging to reduce spoilage
- Set up food recycling plants
- Donate excess food to local charities
- Use food scraps as animal feed when appropriate

Although global estimates of waste are reliant so far on a weak evidence base, there is little doubt that the scale is substantial. It has been estimated that as much as 30% of all food grown worldwide may be lost or wasted before and after it reaches the consumer. Some estimates have placed it as high as 50%.

Addressing waste across the entire food chain will be critical in any strategy to feed around eight billion people sustainably and equitably by 2030, and nine billion by 2050. Making the food chain more efficient through waste reduction measures will reduce pressure on resources required for food production, lower greenhouse gas emissions and contribute to other policy agendas, such as cutting the need for further space set aside for landfill, which in turn would reduce greenhouse gas emissions.

Figure 21. Food waste.

Food waste is defined here as edible material intended for human consumption that is discarded, lost, degraded or consumed by pests as food travels from harvest to consumer or, as some put it, 'from field to fork'. This definition includes food that is fit for human consumption but intentionally used as animal feed and spans the entire food supply chain. Whilst such a broad definition is appropriate, it creates problems in gathering accurate estimates of the total global food waste. This is because it is difficult to obtain accurate estimates of all the different kinds of waste. This Report focuses primarily on food waste that is either not used at all or not used productively or sustainably or where the resulting benefits are small compared with the value of the original food product.

Halving the total amount of food waste by 2050 is considered to be a realistic target, in view of the evidence reviewed by this Project. If the current global estimate of 30% waste is assumed, then halving the total could reduce the food required by 2050 by an amount approximately equal to 25% of today's production.

Making waste reduction in the global food system a strategic target would be more easily achieved if there were high-level international political support and an international body willing to act as champion. This is because many diverse organizations would need to come together to tackle the highly variable levels of waste that occur in the food supply chain in different parts of the world. Rising food prices should themselves act as an incentive for waste reduction. However, there are a number of areas where the market alone will not achieve what is possible, and where other interventions will be required. The following are considered particularly promising.

Reducing post-harvest waste, chiefly in low-income countries:

- Deployment of existing knowledge and technology in storage and transport infrastructure. There are many examples of relatively simple and often traditional technologies that can substantially reduce post-harvest waste. One example concerns a Food and Agriculture Organization (FAO) project that provided simple sealed storage drums for grain farmers in Afghanistan and elsewhere.
- Investment in new, appropriate technology to reduce post-harvest waste. An example would be the use of modern scientific advances to produce crops that are less susceptible to pests and spoilage, or better fish-smoking kilns that reduce losses and demand less fuel.
- Infrastructure, financial and market reforms to reduce waste. The use of ICT (mobile phones in particular) could help improve market information and allow producers to make better decisions about timely supply to markets, avoiding or at least reducing seasonal loss.

Reducing waste by consumers, and the food service sector, chiefly in high-income countries:

- Campaigns to highlight the extent of waste and the financial benefits of reducing it. Specific programs aimed at consumers, companies in the food supply chain, and those providing meals in restaurants, firms, hospitals, schools and other institutions.
- The development and use of cheap, mass-produced sensor technology that can detect spoilage in certain perishable foods. This would allow more sophisticated food management than reliance on estimated 'best before' dates in retail food labeling and have the potential to ensure food quality as well as reduce waste.

- Productive recycling of surplus food is deemed as non-premium quality. This could be achieved through redistribution of good-quality surplus food to consumers via schemes such as 'Fareshare' in the UK or the use of food no longer fit for human consumption as animal feed or a source of energy through processes such as anaerobic digestion.
- Spreading best practice. For example, a project in the Netherlands involving modest funding shows how waste in the supply chain from food processing through to the home can be significantly reduced by a combination of education and simple technology.

Chapter 4

Conclusions

As this book is being written, we are experiencing extreme disruptions to the distribution of foods. These disruptions will in effect become more regular due to ongoing climate change conditions. If business continues as usual, it is likely that soon we will pass a point of no-return. What then can be done to reduce the energy gap between food production and food expenditure?

- Increase urban food production
- Increase peri-urban food production
- Reduce the demand for food

Perhaps the most effective measures that developed countries can aim to reduce the environmental impact of their eating habits is to reduce consumption of meat and dairy products (especially beef), to favor organic plant-based produce, and to avoid food products that have been transported by air at both individual and institutional levels (home and public procurement and catering, respectively).

- Eat less
- Waste less
- Shift in eating patterns (plants, fungi, insects)

Far from proposing a recipe to develop a set sustainable food system, we have compiled distinct motivations, measures, ideas, processes and examples that we hope are useful to inspire action towards more sustainable and just food systems for all.

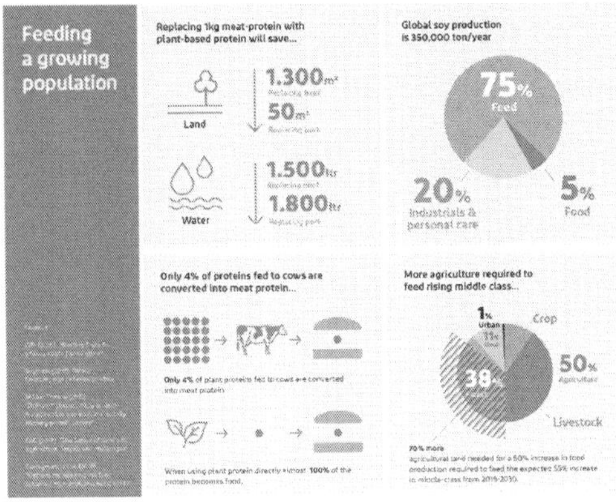

Figure 22. Environmental impact of different food production methods.

Box 15. Edible insects.

Edible insects have always been a part of human diets, but in some societies, there is a degree of distaste for their consumption. Although the majority of edible insects are gathered from forest habitats, innovation in mass-rearing systems has begun in many countries. Insects offer a significant opportunity to merge traditional knowledge and modern science in both developed and developing countries.

Insects are often considered a nuisance to human beings and mere pests for crops and animals. Yet this is far from the truth. Insects provide food at a low environmental cost, contribute positively to livelihoods, and play a fundamental role in nature. However, these benefits are largely unknown to the public. Contrary to popular belief, insects are not merely "famine foods" eaten in times of food scarcity or when purchasing and harvesting "conventional foods" becomes difficult; many people around the world eat insects out of choice, largely because of the palatability of the insects and their established place in local food cultures.

Entomophagy is heavily influenced by cultural and religious practices, and insects are commonly consumed as a food source in many regions of the world. In most Western countries, however, people view entomophagy with disgust and associate eating insects with primitive behavior. This attitude has resulted in the neglect of insects in agricultural research. Despite historical references to the use of insects for food, the topic of entomophagy has only very recently started to capture public attention worldwide.

Edible insects inhabit a large variety of habitats, from aquatic ecosystems and farmed land to forests. Until recently, insects were a seemingly inexhaustible resource obtainable by harvesting from nature. However, some edible insect species are now in peril. A number of anthropogenic factors, such as overharvesting, pollution, wildfire and habitat degradation, have contributed to a decline in many edible insect populations. Climate change will likely affect the distribution and availability of edible insects in ways that arestill relatively unknown. Such efforts contribute to improved habitat conservation.

Box 16. Hypocaloric diets.
The hypocaloric diet is one in which there is a reduction of daily calories or foods with high caloric density usually in order to aid weight loss. The diet varies according to the requirements of each person because everyone has a different metabolism, for example: a growing child, an elite athlete, an elderly person or a pregnant woman. A hypocaloric diet should always be balanced between what is ingested and what energy is expended on daily physical activity.
This diet is based on reduced daily calories total to create an energy deficit that will generate progressive weight loss. The number of calories allowed takes into account the individual's metabolism, their age, sex and existing level of physical activity. For example, a 40-year-old woman with a basal metabolic rate of 1500 who partakes in moderate exercise (activity factor 1, 2) would need about 1900 kcal to maintain her weight. If she intends to lose weight, she would need to follow a diet of approximately 1300 Kcal creating a deficit of 600 Kcal per day. The body ,therefore, consumes stored body fat to make up the 600Kcal and thus leads to progressive weight loss.
It has been shown that every time we eat there is an increase in glucose and an insulin discharge to compensate for that glucose. These sudden discharges of insulin create hunger, so when we eat three large meals a day, binge eat, or simply that we are very hungry, the discharge of insulin is much higher, causing a shorter time between feeling hungry.
However, if we break up the meals into five, we will discharge some insulin, but not an exaggerated amount, and it will help us to maintain ourselves without the peaks and troughs of hunger and satiety.
Meal plans for the hypocaloric diet take the following into consideration:
There should be a robust breakfast, as it is the first meal of the day and it should be abundant and varied (fruits, cereals, some dairy, etc.). By midmorning, we introduce a portion of fruit or some dairy (made from skimmed milk).
Carbohydrates (pastas, rice, potatoes and vegetables) which release energy more slowly are introduced at lunchtime, so their energy is available for consumption later in the day.
The ideal snack is a small portion of seasonal fruit. Dinner should be also light because there are fewer hours for the body to burn fat. In this way, insulin and glucose levels are managed.

4. Diversify Crops

Crop diversification refers to the addition of new crops or cropping systems to agricultural production on a particular farm taking into account the different returns from value-added crops with complementary marketing opportunities. Major driving forces for crop diversification include:

- Increasing income on small farm holdings
- Withstanding price fluctuation
- Mitigating effects of increasing climate variability
- Balancing food demand

- Improving fodder for livestock animals
- Conservation of natural resources
- Minimizing environmental pollution
- Reducing dependence on off-farm inputs
- Depending on crop rotation, decreasing insect pests, diseases and weed problems
- Increasing community food security.

Breeding new and improved crop varieties enhance the resistance of plants to a variety of stresses that could result from climate change. These potential stresses include water and heat stress, water salinity, water stress and the emergence of new pests. Varieties that are developed to resist these conditions will help to ensure that agricultural production can continue and even improve despite uncertainties about the future impacts of climate change. Varieties with improved nutritional content can provide benefits for animals and humans alike, reducing vulnerability to illness and improving overall health.

The aim of crop diversification is to increase crop portfolio so that farmers are not dependent on a single crop to generate their income. When farmers only cultivate one crop type they are exposed to high risks in the event of unforeseen climate events that could severely impact agricultural production, such as the emergence of pests and the sudden onset of frost or drought. Introducing a greater range of varieties also leads to diversification of agricultural production which can increase natural biodiversity, strengthening the ability of the agro-ecosystem to respond to these stresses, reducing the risk of total crop failure and also providing producers with alternative means of generating income. With a diversified plot, the farmer increases his/her chances of dealing with the uncertainty and/or the changes created by climate change. This is because crops will respond to climate scenarios in different ways. Whereas the cold may affect one crop negatively, production in an alternative crop may increase.

A detailed dive into crop diversification science would go far beyond the constraints of this book, but Figure 23 gives a short overview about different methods researched in 193 related publications analyzed in the 'Agronomy for Sustainable Development'(2020).

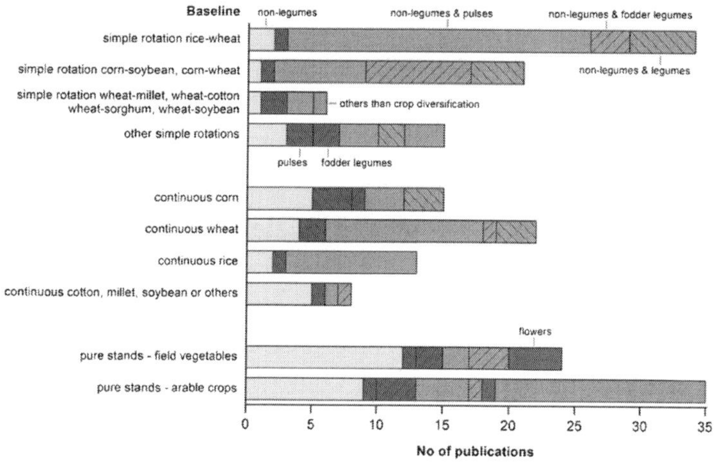

Figure 23. Crop Diversification Approaches in Agricultural Research.

Source: Hofnagel et al ,2020

Box 17. Ancient grains.

There is no fixed definition of 'ancient grains.' All whole grains in the larger sense are "ancient" — they all can trace their roots back to the beginnings of time.

However, according to the Whole Grains Council, ancient grains are generally defined as grains that are largely unchanged over the last several hundred years.

This means that modern wheat (constantly bred and changed) is not an ancient grain, while einkorn, emmer/farro, Kamut®, and spelt would be considered ancient grains in the wheat family. Heirloom varieties of other common grains — such as black barley, red and black rice, blue corn — might also be considered ancient grains. Other grains largely ignored until recently by Western palates (such as sorghum, teff, millet, quinoa, amaranth) would also be widely considered to be ancient grains. Sometimes less common grains, like buckwheat, or wild rice, are also included.

Ancient grains are certainly more nutritious than refined grain products (like white flour or refined crackers). But healthy whole grains need not be exotic. Common foods like brown rice, whole grain pasta, oatmeal, popcorn, and whole wheat bread offer the same whole grain goodness, and often at lower price points.

Many ancient grains thrive with lower levels of pesticides, fertilizers, and irrigation, making them an attractive choice to consumers who choose to shop with their carbon footprint in mind. However, the best way to ensure that you're getting the full spectrum of nutrients available in nature is to eat a variety of different grain foods. After all, each whole grain has something different to offer (from the calcium in teff, to the soluble fiber in barley), making it impossible to play favorites.

While there's not necessarily a fixed and firm list of what qualifies as an ancient grain and what is just a plain whole grain, the list below is a good place to start exploring ancient grains. Here's a list of a few healthy ancient grains to try:

- Amaranth - This gluten-free ancient grain is actually a type of grass and not a grain at all.
- Barley
- Buckwheat - Gluten-free and popular amongst raw foodists since little processing is needed.
- Farro
- Freekeh
- Kamut
- Kaniwa (sometimes called "baby quinoa")
- Millet - Another gluten-free ancient grain that is actually a seed and not a grain.
- Quinoa - Gluten-free seed
- Rye
- Spelt
- Teff - Gluten-free

Like other whole grains, ancient grains can be used whole in pilafs, soups, and salads or paired with chili or stir-fry, like rice, or be ground into flours and used for baking breads, making pancakes or just about anything you would use flour for.

We have two recommendations for the novice. First off, shop for whole ancient grains in the bulk food section of your local natural grocer, and buy only enough for a small portion. You'll spend only a dollar or two, so, if you don't like them, there's little loss (though we always recommend trying a new food twice, prepared two different ways in order to give it a fair trial). And secondly, prepare your grains in a way you know you'll like. For example, if you like risotto, try quinoa "risotto." Like sweet breakfast cereals? Try a quinoa breakfast bowl.

Another safe bet is to try ancient grains in processed foods, such as store-bought bread baked with ancient grains and pastas. Note that some types of bread which claim to be made from ancient grains are made from the whole grains themselves, while others are made from refined flour made from the grains. Refining and processing ancient grains may seem a bit counterproductive, but breads and pasta made with ancient grains offer some nutritional benefit over those made with regular or refined white wheat flour. Read the labels of your purchases carefully if this is important to you.

5. Consider the Role of Water Management

Agricultural water management (AWM) seeks to use water in a way that provides crops and animals the amount of water they need, enhances productivity, and conserves natural resources for the benefit of downstream users and ecosystem services.

Although AWM includes irrigation, it is not simply about applying water. It includes soil, land, and ecosystem conservation practices, such as drainage and watershed management; fisheries management; and technologies for lifting, storing, and conveying water. Traditional AWM was concerned with improving the efficiency of water use in large-scale irrigation schemes in which the objective was to control, not manage, water. As larger numbers of farmers are investing in small-scale irrigation systems, and regulation is either absent or uncoordinated, there is a need for improved practices. AWM has the potential to improve incomes and food security for poor farmers in priority countries.

The FAO forecasts that by 2050 global water requirements for agriculture will increase by 50 percent to meet the increased food demands of a growing population. Global freshwater is becoming increasingly scarce, due to improper management, indiscriminate use and a changing climate. Water scarcity and quality problems in many parts of the world are a serious challenge to future food security and environmental sustainability.

To ensure food security and sustainable water management for agriculture, there is an urgent need to produce more crops per drop of water used in the agricultural sector and hence ensure that water use efficiency is increased without negative impacts on downstream water quantity and quality.

Improvements in the handling of water resources must be built on an integrated approach to soil-water-plant-nutrient management. This should include optimizing irrigation scheduling and more efficient irrigation systems, such as drip irrigation. Soil fertility needs to be improved to ensure that crop growth is not limited by nutrient or physical constraints and every drop of water can be fully utilized for growth. Efficient water uptake by crops can be achieved through demand-based irrigation scheduling that takes account of different crop's water needs, growth stages and the prevailing environmental conditions.

Agricultural water use efficiency can be improved by minimizing soil evaporation losses relative to plant transpiration in the field. The ability to quantify soil evaporation and plant transpiration provides information on irrigation amounts for specific crop types and growth stages, which play key roles in the conservation and management of water.

6. Education of Kids in Food Production and Processing

Healthy nutrition interventions need to occur early in childhood and adolescence in order to prevent or reverse the adverse health effects of overweight and poor eating habits. Childhood and adolescence is a critical period for diets of high nutritional quality as the physiological need for nutrients is high relative to energy needs. In addition, many core eating habits and behavioral patterns are developed that may persist throughout adulthood. Schools can provide an important opportunity for prevention, because they provide the most effective method of reaching large numbers of people, including youth, school staff, families and community members. Healthy food and improved nutrition should be a high priority on every school agenda because of the positive effect on child well-being, and subsequent enhanced learning ability and academic performance. A single European school food and nutrition policy cannot be formulated due to wide cross-country variation among schooling systems. It is therefore essential for each country, authority or school to decide which of the suggestions for school nutrition and food policy are most appropriate and applicable to their circumstances.

A new tool to help get kids started learning about the food production process from farm to fork is an educational curriculum developed by the Alliance to Feed the Future called "Lunchbox Lessons: Professor G.U. Eatwell and the Journey from Farm to Fork." The curriculum includes lessons about food and agricultural production for kindergarten through 8th-grade students and includes interactive activities, food-focused worksheets, and hands-on assignments to do alone or with classmates or parents. While the kids are learning where their food comes from and about the farmers and other producers who work hard to provide safe, healthful, and convenient options, they are also using their math, science and other core skills to complete the activities, helping teachers meet learning requirements while introducing an important and often overlooked topic to students. Lesson topics include: Where Food Comes From, Food Processing, Eating Balanced Meals, Food Safety, Portion Size, Reading Labels and Energy Balance.

In order to design and implement a school food and nutrition policy, it is important to unite all the different stakeholders. Efforts will be more effective when undertaken by a core action group representative of the broader school community (Kubik et al., 2003). The group should consist of representatives of teachers, parents, pupils, caterers, local retailers as well as health professionals and representatives from the school's governing body. Following a baseline assessment of the current food and nutrition situation, the core action group should develop a food and nutrition policy and action plan specific to the school. The action plan needs to identify specific goals and a strategy for achieving them. The recommendations outlined above, for children of preschool and school age could prove useful tools. The overall policy document should aim to ensure that all direct and indirect nutritional messages in the school are coherent and consistent, including those directed at the curriculum, the school environment, the parents and the local community.

The curriculum needs to cover several broad categories of nutrition, food and eating (Dixey et al., 1999) and pupils need to acquire life skills specific to healthy nutrition (WHO, 2003b). The school environment can be improved by providing healthy meals, breakfast clubs, subscription schemes for fruit, vegetables and milk, healthy options in vending machines and snack bars and water. The establishment of a school health service can also contribute to a healthy environment. To improve children's nutritional behavior patterns and knowledge, the community must also be involved in health promotion. The best way to achieve community participation is to collaborate with different sectors and stakeholders. Parents and caregivers are important stakeholders and need to be involved if school-based initiatives are to be sustainable and have a lasting effect on pupils' health. Other community stakeholders of importance include local farmers, retailers and media.

The Current Food System is not Sustainable

Food production is a resource-intensive activity with profound impacts on the environment. It consumes large amounts of natural resources such as water and energy, results in the loss of biodiversity, and contributes to climate change. Food production is responsible for 21-37% of greenhouse gas emissions (Mbowet al. 2019). Despite the overall level of economic prosperity in Europe, access to safe and nutritious food is still problematic for parts of the population. Obesity and diabetes – often related to unhealthy food offerings and poor dietary choices – have become a major public health issue in the EU, with additional negative effects on economic productivity.

Farming and fishing communities sometimes struggle to earn a living, and profit margins are very narrow in parts of the food network.

The food system is already undergoing major transformations that will affect sustainability. The global population is growing: it is expected that there will be around 10 billion people on the planet by 2100. Climate change will affect production, processing, distribution and storage of food. The current European food system is deeply intertwined with global food systems, and because of this globalization it is also affected by geopolitical instabilities, including protectionist trade barriers and volatility of the energy market (STOA 2013; WRR 2016; JRC 2016; SAPEA 2020a: 2.2).

Technological and social innovation has an impact on the food system (SAPEA 2020a: 6), as it can alter power relationships, feedback mechanisms and interactions between subsystems, thus causing the food system to change and evolve. Examples are the use of renewable energy, gene editing through CRISPR technology, further development of aquaculture and new processing technologies for the stabilization of 'fresh' food products. The use of digital technologies changes the interactions between participants in the food system and enables precision farming (STOA 2013; EASAC 2017; SAPEA 2020a: 6.5).

Although there are different views on the exact type of actions and approaches to be taken, there is a broad consensus that a synergistic combination of policies and actions is required (SAM 2019), which:

- promote sustainable intensification and/or scale-up agro-ecological approaches: increasing or maintaining yields and efficiency, while decreasing environmental burden (on biodiversity, soils, water and air);
- reduce food loss and waste, while encouraging the reuse and recycling of unavoidable food waste;
- stimulate dietary changes towards healthier, less resource-intensive (i.e. more plant-based) diets;
- improve the resilience and robustness of the food system in particular by diversification, to cope with shocks from geopolitical developments and to adapt to the effects of climate change
- increase the accountability and stewardship of producers and consumers on the environmental, economic, social and public health effects of the food system through, among others, participatory policy development and monitoring, increasing

transparency, training/education and improving labeling to better inform consumer choices (ibid).

For most people involved in the current food system, 'food' is considered predominantly 'a tradable good', the value of which is determined by its market price. In other words, the current food system is dominated by a 'framing' of food as a commodity (SAPEA 2020a: 3.2). This framing refers to 'citizens' as just 'consumers', while people are obviously not just individuals who act on a market (SAPEA 2020a: 6.5). The current system's goals are aligned to this framing: maximizing food production – in particular calories-rich food – while minimizing costs. It is clear that feeding people healthily is just a subordinate goal in this framing, and that viewing food mainly as a commodity is not compatible with a sustainability focus. A transformation to a sustainable food system, therefore, requires a framing that puts sustainability at its centre, to view food more as a common good (SAPEA 2020a: 3.2).

Reframing food in a way that clearly supports sustainability sends a clear signal to all involved in the food system. It offers an integrated narrative, a coherent, evidence- based framework for policy interventions (SAPEA 2020a: 3.2), and a clear direction in international negotiations and when developing or revising policies and legislation, such as competition and trade law. It defines the overarching goal while leaving space for diversity, context-adapted action, experimentation, learning and 'reflexivity'.

A sustainable food system is one that contributes to all three pillars of sustainability – environmental, economic and social – in a balanced manner, and requires the system to be 'just' (fair). To achieve such a system for the EU, the central goal of all relevant policy assessment and development must be to ensure food sustainability in all three pillars.

Food and agriculture stand today at a crossroad. Major improvements in agricultural productivity have been recorded over recent decades to satisfy the food demand of a growing global population. But progress has often come with social and environmental costs, including water scarcity, soil degradation, ecosystem stress, biodiversity loss, decreasing fish stocks and forest cover, and high levels of greenhouse gas emissions. The productive potential of our natural resources base has been damaged in many places around the globe, compromising the future fertility of the planet.

In addition to the FAO's 5 Principles of Sustainable Food and Agriculture, 20 actions, each describing approaches, practices, policies and tools that interlink multiple SDGs, integrate the three dimensions of sustainable development – economic growth, social inclusion and environmental protection – and involve participation and partnerships among different actors have been prioritized. Context-specific but universally relevant, the actions are designed to support countries in selecting and prioritizing resources to accelerate progress. They identify sectoral synergies that can catalyze achievement of national objectives and deliver results across multiple goals and targets of the 2030 Agenda:

- Facilitate access to productive resources, finance and services
- Connect smallholders to markets
- Encourage the diversification of production and income
- Build producers' knowledge and develop their capacities
- Enhance soil health and restore land
- Protect water and manage scarcity
- Mainstream biodiversity conservation and protect ecosystem functions
- Reduce losses, encourage reuse and recycle, and promote sustainable consumption
- Empower people and fight inequalities
- Promote secure tenure rights
- Use social protection tools to enhance productivity and income
- Improve nutrition and promote balanced diets
- Prevent and protect against shocks: enhance resilience
- Prepare for and respond to shocks
- Address and adapt to climate change
- Strengthen ecosystem resilience
- Enhance policy dialogue and coordination
- Strengthen innovation systems
- Adapt and improve investment and finance
- Strengthen the enabling environment and reform the institutional framework

Improving productivity is key to transforming the livelihoods of hundreds of millions of people across the globe. Yet many smallholder family farmers continue to lack access to resources and services. Without extensive rural infrastructure, the world's chief food producers are hindered from fully participating in the local economy, debilitated in pursuing entrepreneurial activity and limited in hopes of raising their income. Stuck in a vicious cycle of poverty, they are vulnerable to climatic shocks and often pushed into short-term practices that compromise natural resources.

Creating the conditions for inclusive rural transformation requires investing in basic infrastructure: roads, markets, land and water transportation, telecommunications and storage capacity. It means providing greater access to land, resources, services, finance, technologies and modern tools to generate energy.

- Enhancing productivity can be achieved by providing small-scale farmers with access to affordable, quality seeds and planting materials of suitable crop varieties.
- Bringing rural youth back into agriculture can be promoted by investing in mechanization and advanced technologies in rural locations. This has the potential to increase market-oriented and profitable farming. Greater income and opportunities in rural areas address the issue of youth migration.
- Reducing a community's reliance on distant markets, intermediaries and food price fluctuations can be met by decentralizing access to resources, finance and technology. Local food systems will be strengthened while higher value and certified products can be sent to larger markets.
- Directing resources to rural areas promises benefits that go beyond the countryside, rewarding the lives of a whole population and the growth of a nation. As the rural landscape transforms, both on-farm and off-farm economic activity can thrive, with schools, health centers and social services springing up to sustain new communities.

There is widespread consensus that going forward, farmers must produce more food per unit of land, water, and agrochemicals. They will also have to do this while ensuring the provision of various critical ecosystem services. These expectations pose quite a challenge and the outcome depends considerably on the response from millions of mostly small and medium farmers. Yet, civilization's great advances often occur in the face of challenges and when a new paradigm is explored. Marconi's radio made telegraphs obsolete and motor vehicles made the idea of faster animal-drawn carriages unnecessary. Similarly, the supply-oriented paradigm of "more" is in itself clearly inadequate to meet the challenges that we face. In fact, our supply orientation is so outdated and unresponsive to our current needs that it is causing its own problems, particularly for our environment and natural resources. We have a pressing need for new paradigms from which to create the policies and structures that reduce the formidable environmental impacts and consider the social consequences of our evolving agri-food systems. Rather than simply "more" production, we must also consider what would be "better" production and better food systems.

It is not easy in our current economic system to combine the goals of more food, better environment, and reduced poverty, particularly where the private sector has few incentives to provide public benefits. Visionary companies are important but they are not enough. Without strong policy support, even strong managers are less likely to risk short-term gains or market share for long-range benefits.

There are many who advocate a profound re-thinking of our current models and, to better serve our coming needs, would re-imagine and transform the world's major agriculture and food systems, not just modify them incrementally. Recent decades have seen such re-imagining result in radical and world-changing innovations in every field from politics (social network media) to healthcare (nanotech-based diagnostics and drugs) and communication (mobile telephony).

Both food security and environmental benefits, especially in developing countries, will continue to depend upon increased and more secure production among small and medium farmers. And they have proven that they can do it. In parts of peri-urban China, the yields of food crops on small parcels of land (less than one hectare) provide not only diversified subsistence for the household but also substantial supplies of marketable produce as well — all without excessive agrochemical use. Even where markets are lacking in urban areas, such as Havana and Dar el Salaam, for example, a substantial percentage of the cities' total fresh food comes from very small intensely farmed urban plots within both cities. So, farm-scale itself is less the problem than the ability to cooperate and get access to necessary resources such as knowledge, financing, markets, and inputs.

Agriculture policy and investment will be smarter to focus on improved human health and access to nutrition, and not only on increasing food supply. We are simultaneously faced with record numbers of malnourished people and an explosion of obesity and diet–related diseases. Since food crises and malnourishment occur even in countries that have adequate production and are net exporters, access to nutrition is a vital issue. Yet, the consistent failure of structural mechanisms to shift food from abundant sources to areas of need reflects both persistent market imperfections and policy failures.

It makes sense not to completely rely on them for all the solutions to this complex problem. If food security is also perceived as a national security issue, then it is smart to have balanced policies that — while continuing to refine and improve the trade regimes and market delivery systems — also stimulate more localized resiliency and self-provision of at least some foods. They will also need more training, information, and credit. If done with care for environmental and social concerns, localized systems can also offer an opportunity to improve rather than having marginal groups rely solely on purchasing and markets. Local well-being can befostered by greater crop and nutrition diversity.

Agriculture will become a central feature in the management of healthy ecosystems and multifunctionality will become a key consideration as we evolve beyond just 'yield per hectare' to broader working definitions of 'productivity' in agricultural landscapes that encompass valued ecosystem services such as water infiltration, carbon sequestration, and conservation of biodiversity.

Invest in water-conscious agricultural systems. Water's role in agriculture is pivotal, particularly to generate the necessary increases in productivity. There is complete agreement that many freshwater sources are in decline and agriculture is increasingly competing for water resources while water quality is also deteriorating in many parts of the world. The adoption of conservation tillage, modern genetics (not necessarily GMOs) and mechanical or drip irrigation can further increase the amount of 'crop per drop'. Policies that support the concept of multifunctional agriculture can contribute to water quality at the landscape level and remedy contamination with improved management of erosion and of nutrient or biocide applications. Fair allocation and sometimes pricing of scarce water resources can encourage increased efficiency by all users.

To conserve our remaining biodiversity, the best option is to focus on rehabilitating agricultural and pastoral areas that have been eroded and degraded, rather than converting new lands since the most suitable new land is a repository for important biodiversity or otherwise fragile. Soil health determines the productivity and resilience of agriculture and, along with valuable soil organic matter, soil health is in decline in many agricultural areas.

Climate-smart production systems will be vital for necessary adaptation. Agriculture both contributes to climate change (GHG emissions mostly via livestock, deforestation, and fertilizers) and is also in turn affected by the shifts in climate. Impacted areas will need to rely on food from healthy regional and international markets. At the same time, food production must adapt and become more resilient. Even where agricultural conditions could benefit from climate change (i.e., more rain in semi-arid areas or higher temperatures in cold regions) the near-term benefits are still likely to be very limited as farmers adapt to new conditions, soils, and cultivation methods. This will require considerable investment in more adaptable crop varieties and expanding farmer training in appropriate methods. Considerable opportunities exist for improving indigenous crops, many of which are already adapted to harsh environments and resistant to disease.

Technology matters most if it is affordable and if it is appropriate to scale and conditions. Developing countries are littered with decades of failed projects that do not take that into account. Technologies need to become increasingly democratized and more widely available in low-cost forms to small and medium producers. From the re-discovery and re-application of integrated indigenous systems to new scientific breakthroughs we already have many useful tools and technological resources that need to be made more available to small and medium farmers. These include:

- improved breeding for new traits
- climate-resilient agricultural systems, such as precision farming and remote field sensing that more efficiently utilize irrigation and inputs, sequester carbon and reduce GHG emissions.

Technology can facilitate the sort of swift adaptability that will be increasingly necessary as climate change and other pressures mount. Information and communications technology is enabling innovation to both reach users in all but the most remote areas with information and methods and also emerge from them in the form of novel practices. Creating more local capacity to access and use very low-cost information systems is an area of broad consensus. Globally- integrated monitoring systems can now produce timely public information with forecasts of food sufficiency in every country around the world.

What the Future Holds

ROBOTICS AND ITS ROLE IN FOOD PRODUCTION

Food manufacturing has grown into rather complex processes involving preparing, cooking, sorting, packaging and palletizing. Industrial robots are increasingly being integrated in order to save time and space, as well as improving cleanliness and safety.

Food manufacturing robots are commonly used in the dispensing, feed placement, cutting, packaging or casing of food, pick-and-placing products into containers, and sorting. Newer developments also allow for order picking, where an employee or customer is able to place an order electronically, and the food robot automatically fills that specific order.

For the packaging of food items, where speed, consistency or high levels of repetition are concerned, the food robots almost always win over humans in terms of efficiency. Robots are equipped with intelligent vision systems allowing the very specific placement of products on a belt to be done with incredible accuracy. Vision system robots are also utilized in sorting by color, shape or size.

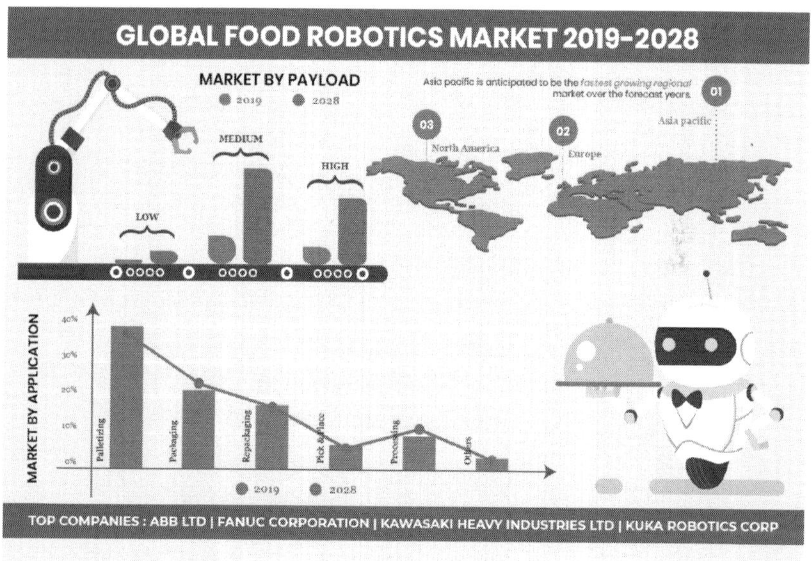

Figure 24. Global Food Robotics Market 2019-2028.

RobotWorx integrates industrial robots into many manufacturing processes, including food. The type of application and requirements such as payload, work envelope, speed, accuracy, and whether vision controls are needed, determine which one is right for you. If your process requires a cleanroom environment, RobotWorx carries robots that meet cleanroom specifications as well.

- Dispensing Robots
- Pick and Place Robots
- Palletizing Robots
- Sorting iRVision Robots
- Order Picking Robots
- Clean Room Robots

There has also been further development in the grippers and vacuum tools used by these robots. The airflow vacuum tool is ideal for handling goods with damageable surfaces because it can pick up products without touching them. The suction cup is ideal for handling many kinds of products, especially those with an uneven surface such as biscuits and frozen pizzas. Using pressure difference, the vacuum gripper holds the product by using, which allows for fast pick up. Finger grippers are best used for products that cannot be handled by suction, such as cakes with loose particles on top. All gripper and suction tools should be easy to clean, change over and made from materials suitable for the application.

An agricultural robot is a robot that is used for specific agricultural purposes. The main application with the agricultural industry would be regarded within the harvesting stage, monitoring the environment, and soil analysis.

Robotics business review explains that advanced robotic systems will take care of and harvest plants, as well as carry out on-farm data collection, increasing crop yields.

Agricultural robots, sometimes known as agribots, are seen as one of the key trends that will deeply influence agriculture.

BIG DATA AND ITS ROLE IN FOOD PRODUCTION

With their ability to collect data, agriculturally used robots play into the other arguably biggest trend of technology-based evolution. Just like any other branch, the food industry in recent years has been heavily impacted by the frontrunner of the digital revolution: “Big Data” - the science of collecting and analyzing massive data amounts in order to gain insights for business relevant decision making. Nowadays this increasing use of data-analytic-tools is paramount for competitive ("informed") decision making in developed countries not only in food production and processing but also in its distribution. Among the many different use-cases of Big Data along the food-supply-chain, at this point we shall focus on relevant cases that contribute to the reduction of waste as well as the broader challenge of sustainable and secure food supply, therefore neglecting data-driven approaches to bolster the food industry firms individually by giving them critical decision-making insights when it comes to the areas of marketing, pricing, product promotion and improvement of customer loyalty.

Benefits and use-cases of Big Data in the food industry:

- Demand forecasting

As the king of all perishable products, food can benefit from advanced insights into demand and supply like no other. Precise predictions about demands for specific food items can nowadays easily be derived with the right data and have been proven to eliminate huge chunks of food waste due to consistent overproduction.

- The power of data analysis in food logistics

Timing is everything - especially in the food industry. Food loss due to timing issues during the transport from producer to processor to distributor all the way to the plate and finally the mouth can nowadays be mitigated with the help of data science. Courier, logistics and delivery service providers currently have advanced technologies at their disposal that enable them to monitor elements such as traffic and routes, weather, fuel, distance and even climate changes during transport. In combination with new artificial intelligence technologies such as Deep Learning a comprehension of said data is facilitated in a way that grants an immense reduction of delivery-related food supply issues. This gains even more importance, when it comes to the cold supply chain during transportation that involves various temperature-sensitive products which require highly suitable and precise environmental conditions and can be tarnished in case of any variations.

Examples for companies that internalize or outsource these Data-Science-Services in order to monitor data about product status, environmental conditions during transportation and other variables are FreshDirect or Blue Apron. The low entry thresholds and advances in data-processing are very likely to increase the number of use-cases in the future significantly.

- Sentiment Analysis

The increasing use of Social Media provides opportunities for data-scientists to gain insights on the general public's opinions or sentiments about specific topics via automated text analysis. The use of such sentiment analysis by individual businesses in order to drive sales activities shall be neglected in this context. The opportunity to analyze consumer attitudes towards sustainable food consumption on the other hand can be useful on a macroeconomic level in the attempt to intensify sustainability research and exert influence on said consumer attitudes (Jantke et al., 2016).

- Quality Control

Big Data also opens new opportunities in biochemical research. Fields such as metagenomics, ergo the extraction, sequencing and analysis of genetic material, are accelerated by the advances in data-science. The complex combinations of microbiological factors that determine food spoilage can therefore be monitored and processed precisely leading to a decrease in spoilage. Such big data applications in food safety and microbial spoilage foster enormous potential since only a small amount of the relevant data generated and available in food science is currently used. A comprehensive multidisciplinary approach across industry, government, and academia to develop the infrastructure to facilitate the application of big data in food science will be needed to unleash the full potential of Big Data in this context.

This path presents challenges ranging from rather mundane tasks, such as switching from paper-based to digital record-keeping schemes, to the complex, such as the implementation of computational tools that can integrate and analyze data to reveal food-safety-relevant associations (Strawn et al., 2015).

- Crop protection

Despite all advances in agriculture, crops are still vulnerable to weeds and insects. The usage of herbicides to protect crops is a far-spread practice in agriculture. The challenge for farmers in order to increase the sustainability of their fields is to administer the correct herbicide instead of the currently "use it all" approach. In order to do so, they need to be able to identify the exact species of insect they are fighting. A recently developed application from the Bayer Group uses machine learning and Big Data in order to match an uploaded photo against a comprehensive database to recognize the species.

- Yield forecasting

Not only demand forecasts, but also supply forecasts can be augmented by the use of data-science. Companies like DTN, the current farming industry standard for agribusiness information sharing in the United States, combine critical weather and agronomic data from fields to forecast future yield and to improve food security. The practice of using data in order to monitor and plan crop harvests is called precision farming.

An applicable European example for precision farming is SMAG, a subsidiary of France's leading agricultural cooperative group InVivo with 220 members, and the French leader in agronomic information systems. 80% of cooperatives and 50% of merchants in France use their complex agronomic Data Crop algorithm for precision farming, utilizing 30 years of weather data history, satellite and drone images, and soil types — to make informed decisions faster.

The array and preferably the combination of Big Data Applications combined with machine learning algorithms for logistics-related planning, demand and yield forecasting, crop protection and chemical data evaluation provide a base for professionals in the food supply chain to tweak parameters such as crop rotation , irrigation, fertilization and others in a way that decreases food loss and insecurity substantially. Yet the potential of the digital revolution needs to be further explored and applied in order to address the food-supply-related issues presented in this book.

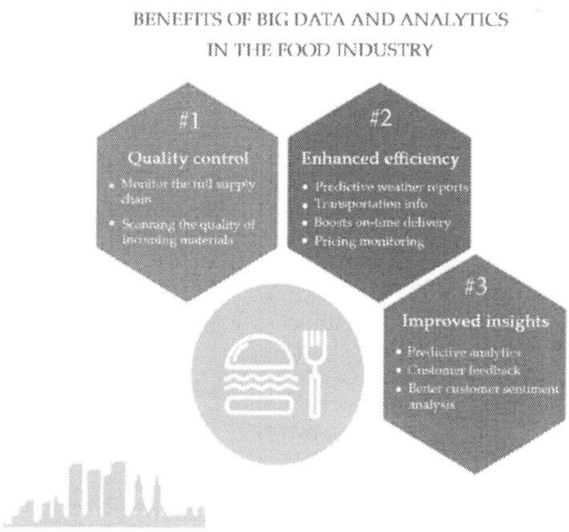

Figure 25. Benefits of Big Data in the food industry.

Source: https://www.byteant.com/blog/how-big-data-is-boosting-food-industry-the-best-examples/

LAB-GROWN FOOD AS AN ALTERNATIVE FOR PROTEIN INTAKE

Since the world's population is expected to reach 9 billion by 2050, there is renewed focus on how to create a food supply that can sustain this amount of people without destroying our planet. According to the U.N. Food and Agriculture Organization (FAO), industrialized agriculture is responsible for a significant portion of our air pollution, biodiversity decline, climate change and land degradation. Growing food in labs is one solution that creates more food with less space and damage to the environment if we can find a way to produce it cost-effectively at scale.

Additionally, developing countries are increasing their meat consumption, so they could quickly reach the consumption levels of North America and Australia. Additional food production increases emissions, which then can ruin the ecosystem required to sustain the animals and crops we need to feed them before they get slaughtered and processed for our consumption.

Researchers from a variety of start-ups are now tackling the problem to create meat without using an animal to help meet future demand. Growing meat in a lab could cut greenhouse gas emissions caused by agriculture to drop 78-96 percent while using 99 percent less land. Often referred to as cellular agriculture, researchers take stem cells from an animal—cow, pig, chicken and sea creatures—and then place it in a growing medium in a bioreactor to produce "cultured meat." While science can't yet create the texture of a fine steak, processed meat such as burgers, chicken nuggets and meatballs are getting good reviews and are expected to be available on supermarket shelves in five years.

In an effort to sway popular opinion about the benefits of cultured meat, a fictitious website called Bistro In Vitro helps educate people about the benefits of meat grown in a lab. Fast-food chain Burger King recently launched a Whopper sandwich made with an Impossible™ patty—a patty made from plants, but that has the flavor and aroma of beef. While not grown in a lab, the Impossible burger exposes consumers to more meatless alternatives. This, along with other initiatives, might eventually get more people prepared to accept meat alternatives when they are available.

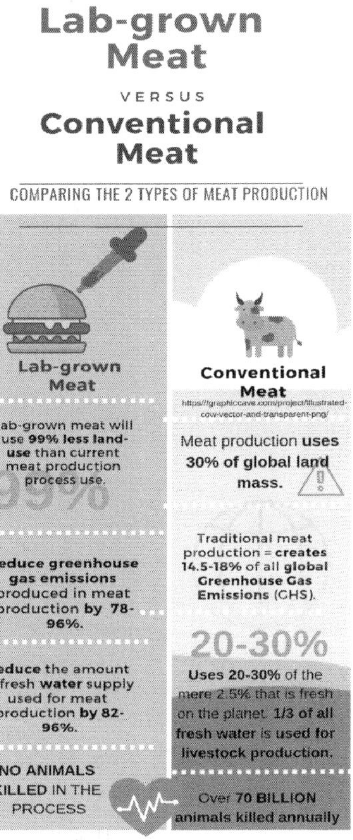

Figure 26. Lab Grown Meat vs Conventional Meat.

There are other companies focused on cell-based seafood, including BlueNalu and Finless Foods. Just like Professor Post, BlueNalu employees extract muscle cells from a particular fish to grow in a lab. Ultimately the vision for these cells is to be cultivated in a lab until they grow large sheets of whole muscle tissue that can then be packaged for sale. This vision is not yet a reality as few of the seafood-focused companies have seafood that's available to sample yet. But when they do, this seafood won't have heads, tails, bones, blood or contaminants such as mercury, parasites and plastics.

With a continued focus on improving health and nutrition, a new sector is growing in the food industry—smart food. Smart food is not only pre-packaged and convenient, but it's also nutritionally optimized. Companies around the world, including Soylent (U.S.), Huel (U.K.) and Vitaline (France) are focused on this service. It doesn't seem like it will be in the too far distant future, by 2169 according to a report from Sainsbury, when we could implant food via microchips that are developed specifically for our individual needs.

OTHER FUTURE FOOD DEVELOPMENTS

Using vegetable proteins, the first piece of "meat" has been printed using a 3D printer. This technology also allows for customization of the ingredients to accommodate an individual's dietary needs. Part of the challenge is to create a piece of meat that tastes, feels and looks like what consumers expect, and the results are getting better.

In the coming years, there will be a continued focus on food as medicine and plant-friendly food. More people will reduce their consumption of meat due to animal welfare, health and environmental concerns. The alternative proteins market is expected to grow by 25 percent—algae milk or cricket flour, anyone?

Further, into the future, it might be the norm that we enjoy a perfect fillet steak or seared piece of tuna, 3D printed on demand, that includes not only everything we need to keep us healthy but won't require us to kill any animals.

Algae as a protein source

Seeking better nutrition for better health, consumer interest in protein products has continued to increase over the past decade. However, the sheer number of protein products and products enhanced with protein is mind-boggling and overwhelming to the average consumer. A trip to the health food store or healthy food aisle of the grocery store will show you products with protein sourced from various sources, including animal, brown rice, dairy, whey and soy sources. What you might be missing in the deluge of products is a smarter plant-based protein source that stands out from the crowd. Algae protein is gaining prominence as a smarter choice for your healthy lifestyle.

Organic blue-green algae, including spirulina, Chlorella and Aphanizomenon flos aquae (AFA) are considered super foods because of their high concentrations of complete protein, vitamins, amino acids, omega-3 and other essential fatty acids. AFA naturally contains the highest level of biologically active chlorophyll than other known foods. Chlorella and spirulina are composed of 70 percent protein and contain over 65 vitamins, minerals and enzymes.

If you have not tried algae protein, it is time to consider the benefits of adding it to your diet.

1) Digestibility of Single Cells

Algae are simple, single-celled photosynthetic organisms with superior bioavailability. They contain organelles called chloroplasts that function to store chlorophyll. The chlorophyll captures the energy from the sun. Through photosynthesis, that energy is converted into sugars that feed the algae making it self-sufficient with only requiring water and sun to survive.

Algae's nutritional value is not compromised by other ingredients despite its simple cellular construction. Its protein and other nutrients are easily digested and absorbed causing little gastric disturbance in comparison to whey proteins. Any leftover nutrients and undigested fiber travel through the small intestine to the colon where they help stimulate immune response and gut health with their fermentation.

2) Building Blocks of Protein

Amino acids are powerful protein building blocks that are crucial for every metabolic process in your body and make up most of the body's cells, tissues and muscles. Algae contain all essential and non-essential amino acids making them a complete protein source. There is over three times the amount of the amino acid arginine than what is found in whey protein and almost the same amount of glutamine. Research has shown that arginine helps improve circulation by increasing nitric oxide in the blood, while also helping to decrease cholesterol levels. Glutamine is important for muscle growth and cellular support that no other single amino acid can provide.

3) Omega-3s and Essential Fatty Acids

Diets high in omega-3s and other essential fatty acids are important for good health and for your body to function properly. These nutrients play a vital part in heart health, brain function and reducing inflammation. But some diets, especially vegan diets, can be lacking in these crucial nutrients. The body cannot produce omega-3 fatty acids on its own. Plant-based protein such as algae can be a better source of omega-3's EPA and DHA than fish.

4) Loaded with Healthy Antioxidants

AFA is rich in compounds that are loaded with antioxidants. Studies have shown that adding AFA, spirulina and Chlorella to your diet acts as a defense against oxidative damage to your red blood cells. As an effective adaptogen, the antioxidant activity of blue-green algae can protect your body from stress (including tension on the body from exercise) while also boosting your immune system with its natural anti-viral properties.

5) Our Ancestors Knew the Value of Plant-Based Proteins

Asian societies and ancient cultures, including the Aztecs, recognized that plant-based foods derived from algae were a rich source of protein and other important nutrients. Chlorella, spirulina, kelp and Aphanizomenonflosaquae (AFA) are foods that are derived from different strains of algae that are known for their nutritional value. But the benefits of algae surpass its nutritional value.

Today, there is an increased focus on the need for sustainable resources and ethical practices. A plant-based diet is more in-line with these higher standards for sustainability and ethicality. Algae make a great protein source that not only provides health benefits of plant-based proteins, but also helps with sustainable practices because it:

- Grows fast. Because algae grow continuously, they can be harvested daily at a rate much greater than some of agriculture's most productive crops
- Consumes carbon dioxide. When grown in sunlight, algae absorb carbon dioxide and release oxygen into the air, just like any other plant
- Does not compete with agriculture. Algae cultivation does not compete with land that is traditionally used for agricultural crops. It can be grown on land that is not suited for traditional crops such as within quality controlled ponds and/or natural pools
- Has many uses. While microalgae can be cultivated for their nutritional powerhouse for human nourishment, they can also be used to produce biofuels and livestock feeds
- Creates jobs. Because algae can be grown in a variety of climates using multiple production methods, the algae industry has great potential for growth. The Algae Biomass Organization projects that up to 220,000 jobs will be created by 2020 in the algae industry including research, engineering, construction, and farming jobs

Insects as a protein source

Several projections have suggested that the world population will reach over 9 billion by 2050 (Grafton et al., 2015; Park and Yun, 2018). This increase in population requires approximately double the current food production

(Belluco et al., 2013). Alarmingly, global warming is gradually decreasing the areas used for food production worldwide (Dobermann et al., 2017). The climate change and the environmental destruction from industrial development also negatively affect food productivity (van Huis and Oonincx, 2017). In light of worsening resource shortage, several foods have been proposed as alternatives, with insects receiving the most attention (Patel et al., 2019). Insects are institutionally accepted as a food in many regions and historically consumed (Murefu et al., 2019), providing sufficient nutritional value for humans (Zielinska et al., 2018). However, the rapid increase in food production through technological advancement has largely eliminated insects from our diets (Gao et al., 2018).

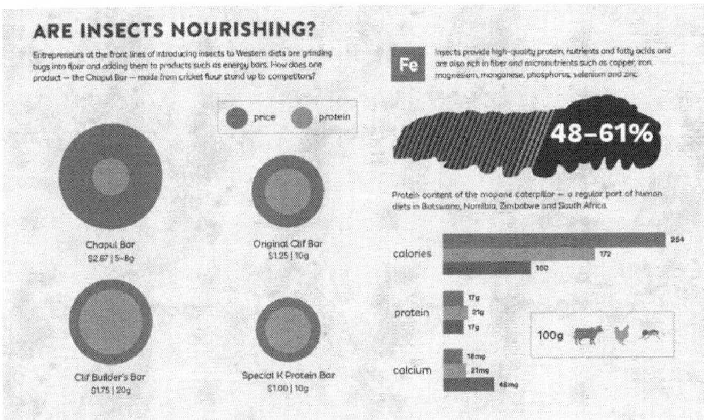

Figure 27. Insect Nutrient Facts.

The reappearance of insects as a viable food group can be attributed to their nutritional, environmental, and economic value (Nongonierma and FitzGerald, 2017). The increased scrutiny of edible insects is part of a multifaceted strategy for achieving global food security (van Huis, 2015). In general, insects have high protein content and excellent production efficiency compared with other conventional food groups (Kohler et al., 2019; Nongonierma and FitzGerald, 2017; Zielinska et al., 2015). This characteristic is particularly valuable given that future protein consumption is expected to increase, but food supply declines (Gao et al., 2018; Kohler et al., 2019; Patel et al., 2019). Currently, Europe and the United States have the fastest-growing edible-insect industry, where a trend is associated with high meat intake (Mlcek et al., 2014). Moreover, it is recognized that a steady increase in the global market size of the insect industry, with applications reaching beyond food into the material and drug development (van Thielen et al., 2019).

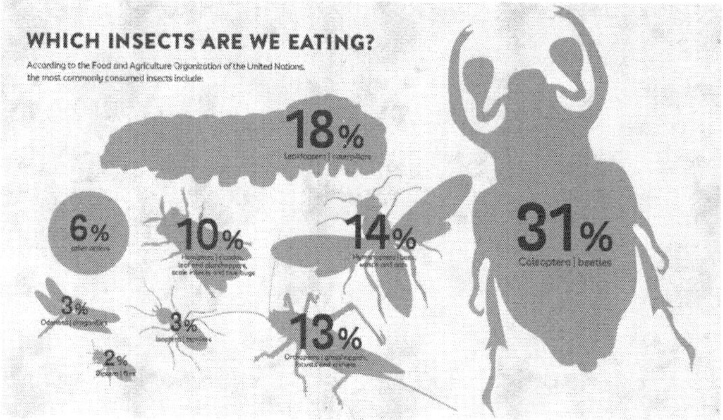

Figure 28. Types of Insects in current Nutrition.

Despite the numerous practical advantages, many barriers remain in insect-food development because the concept of insect foods is not similar to conventional Western eating habits (Murefu et al., 2019). Currently, insect foods are in a transitional stage, and a promising new technique involves developing new food products via combining protein-processing technology with insects (Kohler et al., 2019; Patel et al., 2019).

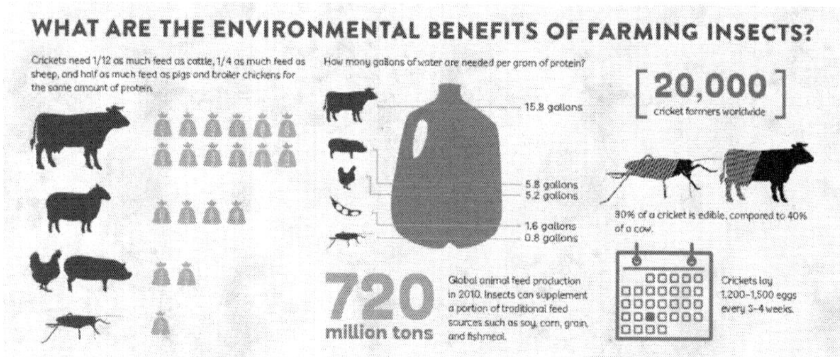

Figure 29. Environmental Benefits of Insect Farming.

The demand for sustainable food production

From Slow Food and farmers' markets to ecolabels and fair trade, an unprecedented number of consumer-based alternative food movements have risen in response to concerns about the environmental and social effects of industrialized agriculture. Some research suggests that these movements are successful in their efforts to reconnect communities, demystify global food chains, and produce sustainable foods, which are healthier for the planet and human bodies. Yet other scholars argue that the contemporary focus on consumer responsibility in policy and practice indicates much more than a process of reflexive modernization. The devolution of responsibility to consumers and the dominance of market-based solutions, these scholars argue, reflect the growing influence of neoliberal environmental governance. From this perspective, these movements are naive in their assumption that consumers have the power necessary to overcome the structural barriers that inhibit significant change. These critics argue that the focus on consumer responsibility excludes those without access to consumer choice, reproduces social hierarchies, and fails to deliver the political and redistributive solutions necessary to achieve sustainability.

Food supply chains

Sustainability and protecting the environment have, of course, been in the news for a while. Driven primarily by consumers who want healthier food that doesn't damage their surroundings, sustainability is having a profound effect on the global food supply chain. In most of the world, eating habits have long been dependent on a mixture of local production and imported conserved foods. More recently, manufactured foods have become an important part of many people's diets, and many of the world's staple foods are now traded internationally as commodities.

Local food supply chains are often considered to be relatively sustainable (e.g. Nestle 2002; Sustain 2002) partly because they support 'mixed' and organic farming and reduce emissions and externalities created by long-distance transport and high 'food miles' (Jones 2001; Pretty et al. 2005). Local food supply chains are also valued for their capacity to generate rural enterprise and regenerate rural communities, break agribusiness monopolies and create spiritual links between man and nature (e.g. Pretty 2002, 2004; Halweil 2004).

Food conservation is important for reducing losses and degradation during transport from rural areas to urban populations (Hulse, 2004) and allowing people to enjoy a nutritious and varied diet throughout the year. Stable food products created by drying, salting, smoking and fermenting have been stored and traded outside the local area in 'conserved' food supply chains for thousands of years. Canning, pasteurization and freezing increased the variety of foods that could be conserved, and more recent technologies such as chilling, aseptic and controlled atmosphere packaging (combined with rapid inexpensive transport) have enabled many 'fresh' fruit and vegetables (Wu Huang et al. 2004) and dairy produce to be traded as 'conserved food', with considerable impact on national and international patterns of agricultural production and trade.

Manufactured foods usually contain ingredients from different origins and production systems. Although some may be derived from simple supply chains and others may involve many transactions between farmers and manufacturers, it is probable that the total number of transactions involved in any one product is high. Some ingredients (e.g. herbs, spices, dried fruit) may make up only a tiny proportion of the finished product or may be required only for the short product life of a particular variety of product (e.g. bakery product, sauce, meal) and major ingredients may be derived from dynamic international supply networks that overlap with those of business competitors; vegetable oils, for example, are often mixed or substituted to compensate for seasonal unavailability or variation in quality and price. Mixing and substitution along complicated dynamic supply networks may limit not only traceability but also the flow of information and influence along the chain.

Traceability, knowledge and influence only trickle along many commodity supply chains, where foods, bought and sold to standard specifications worldwide, are often bulked for low costs and ease of transport and storage. Commodities are usually simple conserved foods that can be stored and traded internationally, often using long-distance sea transport. Prices are dependent on market mechanisms and may be subject to future trading. Since production often exceeds demand for traditional food commodities, prices tend to be low, unstable and declining (FAO 2004), making commodity-based foodstuffs (e.g. bread, sugar, rice and beverages) available to consumers from all sectors of society, but having a catastrophic impact on the lives of farmers when prices fall dramatically (Fairtrade 2005, http://www.fairtrade.org.uk/about_what_is_fairtrade.htm).

Several, often contradictory, trends have emerged in the last 20–40 years. The removal of trade barriers, relatively inexpensive transport and technical advances in food conservation have encouraged international standardization and commoditization of conserved food, as producers of, for example, frozen chicken, wine, orange juice, fruits and vegetables, often in developing countries, compete internationally in 'buyer-driven' markets (Gereffi, 1994). Meanwhile, manufacturers and retailers have been demanding differentiated specific attribute products, rather than traditional commodities, from farmers (Martin, 2001b) in order to enhance their own product quality, brand reputation or range of specialty products, and political and social movements towards more local food supplies have emerged in some parts of the world.

Traceability

Traceability of ingredients in food supply chains has become paramount in a world in which markets become global, heterogeneous, and complex and in which consumers expect a high level of quality. The food supply chain consists of many organizations having different interests and are often reluctant to share traceability information with each other. Blockchain has been advocated for improving traceability by providing trust. Yet, practice proved to be more stubborn.

Food traceability has its roots in 1930s Europe, where countries wanted proof that high-end products like French champagne were indeed products of the regions claimed on labels.

Today, traceability takes on many different forms. Food manufacturers need to have powerful systems in place to manage traceability, Why? There are increasing regulatory requirements to protect consumers from food borne illnesses and respond to recalls promptly. Like citizens 80 years ago, traceability is also needed to satisfy consumer demand for ingredients and foods from a global market.

Traceability has two essential components:

- Tracing provides a history of each food product's journey throughout the supply chain, from farms that produce ingredients to how those ingredients are combined to where those finished goods are inventoried on-site. Tracing offers a transparent picture of a product's history from its origins forward.
- Tracking allows for the accurate identification of a product's journey after it leaves a manufacturing facility up to its final destination, whether that is a restaurant, grocery store, or consumer.

Both tracking and tracing can be done on an individual unit or batch basis. No matter what process is used, these weighty responsibilities require technology solutions that monitor processes, from ordering to production to inventory to transportation. These same solutions need to allow for powerful, real-time track and trace functions throughout the supply chain. With so many requirements and pressures facing food and beverage makers, it is important to understand deeply why traceability is essential and what companies can do to ensure they are compliant and responsive to demand.

MARKET-ORIENTED INITIATIVES FOR ENVIRONMENTALLY SUSTAINABLE FOOD PRODUCTION

European food is safe, nutritious and of high quality. This is the result of years of EU policy aimed at protecting human, animal and plant health. However, climate change, biodiversity loss and the degradation of land and sea are a reality despite farmers' and fishers' current efforts. Extreme weather events around the globe, which are set to increase significantly with higher temperatures, severely affect agriculture, forests, fisheries and aquaculture, including through the spread of animal and plant diseases and invasive alien species. Food systems are globally responsible for around 21-37% of total greenhouse gas (GHG) emissions, have a profound effect on biodiversity, water and soil pollution, carbon sinks and are one of the principal causes of resource depletion and degradation of natural ecosystems. Livestock supply chains account for 14.5% of global GHG emissions. In the European Union, 71% of farmland is dedicated to meat and dairy production and almost half of the European Union's agricultural GHG emissions come from the animal sector. In addition, manufacturing, processing, packaging and transportation of food greatly contribute to pollution of air, soil and water and produce GHG emissions.

Nevertheless, citizens' demand is evolving. Consumers' habits are driving significant change to the food market. Citizens increasingly pay attention to environmental, health and ethical issues. They want green, organic food, with less pesticides, sugar and additives. Even as societies become more urbanized, citizens want to feel closer to their food, having it fresher, less processed and locally sourced. Consumers expect transparency across the entire supply chain to be sure that they are buying "healthy food from a healthy planet". Food processors and retailers play a key role in ensuring that such demand is met. In recent years, consumer trust has been eroded through intentional violations of food supply rules. Achieving a sustainable food system requires a zero-tolerance policy as regards food fraud.

The EU is the largest importer and exporter of agri-food products and the largest seafood market in the world. Imports of certain commodities may however result in negative environmental and social impacts in third countries, including deforestation, air and water pollution and labor conditions including workers' safety. Therefore, efforts to increase the sustainability requirements of the EU food system should be accompanied by policies helping to progressively raise standards globally, in order to avoid the externalization of unsustainable practices.

All citizens and economic players across value chains, both inside and outside the EU should benefit from a just transition. A shift to a sustainable food system can bring environmental, social and health benefits and offer economic gains. At the global level, it is estimated that a food and agriculture system in line with the Sustainable Development Goals (SDGs) could create a new economic value of more than EUR 1.8 trillion by 2030. Ensuring sustainable livelihood for primary producers, who still lag behind the rest of the EU economy in terms of income, is essential for the transition to sustainable food systems. For example, the average EU farmer currently earns around half of the average worker in the economy as a whole. Research, innovation, digitalization, technology, knowledge sharing and financial investments will provide solutions that deliver better environmental results and higher profits and will open up new business and job opportunities.

The EU's ultimate goal is to reduce the environmental and climate footprint of the food system, lead a global transition towards competitive sustainability from farm to fork and tap into new opportunities. This means:

- Ensuring that the way that food is produced, transported, distributed and marketed has a neutral or positive environmental impact, preserving and restoring the land and sea-based resources on which the food system depends; contributing to mitigating climate change and adapting to its impacts; protecting land, soil, water, air, plant and animal health; and stopping the loss of biodiversity.
- Ensuring food security and citizens' health: making sure all people have access to sufficient, nutritious, sustainable food that meets high standards of food safety and quality, plant health, animal health and welfare, while meeting their dietary needs and food preferences.
- Preserving affordability of food while generating fairer economic returns in the food supply chain, promoting competitiveness of the food supply sector, fair trade and creating new business opportunities linked to the transition, while ensuring occupational health and safety.

In championing the global transition, the EU can make sustainability its key trademark and gain a competitive first mover advantage. To achieve a fair, healthy and environmentally friendly food system, an integrated approach covering the entire food chain from farm to fork is needed. To that end, targets in priority areas are set for the EU as a whole. To reach those targets, different starting points and differences in improvement potential between the Member States should be duly recognized to ensure a fair transition. By the end of 2023, a legislative framework for sustainable food systems will be proposed to recognize the performance of front-runners and gradually raise sustainability standards so as to become the norm for products placed on the EU market.

To achieve sustainable food production, farmers, fishers and aquaculture producers need to transform their production methods, making the best use of nature-based, technological and digital solutions to deliver better environmental results, increase climate resilience and reduce input use (e.g. pesticides, fertilizers). Such solutions will require human and financial investments but also promise higher returns by allowing direct marketing or sales of high value-added products. New business models, better advice and knowledge transfer, as well as adequate pricing signals, will improve the way primary producers are working and increasingly put them at the center of a food value chain that promotes circular use of food resources.

URBAN FARMERS

Urban agriculture is often confused with community gardening, homesteading or subsistence farming. What distinguishes urban farming is that urban agriculture assumes a level of commerce, the growing of products to be sold as opposed to being grown for personal consumption or sharing. In community gardening, there is no such commercial activity.

It is not necessary to be a corporation to be an urban farm or have a large tract of land. An individual, a couple of friends, a nonprofit entity, or neighborhood group can start and run an urban farm. There is no one correct sales outlet for an urban farm. Food can be then sold to restaurants or at a farmers market, given to a local soup kitchen or church, but the food is raised primarily to be moved (through some form of commerce) from the grower to the user.

As more of us begin to understand our food system, more of us seek to have more input into how food is grown, how it is treated after being harvested and how it moves from one place along the food route to another.

People have begun to understand how far food travels, and that they, as the consumer, have had no say in what is grown or how it is grown. Urban agriculture can change that and in doing so it can take a rightful place in the larger food system.

Urban agriculture has become a means to increase access to locally grown food and a way of reintroducing the public to the many aspects of food that we have lost as a culture. How food grows, what grows regionally and seasonally are all important lessons and make a better informed urban consumer. Urban farms can be the front line of the food system.

For some, the term urban implies inner city. For others, urban has come to mean areas that are on the perimeter of cities (what some refer to as peri-urban). There is no single characterization of size or placement; some are on rooftops, on landfills, brown fields, or areas where housing or industry may have been demolished. Some cities are giving up part of their park systems to allow urban farmers to plant their seeds. Every urban farm is different just as every rural farm is different.

Zoning plays a big role in urban agriculture. It can dictate what kind of growing may be allowed, whether animals, retail sales, and even education can be part of the operation. Many cities have multiple restrictions on raising animals with the result that most urban farms don't keep animals for production purposes. Farming, big or small, is almost always a regulated activity. The production and selling of a food item are potentially rife with safety and liability issues, as well as commerce, zoning and cultural issues. Producing food for people to eat is a big responsibility and not to be entered into without a great deal of thought and planning.

Some urban farms are built exclusively for education, training or re-entry programs. Many are built to improve food access in a specific community or to continue traditional culinary cultures. Some are built as for-profit concerns, recognizing that the savings on food transportation can make urban farming financially viable as well as more environmentally responsible. For others, food justice is the reason to develop urban farms in their communities, which means improving the access to fresh food for economically disadvantaged communities.

Urban farming includes a wide array of food-producing projects and activities. And with the recent resurgence of farming in and around cities, people have been reconnecting to agriculture by growing food themselves and visiting farmer's markets. This fast-growing phenomenon has the potential to nourish communities and create economic opportunities. Urban farming is popular for several reasons such as sustainability, affordability, health, and convenience.

Today urban agriculture exists in many forms including: community and backyard gardens; rooftop and balcony gardening; growing in vacant lots, parks the list goes on.

The trouble with urban agriculture

Looking at most farms that produce roof- and indoor-grown vegetables at commercial scales, it has been found that the biggest of these commercial farms are around a third of an acre in size. Most are on roofs spread across cities, and some are inside buildings and shipping containers. Mainly, these farms are producing impressive amounts of leafy greens such as lettuce, and herbs; some also produce fish.

But while rooftop farms rely on natural sunlight to feed the crops, indoor farms use artificial lights. These farms potentially have a greater energy footprint even than conventional outdoors farms, challenging the assumption that urban farms are less impactful than conventional ones.

Some farms also embraced high-tech systems, such as wind, rain, temperature, and humidity detectors and indoor heating, to enhance growing conditions in environments that aren't naturally suited to agriculture. These elevate the energy costs of the food produced, and maybe giving an unexpectedly high carbon footprint.

Furthermore, the predominantly grown foods–such as lettuce–aren't of great nutritional value for the urban population, especially those threatened by food insecurity. Most produce from CEAs is sold at a premium, something that partly reflects the cost of the real estate used to grow the food. Consequently, that produce is typically grown for high-end food stores and restaurants, meaning it's unlikely to reach low-income urban populations who need it most.

The rising cost of real estate might put these urban acres beyond the reach of new farming start ups, they think. These companies also face increasing competition from a growing number of farms springing up on the outskirts of cities–where land is cheaper and there's space to produce more food, while also benefiting from urban proximity. More thought might also be given to the nutritional value and cost of foods grown, to generate benefits for all the city's residents, not just high-income ones. It is questionable whether smaller, community-driven plots of urban agriculture–like community gardens, school, and prison farms–might actually do a better job of providing food to at-risk city residents, compared to commercial urban farms that inevitably have to focus on profits.

Farming requires new models, tools and information

Farming in the city presents unique challenges. These challenges are common to every city everywhere. Here are what the authors consider the most common urban farming challenges:

Challenges

- Limited lateral space
- High land values
- Contaminated soils
- Theft and vandalism
- Pavement
- Loss and damage of crops from birds and rodents
- High costs (water, infrastructure, permits, housing, etc.)
- Lack of experienced skilled labor and management

And yet, farming in the city offers distinct advantages for the farmer and for those eating his or her food that far outweigh the challenges.

Advantages For the Farmer:

- Proximity to markets
- Proximity to a large customer base and labor
- Lower weed (and some pest) pressure
- Warmer conditions, due to the urban heat sink, which provide earlier production

Advantages For the Neighborhood:

- Direct visual and participatory connection to the farm and the farmer
- Improved food quality
- Access for children to food and how it is grown
- Greening of neighborhoods
- Job opportunities

The ability to secure a stable and accessible supply of food for a global population of 9.7 billion by 2050, whilst limiting contributions to climate change and conserving the world's limited water, land, and energy resources, is one of the most pressing and complex challenges facing the world today (FAO 2015; UN Department of Economic and Social Affairs 2019). The current agri-food system is responsible for up to 30% of the world's greenhouse gas emissions (Vermeulen et al. 2012), as well as the destruction of important ecosystems, loss of biodiversity, pollution of land and water bodies, and depletion of non-renewable resources (Newbold et al. 2015; Dalin et al. 2017; Goucher et al. 2017; Sánchez-Bayo and Wyckhuys 2019). As the world's population becomes increasingly urbanized, with an estimated 68% of the global population living in urban areas by 2050, agricultural land will continue to be strained further to meet the nutritional needs of these densely populated areas (Eigenbrod and Gruda, 2015; FAO, 2015; UN Department of Economic and Social Affairs, 2018; Wilhelm and Smith, 2018).

Current agricultural land has seen extensive degradation via erosion, loss of fertility, loss of biological life, and increased prevalence of resistant soil-borne pathogens, pests, and weeds (Bridges and Oldeman, 1999; Bai et al. 2008; FAO, 2015). Much of this can be attributed to the widespread utilization of unsustainable, intensive farming practices, such as the farming of high-yielding crops in monocultures with low genetic diversity and the use of excessive inputs of synthetic fertilizers and pesticides (Woodhouse, 2010; Holt-Giménez and Altieri, 2013; Horton, 2017; Sánchez-Bayo and Wyckhuys, 2019). Despite the negative environmental consequences of these practices, the dominant discourse on achieving global food security still perpetuates a productionist view of further intensifying agricultural production as the mainstream solution (The Royal Society, 2009; Godfray et al. 2010), although the main problems of hunger and malnutrition are generally not associated with a lack of food supply, but rather affordability and access (Lang, 2010; Holt-Giménez and Altieri, 2013; Sage, 2013; Tomlinson, 2013; Bernard and Lux, 2017; Kennard, 2019). Thus, finding ways to empower and support regenerative, biodiverse smallholder farms and local food systems should be prioritized in any discourse on sustainable agriculture and food security (FAO 2017). In light of this, urban agriculture (UA) has emerged as one approach to contribute to local food security by increasing the availability and accessibility of fresh and healthy produce in food-insecure areas in cities (FAO 2007, 2011; Zezza and Tasciotti, 2010; Martellozzo et al. 2014; Mack et al. 2017).

Creating spaces for people to grow and sell their own produce within cities allows for the generation of local food economies which shorten the food supply chain and circumvent the corporate-controlled food system that supports unsustainable industrial agricultural practices (Mariola, 2008; Altieri, 2009; van der Ploeg, 2010). Shifting some food production to areas of high demand can also reduce the greenhouse gas emissions associated with food supply chains, provide fresher and more nutritious produce than imported foods due to lower transport times, and help reduce pressure on current agricultural land (Kulak et al. 2013; Eigenbrod and Gruda, 2015; Wilhelm and Smith, 2018).

In 1996, it was estimated that 800 million people worldwide (15% of the world population at that time) were involved in UA activities in some way, ranging from household gardening to larger-scale commercial urban farms, with 200 million producing for the urban market (UNDP 1996). Many different types of UA exist; as shown in Table 1, these can include activities on the personal scale in privately owned areas (household gardening or part-time subsistence farming), on the community scale in interactive environments (community gardens, institutional gardens, allotments, guerrilla gardening, urban foraging, and public food forests), and on the commercial scale (for-profit or non-profit urban farms, indoor farms, and vertical farms) (Brown and Carter, 2003; Pearson et al. 2010; Poe et al. 2013; Adams and Hardman, 2014; Mok et al. 2014). UA has long been used for subsistence and as a mode to supplement household food security in developing countries, while in developed countries it most commonly serves recreational purposes, although is more recently being used as a tool to improve food access in marginalised communities (Pearson et al. 2010; Hamilton et al. 2014;Mok et al. 2014).

Indeed, UA can contribute to each of the four dimensions of food security. UA can provide an extra supply of produce in urban areas, increasing the availability of locally grown foods (Grewal and Grewal, 2012). UA sites and markets can be preferentially located in food insecure and food desert areas to increase access to fresh produce (Mack et al. 2017). Improvements in personal nutrition, health, and wellbeing have also been documented for people involved in UA activities (Armstrong 2000; Twiss et al. 2003; Wakefield et al. 2007; Kortright and Wakefield, 2011). Finally, UA can be used as a strategy to increase the food self-sufficiency of a city, thereby increasing resilience to breakdowns in the national or global food supply chain which may be heightened with extreme weather events and political crises associated with climate change (Altieri et al. 1999; Grewal and Grewal 2012; Barthel and Isendahl, 2013; Hamilton et al. 2014; Barthel et al. 2015).

Integrating agricultural spaces into the built environment can also provide a wide variety of ecological, provisioning, and cultural services for cities, whilst leveraging synergies for other urban problems such as waste and water cycling (Pearson et al. 2010; Lovell and Taylor, 2013; Ackerman et al. 2014; Proksch 2017). For example, UA spaces in cities can be important for reducing local air temperatures, improving air and water quality, intercepting stormwater, remediating soils, sequestering carbon, and enhancing biodiversity via habitat creation for wildlife (Oberndorfer et al. 2007; Pearson et al. 2010; Beniston and Lal 2012; Lovell and Taylor 2013; Lin et al. 2015; Goldstein et al. 2016; Clinton et al. 2018). In addition, UA provides social benefits by creating an interactive space for urbanites to reconnect to their food system and the natural environment, improving personal health, creating feelings of relaxation and well-being, and providing areas for community engagement and education (Tzoulas et al. 2007; Wakefield et al. 2007; Pearson et al. 2010; Turner, 2011).Thus, while UA is not a viable solution to provide for all food needs of urban residents, shifting some food production within cities can help reduce pressure on current agricultural land and increase the access and availability of healthy foods, while also providing other benefits to the urban landscape (Clinton et al. 2018; Wilhelm and Smith, 2018).

Urban Agriculture & Local Food Supply

UA can provide a source of fresh and healthy produce for individual families, community groups, and urban markets. However, it is difficult to quantify just how much UA contributes to the global food supply. A commonly cited figure used by the FAO estimates that urban agriculture provides 15-20% of the world's food (Armar-Klemesu, 2000; FAO 2007), although this has more recently been regarded as a gross overstatement (Clinton et al. 2018). Indeed, a recent mapping assessment predicted that, with maximal use of available space and intensive production practices, UA could potentially produce 5% of the global agricultural production of pulses, roots and tubers, and vegetables, but likely only contribute to 1% of this production currently (Clinton et al. 2018).

However, many cities across the world have long reported high degrees of food self-sufficiency, which refers to the extent to which a specific area can satisfy its population's food needs from domestic production (Thomson and Metz, 1998; Clapp, 2017). Shanghai, China is able to meet 50% of vegetable demands from production inside city borders (Lang and Miao, 2013), while Dar-es-Salaam, Tanzania produces 90% of leafy vegetables and 60% of milk consumed within the city (Jacobi et al. 2000). The city of Sydney, Australia produces 24% of total vegetables and 99% of Asian vegetables out of the state's total production (Mok et al. 2014).

In many cases, political crises have spurred both personal and urban food production. Indeed, during World War II, 20 million 'victory gardens' in the U.S. provided 40% of the nation's fresh vegetables (Bassett 1981). Cuba's agri-food system in particular is a primary example of the utilization of UA to enhance food self-sufficiency following a political crisis. UA in Cuba grew out of necessity following the fall of the Soviet Union in 1989, which led to an economic crisis characterized by fuel, food, and material shortages as well as a drastic reduction in export markets (Altieri et al. 1999; Koont 2008; Fernandez et al. 2018). Limits in trade caused a shift from the dependence on industrial agricultural methods of mechanization and use of agrochemicals to more agroecological methods, focusing on traditional farming knowledge, higher use of human and animal labor, the use of organic matter amendments as fertilizers, and smaller, diversified farms (Altieri et al. 1999; Koont 2008; Woodhouse 2010). In many cases, large, industrial farms were redistributed to small farmers and cooperatives (Altieri et al. 1999; Fernandez et al. 2018). The government was critical in promoting UA to supplement the island's food production, providing training and extension services in urban areas, increasing land access rights of individuals and cooperatives to grow on state and vacant land, and supporting local markets and workers cooperatives (Koont, 2008). In 2014, 560 km2 of urban and peri-urban agriculture in Cuba produced 50% of all fresh produce for the country (over one million tonnes) and generated 300,000 jobs, making this country a global leader in UA (Hamilton et al. 2014; Companioni et al. 2016; Altieri and Nicholls, 2018). Indeed, in soil-based urban farming, the highest reported yields (15-25 kg m-2 yr-1) have been from intensive, agro ecologically managed farms in Cuba (Ministerio de Agricultura, 2002; Funes and Vázquez, 2016).

However, the ability of certain cities and countries to use UA to provide significant contributions to their local food supply is highly variable. A mapping study by Martellozzo et al. (2014) showed that, on average, UA would require 30% of the area of cities globally to provide for the total vegetable consumption of urban dwellers (Martellozzo et al. 2014). However, this average hides a wide range, with 11 countries in the assessment not having enough urban extent area to satisfy the consumption demands of their citizens and 22 countries needing less than 10% of their urban area to do so. For countries that are lacking in available urban space, an option could be the possible use of rooftop gardens, vertical farming, and indoor growing methods, which was not assessed in this mapping study and could circumvent the need for large amounts of land area for urban growing (Despommier, 2011; Martellozzo et al. 2014).

In the U.S. and Canada, there has been a wide range of mapping studies aiming to evaluate the potential food production and food self-sufficiency that could be achieved from UA in various cities (Colasanti and Hamm 2010; MacRae et al. 2010; Ackerman 2012; Grewal and Grewal 2012; McClintock et al. 2013; Saha and Eckelman 2017). Table 2 provides a summary of recent studies in this area. Results are variable and largely based on the amount of available vacant land that could be used for food production in each city. For example, Detroit and Cleveland, as post-industrial cities with declining populations, have significant amounts of vacant land to dedicate to UA, and even under conservative estimates, could produce at least a quarter of fresh vegetable and fruit demand within city borders using vacant land (Colasanti and Hamm, 2010; Grewal and Grewal, 2012; United States Census Bureau, 2018). However, for larger cities with growing populations such as New York City and Toronto, vacant land comprises a much smaller portion of total city area; indeed, the percentage of available vacant land per total city area in Detroit (5.5%) and Cleveland (6.9%) is at least double the amount available in New York City (2.6%) and Toronto (1.7%) (MacRae et al. 2010; Ackerman, 2012; Statistics Canada 2016; United States Census Bureau, 2018).

Using only vacant land and conservative production values, New York City and Toronto would only be able to meet less than 5% of each city's fresh fruit and vegetable needs (MacRae et al. 2010; Ackerman, 2012). Thus, for densely populated, highly built, and growing cities, the utilization of other unused areas, such as rooftops, will be crucial for expanding food production. It should also be noted that for these mapping studies, results are largely based on yields reported from commercial farms or biointensive gardens rather than actual, climate-specific UA yields, due to the lack of research in this area. Some studies have aimed to quantify yields for UA, but they range widely between 0.06-25 kg m-2 yr-1 depending on the production method, management technique, and location; in addition, most of these studies relied on self-reported yields by growers with little ground truthing (Altieri et al. 1999; Ministerio de Agricultura 2002; Duchemin et al. 2008; Vitiello and Nairn 2009; Vitiello et al. 2010; Smith and Harrington 2014; Pourias et al. 2015; McDougall et al. 2018). Additionally, there is a severe lack of data on yields from commercial urban farms, with only one study in

East Bay, CA, USA aiming to quantify this (Altieri et al. 2014). Thus, there is a need for more UA yield data, especially for commercial urban farms, in order to accurately estimate the potential contribution UA could make to meeting the consumption demands of city dwellers.

Urban Agriculture & Food Access

Increasing food production does not necessarily translate to reducing hunger, and the lack of access to and affordability of healthy food for many has resulted in health-related issues of both malnutrition and obesity (Larson et al. 2009). Healthy food access is a precursor for healthy food consumption, which is necessary for improvements in overall health (Mack et al. 2017). The global agri-food system is host to stark inequalities, with nearly 1 billion people suffering from undernutrition in developing countries (FAO, 2014) whilst nearly a quarter of children and adolescents in developed countries are overweight or obese (Ng et al. 2014). Within developed countries, there are many inequalities in terms of access to fresh, healthy foods.

Areas that suffer from issues associated with food access have been collectively cited under the term 'food deserts.' Definitions for food deserts vary; simply, they are areas where fresh, nutritious foods such as fruits and vegetables are not available or accessible to the average person (Wrigley, 2002). The United States Department of Agriculture (2017) provides a more specific definition, where food deserts are low-income communities in which a significant share of the population (at least 33%) lives at least one mile (in urban areas) from a source of fresh produce, such as a supermarket.

It has been shown that low-income and non-white urban neighborhoods in the U.S. tend to have higher densities of liquor stores, fast food restaurants, and convenience stores and lower densities of supermarkets than higher-income, white neighborhoods (Morland et al. 2002; Block et al. 2004; Larson et al. 2009). The racial segregation of healthy food resources is especially apparent in the U.S., with one study showing that across four different states, white neighborhoods had 4x more supermarkets than black neighborhoods (Morland et al. 2002). Thus, lower-income and minority communities are disproportionately affected by the lack of access to supermarkets and healthy food. Because of this, residents in these areas must often shop at convenience stores that have limited access to fresh produce, limited food selection, lower quality foods, higher prevalence of energy-dense foods, and often higher prices compared to large supermarkets; this has been shown to lead to unhealthy diets and increased levels of obesity for people living in these areas (Larson et al. 2009; Zenk et al. 2011).

UA has emerged as one way to potentially increase access to fresh and healthy foods in food desert areas. Indeed, a variety of community gardens, non-profit urban farms, and even for-profit urban farms have missions dedicated to increasing food access in food deserts (Block et al. 2012; Biewener 2016). Community gardens can improve access to wholesome, healthy foods for local citizens (Wakefield et al. 2007; Kortright and Wakefield 2011). In addition, various people engaged in UA may donate a portion of their harvests to charity organisations such as food banks in order to provide fresh produce to those in need (Blaine et al. 2010; Poe et al. 2013; Ackerman et al. 2014). In some cities, programs have been put in place to increase the affordability of locally grown produce for the food insecure; for example, in Atlanta, GA, USA, those who require government aid to purchase food under the Supplemental Nutrition Assistance Program (SNAP) can buy local produce at farmers' markets with SNAP dollars (previously known as food stamps) under the "Georgia Fresh for Less" program, which doubles the value of their SNAP dollars (Wholesome Wave, 2019). In addition, another city program in Atlanta, called the "fresh MARTA markets", has been established to sell produce from urban farms in pop-up markets in the underground transport stations located in food desert areas, aiming to intersect transit with healthy food access (Food Well Alliance, 2018).

The overall effect of UA efforts to increase healthy food access has not been extensively researched and is difficult to quantify. Some mapping studies have attempted to understand the spatial distribution of community gardens in relation to household income. In Philadelphia and Madison, USA, similar trends were observed in that the majority of community gardens were located in census tracts with a median household income below the city average. For example, in Philadelphia, Kremer and DeLiberty (2011) showed that over 50% of community gardens were located in the lowest income neighborhoods (annual household income $18,000 USD or less compared to a city average of $42,000 USD). However, in Chicago, community gardens were more equally distributed over lower and higher-income census tracts, with over 50% being located in census tracts with a median household income of $33,000 USD or more compared to a city average of $47,000 USD (Taylor and Lovell, 2012). Still, the majority of Chicago residents live in a census tract with no community gardens at all, and 45% of these census tracts have a poverty rate that exceeds the city average (Taylor and Lovell, 2012).

However, the spatial distribution of community gardens does not necessarily indicate that people living in these areas have greater access to local produce. Indeed, in Madison, it was found that many community gardens were used by people living outside of that community, some traveling more than 30 minutes by car to reach the garden; in these cases, gardeners had largely chosen the community garden based on proximity to their work commute (Smith and Harrington 2014). In Philadelphia, although the majority of community gardens are located in lower-income neighborhoods, the majority of farmers' markets (53%) were located in middle-high income neighborhoods (with annual household incomes of $30,000 USD or more) (Kremer and DeLiberty, 2011). The farmers' markets that did exist in low-income neighborhoods were either located next to major institutions (city halls, hospitals, etc.) or were specifically part of food access improvement programs. Thus, while a large majority of urban-produced food may be grown in lower-income neighborhoods, likely due to greater availability of space and lower rent prices, this may not be where the majority of it is sold or distributed (Kremer and DeLiberty, 2011; Taylor and Lovell, 2012).

Another mapping study in Phoenix, USA aimed to understand how community gardens could be preferentially located to serve food desert areas (Mack et al. 2017). They found that the current 68 community gardens in the city only provided coverage to 8.4% of food desert residents; however, introducing 53 community gardens in vacant lots across the city would provide coverage to 96.4% of food desert residents. Thus, the spatial distribution of growing spaces, as well as the distribution networks associated with urban-produced foods, impact the ability of UA to improve food access and food security in communities. More research is needed in tracking where urban-produced foods are sold and who they are sold to, in order to understand the contribution UA is making to issues of food access and security (Siegner et al. 2018).

Urban Agriculture, Nutrition, & Health

The role UA can play in improving nutrition, health, and wellbeing has been well-documented.

Studies have shown that gardening improves physical and mental health through increased levels of fruit and vegetable consumption, improved dietary diversity, increased physical activity, and by providing a source of stress-relief and relaxation for gardeners (Armstrong ,2000; Twiss et al. 2003; Wakefield et al. 2007; Kortright and Wakefield, 2011). Indeed, green spaces in cities enhance the aesthetics of a community, providing relaxation and reducing mental fatigue, and contributing to positive emotions and self-reflection (Tzoulas et al. 2007). UA can also contribute to one's sense of place, with natural spaces often being important for self-reflection and agricultural spaces allowing urbanites to reconnect with typical rural views and methods of food production (Tzoulas et al. 2007; Pearson et al. 2010; Turner, 2011). Gardening can provide a way for people to connect with their personal, cultural, and community history, and can contribute to transmitting knowledge systems through intergenerational learning (Hancock, 2001; Galluzzi et al. 2010). In particular, community gardens can be important places for individuals to grow culturally relevant foods that cannot be found in local supermarkets, and this has shown to be especially important for migrants and refugees to connect to their cultural food and growing traditions (Baker, 2010; Kortright and Wakefield, 2011).

In addition, the availability of locally produced foods in cities can possibly encourage the consumption of fruit and vegetables by typical consumers (Opitz et al. 2016). Locally produced foods may be perceived as higher quality by consumers, as food quality perception relates to aspects of origin, trust, freshness, and flavor; indeed, being able to visit the farm and meet the growers provides a high level of transparency about the production of the food, which can be important for those who are suspicious of the origins of products in supermarkets (Kortright and Wakefield 2011; Block et al. 2012). However, potential issues with food safety for urban-produced foods can also adversely influence the perception of food quality, and these risks must be addressed and minimized by urban growers (Witzling et al. 2011; Mok et al. 2014).

This is especially a problem in many developing countries, where authorities see UA as having a negative impact due to claims that it increases the incidence of malaria and diarrhea (Hamilton et al. 2014). Research in Ghana has shown that agronomic practices such as open irrigation and overuse of insecticides may create mosquito habitats and resistance development (Klinkenberg et al. 2005, 2008; Matthys et al. 2006). Furthermore, the use of fecal sludge as a nutrient source and contaminated wastewater as irrigation is likely to cause negative health impacts (Cofie et al. 2005; Hamilton et al. 2014). Indeed, an evaluation of urban-produced vegetables which used wastewater irrigation in Ghana showed that a majority of the samples contained pesticide residues and fecal contamination above maximum limits for consumption (Amoah et al. 2006). These issues have generated a predominant view amongst governments in much of the developing world that UA is simply an archaic practice which should be ignored or even repressed (Kironde, 1992; Thaman, 1995; Hamilton et al. 2014). However, despite these challenges, UA is widespread in the developing world and has been shown to have a positive impact on food security, access, and nutrition, although data is sparse and more research in this area is desperately needed (Eriksen-Hamel and Danso, 2010; Zezza and Tasciotti, 2010; Hamilton et al. 2014).

Thus, understanding the nutritional quality of urban produce and improving food safety guidelines for these foods is especially important. More context-specific research is needed to understand how UA can be used to effectively recycle city wastes, such as compost and wastewater, to produce safe food for citizens (Pearson et al. 2010; Proksch 2017). Since a number of UA operations supply to vulnerable populations such as at food banks, schools, and hospitals, it is of vital importance that food provided by UA is both safe and nutritious (Siegner et al. 2018). In this way, UA can be used as a tool to address specific human deficiencies in micronutrients and vitamins, and in some cases, urban farms have begun supplying produce to hospitals specifically for people with such deficiencies (Pearson et al. 2010; Eigenbrod and Gruda, 2015). Thus, more research is needed to evaluate the safety and nutritional density of urban-produced foods, which will then contribute to understanding on potential impacts in improving nutrition and health for consumers.

Despite the goals of many UA operations to improve healthy food access in cities, it is extremely difficult for commercial operations to do this. Daftary-Steel, Herrera and Porter (2015) have called the various goals urban farms often struggle to balance the 'unattainable trifecta of urban agriculture'; this refers to the sometimes contradicting goals of providing quality food to people at affordable prices, providing jobs and work experience at living wages to those typically excluded from employment or leadership roles, and generating a profit from sales in order to sustain operations.

It is nearly impossible for for-profit urban farms to meet all of these goals and expectations at once, and usually, one aspect must suffer; for example, many urban farms may market fresh, high-quality, local produce to middle-high income individuals at slightly higher prices than one would find in the supermarket in order to gain a profit; in other cases, urban farms may rely on family, volunteer, or part-time labor in order to keep produce prices at more affordable levels (Daftary-Steel et al. 2015; Biewener 2016; Siegner et al. 2018). Indeed, it has been seen that many commercial UA enterprises which are aiming to break away from the industrial food system and improve healthy food access ultimately end up trapped within the same neoliberal capitalist framework on a smaller scale, still perpetuating inequalities in food access (McClintock, 2014). In response, some for-profit enterprises with social missions are now converting to non-profits or creating non-profit arms to coincide with their business in order to meet social missions (Siegner et al. 2018). More research is needed to understand which business models are the most appropriate for urban farms in order to sustain financial viability and contribute to local food security.

Commercial urban farmers also face a variety of other challenges, including a lack of access to viable land, resources, and training. Urban farms and community gardens must compete with residential and commercial developments for space, and this often proves difficult without public or governmental support (Brown and Carter 2003; Cavailhes and Wavresky 2003; Wakefield et al. 2007; Eriksen-Hamel and Danso 2010; Kortright and Wakefield 2011; Erickson et al. 2013). Further, even if land is available, it may not be viable for agriculture, with issues of soil compaction and contamination common in post-industrial and residential urban areas (Eriksen-Hamel and Danso ,2010; Beniston and Lal, 2012). Renting land within the city constitutes a major expense for commercial urban farmers, thus making it difficult to stay profitable whilst keeping produce prices affordable (Daftary-Steel et al. 2015; Siegner et al. 2018). Finding equipment and tools for small-scale production can also be a challenge and buying high-quality organic amendments at affordable prices is difficult as these products are often sold in bulk (Altieri and Nicholls, 2018).There is also a lack of training and agronomic extension services geared toward urban farmers, many of whom are often young and inexperienced (Eriksen-Hamel and Danso, 2010; Food Well Alliance, 2017). Indeed, the success of UA in Cuba can largely be attributed to the support of the government in providing training, land, and extension services for new urban farmers and this should be considered as a model for other cities worldwide (Koont, 2008).

Thus, it becomes apparent that for UA to be successfully implemented in a coordinated, efficient way that allows it to contribute significantly to local food security, infrastructure and institutional support on the city, state, and country levels are necessary (Mok et al. 2014). Food policy plans should be developed which include the management of UA in city planning documents (Mok et al. 2014). The potential zoning of specific spaces, especially vacant lots, for UA could be an effective way of increasing food production in cities. These spaces could have subsidized land rent prices for urban farmers or community gardens, thus improving the financial viability and longevity of UA operations. Indeed, if urban farms are contributing so significantly to overall public benefits and sustainable development of cities, farmers should be rewarded and supported as stewards of the land.

Box 18. Protein requirements.

How much protein do we really need?

Protein is essential to good health. The very origin of the word — from the Greek protos, meaning "first" — reflects protein's top-shelf status in human nutrition. You need it to put meat on your bones and to make hair, blood, connective tissue, antibodies, enzymes, and more. It's common for athletes and bodybuilders to wolf down extra protein to bulk up. But the message the rest of us often get is that our daily protein intake is too high.

The Recommended Dietary Allowance (RDA) for protein is a modest 0.8 grams of protein per kilogram of body weight. The RDA is the amount of a nutrient you need to meet your basic nutritional requirements. In a sense, it's the minimum amount you need to keep from getting sick — not the specific amount you are supposed to eat every day.

For a relatively active adult, a daily protein intake to meet the RDA would supply as little as 10% of his or her total daily calories. In comparison, the average American consumes around 16% of his or her daily calories in the form of protein, from both plant and animal sources.

Unhealthy and un-sustainably produced food poses a global risk for people and the planet. Nearly 1 billion people in the world lack sufficient food and many more consume an unhealthy diet that contributes to premature death and morbidity. Simultaneously, global food production is the single largest human pressure on Earth, threatening local ecosystems and the stability of the entire Earth system.

Present dietary trends, combined with projected population growth to nearly 10 billion by 2050, will exacerbate these conditions. The global burden of non-communicable diseases is set to worsen and the impacts of food production on greenhouse gas emissions, nitrogen and phosphorus pollution, biodiversity loss, and water and land use will erode the stability of the Earth system.

A transformation to healthy diets from sustainable food systems is a prerequisite for attaining the UN Sustainable Development Goals and Paris Agreement, and scientific targets for healthy diets and sustainable food production are needed to guide a Great Food Transformation.

Healthy diets have an appropriate caloric intake and consist largely of a diversity of plant foods, low amounts of animal source foods, contain unsaturated rather than saturated fats, and limited amounts of refined grains, highly processed foods and added sugars.

Transformation to healthy diets by 2050 will require substantial dietary shifts, including a greater than 50% reduction in global consumption of unhealthy foods such as red meat and sugar, and a greater than 100% increase in the consumption of healthy foods such as nuts, fruits, vegetables and legumes. However, the changes needed differ greatly by region.

This means that producing food for nearly 10 billion people should: use no additional land; safeguard existing biodiversity; reduce consumptive water use and manage water responsibly; drastically reduce nitrogen and phosphorus pollution; produce zero carbon dioxide emissions and cause no further increase in methane and nitrous oxide emissions.

Transformation to sustainable food production by 2050 will require at least: a 75% closing of yield gaps; a global redistribution of nitrogen and phosphorus fertilizer use; recycling of phosphorus; radical improvements in fertilizer and water use efficiency; rapid implementation of agricultural mitigation options to reduce greenhouse gas emissions and adoption of land management practices that shift agriculture from carbon source to sink, and a fundamental shift in production priorities.

Dietary changes from current diets towards healthy diets are likely to result in significant health benefits that include averting approximately 7.4 to 10.8 million sustainable food production needs to operate within the safe operating space for food systems

The scientific targets for healthy diets from sustainable food systems that we have described are intertwined across all UN Sustainable Development Goals (SDGs). In particular, this includes eradicating hunger and universal access to high-quality primary health care that integrates family planning and education on healthy diets, with the SDGs on freshwater, climate, land, oceans and biodiversity and achieved through a strong commitment to global partnerships and action.

Achieving healthy diets from sustainable food systems for everyone on the planet will require substantial shifts towards healthy dietary patterns together with large reductions in food losses and waste and major improvements in food production practices. This universal goal is within reach but will require the adoption of scientific targets by all sectors to stimulate a broad spectrum of actions from individuals and organizations working in all sectors and at all scales.

Options for Increasing Food Production without Adverse Land Expansion

Farm Smarter:

Severe limitations on water availability and the already heavy use of fertilizer in most regions limit the current capacity to boost yields simply by adding more inputs. These strategies would in any case fail to meet the sustainability criteria set for the menu. Smarter farming will therefore have to fuel yield growth. In the last two decades, improved use of agricultural technology in the broadest sense maintained a high level of growth in food production even with less growth in agricultural inputs. Globally, increased use of land, water, chemical, and other inputs contributed to roughly 70 percent of the growth in annual agricultural output in the 1970s and 1980s, but less than 30 percent in the 1990s and 2000s. Yet even with these improvements, agricultural land expansion continues, so the need for smarter farming is even greater going forward. Key opportunities for improved farm management include more careful selection of seed varieties adapted to local conditions, more judicious use of fertilizer, more attention to micronutrients, and improved weather forecasting to inform the selection of planting dates.

Breed better seeds:

Improved breeding has always been critical to agricultural progress and will remain fundamental. Genetic engineering can play a role, particularly because improved techniques now allow the insertion of genes in particular locations, reducing the amount of trial and error necessary to produce crops with improved traits (such as pest or drought resistance). In the short run, genetic engineering can most help by enabling faster breeding responses to new pests. More fundamental crop improvements from genetic engineering, such as improved uptake of nutrients and reduced losses of water, are uncertain and will take decades to come to fruition. But the strongest breeding opportunities will continue to rely on conventional breeding, in part because they can take advantage of modern biological methods. Those methods make it easier and faster to identify and select for the combinations of genes that result in higher yields, and justify increases in conventional breeding budgets.

Leave No Farmer Behind:

Yield growth will also rely on "leaving no farmer behind" by closing the gap between what many farmers currently achieve and what they could potentially achieve. Global yield gaps are unquestionably large, but global studies have large methodological limitations. Studying gaps using locally verified crop models is a priority to identify not just where the largest gaps occur, but also the causes of those gaps so they can be addressed.

Crop the Same Land More Frequently:

FAO data indicate that more than 400 million hectares of cropland go unharvested each year, suggesting that this amount of land is left fallow. On the other hand, farmers plant roughly 150 million hectares twice or more each year. Planting and harvesting existing cropland more frequently, either by reducing fallow or by increasing double cropping, could in theory boost production without requiring new land. FAO projects an increase in such planting frequency ("cropping intensity"), which would avert the need to clear an additional 62 million hectares for crops by 2050. Unfortunately, our review suggests that the practicalities of double cropping are little understood. Meanwhile, some fallow "croplands" are either in very long-term rotations or have been abandoned. These lands commonly revert to forest or grassland, helping to store carbon and provide other ecosystem services. Planting them more frequently sacrifices these benefits. Greater cropping intensity is a promising option but requires closer analysis both of double-cropping potential and of the "croplands" that countries now identify as unused.

Boost Yields in Africa in Part Through Improved Soil and Water Management:

Although sub- Saharan Africa today consumes only 9 percent of the world's calories, its likely growth in demand accounts for more than one-third (37 percent) of all additional calories required by 2050. The region also has the highest hunger rate, imports 25 percent of its grain needs, and has the world's lowest staple crop yields. Boosting those yields is therefore critical both for reducing hunger and for avoiding large-scale deforestation.

Soil degradation, particularly the loss of soil carbon, presents a particular challenge to agricultural production in sub-Saharan Africa, and 285 million people now live in dry regions where soil degradation has even harsher effects. Yet in Niger, farmers have rebuilt soil fertility and boosted yields on 5 million hectares of land by husbanding the natural regeneration of nitrogen-fixing trees and other native vegetation. Over sub-Saharan Africa's 300 million hectares of dry cropland, this type of agroforestry has even greater potential to boost yields when combined with water harvesting and microdosing of individual plants with small quantities of fertilizer. Conservative estimates suggest that scaling up these practices could potentially provide the present dryland population an additional 615 kcal per person per day.

Expand Crops into Low-Carbon Degraded Land:

Even if cropland must expand, it can do so with a modest environmental cost if it expands into non-agricultural lands that have low biodiversity value, store little carbon, and are also unlikely to store much carbon in the future. Millions of hectares of such lands exist in Indonesia and Malaysia, where Imperata grasses have overrun logged forests and hold back reforestation. Our analysis suggests that more than 14 million hectares of low-carbon degraded land in Indonesia's Kalimantan region of Borneo may be suitable for palm oil production— enough to accommodate additional oil palm plantations in Indonesia to 2020. Directing oil palm expansion to these lands is critical in the near term because oil palm is now expanding heavily into primary forests and peatlands. Peatland conversion leads to vast, ongoing annual carbon releases as the peat degrades over decades, which could within the next decade or two generate annually 5 to 7.5 percent of all current greenhouse gas emissions.

Globally, most of the lands considered by many analyses as "potential but unused" croplands do not truly qualify as environmentally low cost. Grazing lands produce valuable forage, and tropical savannas and sparse woodlands have high carbon storage and biodiversity value. Abandoned croplands, in areas capable of supporting trees, typically reforest, sequester carbon, and play an important role in holding down climate change.

Intensify Pasture Productivity:

Among relatively wet pastures already converted from natural forests and savannas, large opportunities exist to intensify the output of milk and meat. Standard techniques include adding fertilizer, growing legumes, and confining cattle to small grazing areas and rotating them quickly. More sophisticated systems combine grasses with nitrogen-fixing shrubs and multiple layers of trees. These pasture intensification efforts require far more technical attention and incentives than they now receive because the alternative implies vast deforestation.

Avoid or Manage Shifts in Agricultural Land:

Shifts in agricultural land from region to region and within regions cause millions of hectares of deforestation in excess of net agricultural expansion. The losses in carbon storage and other ecosystem services due to new deforestation generally exceed the gains from eventual reforestation elsewhere. It will be important to avoid shifts in agricultural land, and to restore abandoned lands more quickly when these shifts do occur.

Increase Productivity of Aquaculture:

As wild fish catch has plateaued, aquaculture has expanded rapidly to produce nearly half of all the fish people consume. On average, farmed fish are as efficient at converting feed to food as chicken, making them an environmentally desirable source of animal protein, if produced sustainably. Aquaculture's rapid growth initially led to several adverse environmental impacts, but these effects have since been reduced; for example, by slowing conversion of mangroves to shrimp ponds and by reduced reliance on wild caught fish as feed. To maintain the role of fish in diets, aquaculture production will have to more than double from current levels by 2050. Even with enormous progress in feeding efficiency, the industry still faces a static supply of fishmeal and fish oil, which could limit future growth unless progress is made in algae production or breeding plants to produce such oils. Aquaculture ponds also cover a significant area, and suitable lands for expansion are limited. Future production growth will require increased fish per hectare of a pond, which in turn requires more energy use to circulate and aerate the water. Such intensification has the potential to lead to other adverse environmental and social impacts; minimizing these impacts will be a key challenge.

Final thoughts

Addressing global issues in ways that will result in permanent, widespread change is a tall order. But for companies willing to take a fresh look at their practices and retool or reinvent them to reduce their environmental impact and spur positive social change, the rewards can be big: improved brand image, greater consumer trust, rising revenue, and employees who are proud to work for a company doing its part to preserve the planet for future generations.

Uncertainty in projections makes it difficult to determine the precise impact of climate change on future agricultural productivity, but studies have consistently found that under most scenarios significant negative effects should be expected worldwide and especially in economically underdeveloped regions

References

1. Ackerman K (2012) The potential for urban agriculture in New York City: Growing capacity, food security, and green infrastructure. Urban Design Lab, Columbia University, New York City
2. Ackerman K, Conard M, Culligan P, et al (2014) Sustainable food systems for future cities: The potential of urban agriculture. Econ Soc Rev (Irel) 45:189–206
3. Adams D, Hardman M (2014) Observing Guerrillas in the Wild: Reinterpreting Practices of Urban Guerrilla Gardening. Urban Stud 51:1103–1119. doi: 10.1177/0042098013497410
4. Alexandratos N, Bruinsma J. (2012) World Agriculture Towards 2030/2050: The 2012 Revision(Food and Agriculture Organization of the United Nations, Rome).
5. Altieri MA (2009) Agroecology, small farms, and food sovereignty. Mon Rev 61:102–113
6. Altieri MA, Companioni N, Cañizares K, et al (1999) The greening of the "barrios": Urban agriculture for food security in Cuba. Agric Human Values 16:131–140. doi: 10.1023/A
7. Altieri MA, Nicholls CI (2018) Urban Agroecology: designing biodiverse, productive and resilient city farms. Agro Sur 46:49–60. doi: 10.4206/agrosur.2018.v46n2-07

8. Altieri MA, Pallud C, Arnold J, et al (2014) An Agroecological Survey of Urban Agriculture Sites in the East Bay, California: A report to the Berkeley Food Institute. Berkeley Food Institute, Berkeley, CA, USA
9. Amoah P, Drechsel P, Abaidoo RC, Ntow WJ (2006) Pesticide and pathogen contamination of vegetables in Ghana's urban markets. Arch Environ ContamToxicol 50:1–6. Doi: 10.1007/s00244-004-0054-8
10. Armar-Klemesu M (2000) Urban agriculture and food security, nutrition and health. In: Bakker N, Dubbeling M, Guendel S, et al. (eds) Growing Cities, Growing Food: Urban Agriculture on the Policy Agenda. Deutsche Stiftung fur internationaleEntwicklung (DSE), Feldafing, pp 99–118
11. Armstrong D (2000) A Survey of Community Gardens in Upstate New York: Implications for Health Promotion and Community Development. Health Place 6:319–327
12. Bai ZG, Dent DL, Olsson L, Schaepman ME (2008) Proxy global assessment of land degradation. Soil Use Manag 24:223–234. doi: 10.1111/j.1475-2743.2008.00169.x
13. Baker LE (2010) Tending Cultural Landscapes and Food Citizenship in Toronto's Community Gardens. Geogr Rev 94:305–325. doi: 10.1111/j.1931-0846.2004.tb00175.x
14. Barthel S, Isendahl C (2013) Urban gardens, agriculture, and water management: Sources of
15. resilience for long-term food security in cities. Ecol Econ 86:224–234. Doi: 10.1016/j.ecolecon.2012.06.018
16. Barthel S, Parker J, Ernstson H (2015) Food and Green Space in Cities: A Resilience Lens on Gardens and Urban Environmental Movements. Urban Stud 52:1321–1338. doi:
17. 10.1177/0042098012472744
18. Bassett TJ (1981) Reaping on the Margins: A Century of Community Gardening in America. Landscape 25:1–8
19. Bazilian, M., Rogner, H., Howells, M., Hermann, S., Arent, D., Gielen, D., Steduto, P., Mueller, A., Komor, P., Tol, R., Yumkella, K.. 2011. Considering the energy, water and food nexus: Towards an integrated modelling approach. EnergyPolicy 39(12):7896–7906.
20. Belluco S, Losasso C, Maggioletti M, Alonzi CC, Paoletti MG, Ricci A (2013). Edible insects in a food safety and nutritional perspective:

A critical review. Compr Rev Food Sci Food Saf; 12:296–313. doi: 10.1111/1541-4337.12014

21. Beniston J, Lal R (2012) Improving Soil Quality for Urban Agriculture in the North Central U.S. In: Lal R, Augustin B (eds) Carbon Sequestration in Urban Ecosystems. Springer Netherlands, Dordrecht, pp 279–313
22. Bernard B, Lux A (2017) How to feed the world sustainably: an overview of the discourse on agroecology and sustainable intensification. Reg Environ Chang 17:1279–1290. Doi: 10.1007/s10113-016-1027-y
23. Biewener C (2016) Paid Work, Unpaid Work, and Economic Viability in Alternative Food Initiatives: Reflections from Three Boston Urban Agriculture Endeavors. J Agric Food Syst Community Dev 6:1–19. doi: 10.5304/jafscd.2016.062.019
24. Blaine TW, Grewal PS, Dawes A, Snider D (2010) Profiling community gardeners. J Ext 48:6
25. Blay-Palmer, A. 2008. Food Fears: From Industrial to Sustainable Food Systems. Surrey: Ashgate.
26. Block DR, Chávez N, Allen E, Ramirez D (2012) Food sovereignty, urban food access, and food activism: Contemplating the connections through examples from Chicago. Agric Human Values 29:203–215. doi: 10.1007/s10460-011-9336-8
27. Block JP, Scribner RA, Desalvo KB (2004) Fast food, race/ethnicity, and income: A geographic analysis. Am J Prev Med 27:211–217. doi: 10.1016/j.amepre.2004.06.007
28. Bouwman AF, et al. (2011) Exploring global changes in nitrogen and phosphorus cycles in agriculture induced by livestock production over the 1900–2050 period. Proc Natl Acad Sci USA 110:20882–20887.
29. Bridges EM, Oldeman LR (1999) Global assessment of human-induced soil degradation. Arid Soil Res Rehabil 13:319–325. doi: 10.1080/089030699263212
30. British Cabinet Office (BCO). 2007. Food: An Analysis of the Issues. London: BCO.
31. Brown K, Carter A (2003) Urban Agriculture and Community Food Security in the United States: Farming from the City Center to the Urban Fringe. Community Food Security Coalition's North American Urban Agriculture Committee

32. CA. (2007) Comprehensive Assessment of Water Management in Agriculture (Earthscan, London).
33. Cavailhes J, Wavresky P (2003) Urban influences on peri urban farmland prices. Eur Rev Agric Econ 30:333–357
34. Ceballos et al. (2015)., Accelerated modern human-induced species losses: Entering the sixth mass extinction. Sci. Adv. 1, e1400253 (2015).
35. CIBE (2003). (International Confederation of European Beet Growers) and CEFS (Center for Environmental Farming Systems), "Environmental Report: Beet growing and sugar production in Europe,".
36. Clapp J (2017) Food self-sufficiency: Making sense of it, and when it makes sense. Food Policy 66:88– 96. doi: 10.1016/j.foodpol.2016.12.001
37. Clinton N, Stuhlmacher M, Miles A, et al (2018) A Global Geospatial Ecosystem Services Estimate of Urban Agriculture. Earth's Futur6:. doi: https://doi.org/10.1002/2017EF000536
38. Coff C, Korthals M, & Barling, D. 2008. Ethical traceability and informed food choice. In C. Coff, D. Barling, M. Korthals, & T. Nielsen (Eds.), Ethical Traceability and Communicating Food. pp. 1–18. New York: Springer.
39. Cofie OO, Kranjac-Berisavljevic G, Dreschsel P (2005) The use of human wate for peri-urban agriculture in Northern Ghana. Renew Agric Food Syst 20:73–80. Doi: https://doi.org/10.1079/RAF200491
40. Colasanti K, Hamm MW (2010) Assessing the local food supply capacity of Detroit, Michigan. J Agric Food Syst Community Dev 1:41–58. doi: 10.5304/jafscd.2010.012.002
41. Commission of the European Communities (CEC). 2007. White Paper on a Strategy for Europe on Nutrition, Overweight and Obesity Related Health Issues. COM(2007) 279 Final. Brussels: European Commission.
42. Consmüller, N., Beckmann, V., &Petrick, M. (2012). Identifying Driving Factors for the Establishment of Cooperative GMO-free Zones in Germany. Conference of the International Association of Agricultural Economists. August 18–24, Foz do Iguaçu, Brazil.
43. Corsolini S, Ademollo N, Romeob T, Grecob S, Focardia S (2005) Persistent organic pollutants in edible fish: a human and environmental

health problem. Microchem J 79:115–123. https://doi.org/10.1016/j.microc.2004.10.006

44. Daftary-Steel S, Herrera H, Porter C (2015) The Unattainable Trifecta of Urban Agriculture. J Agric Food Syst Community Dev 6:19–32. doi: 10.5304/jafscd.2015.061.014
45. Dalin C, Wada Y, Kastner T, Puma MJ (2017) Groundwater depletion embedded in international food trade. Nature 543:700–704. doi: 10.1038/nature21403
46. Despommier D (2011) The vertical farm: controlled environment agriculture carried out in tall buildings would create greater food safety and security for large urban populations. J ConsumProt Food Saf 6:233–236. doi: 10.1007/s00003-010-0654-3
47. Diels J, Cunha M, Manaia C, Sabugosa-Madeira B, Silva M (2010). Association of financial or professional conflict of interest to research outcomes on health risks or nutritional assessment studies of genetically modified products. Food Policy; 36:197–203.
48.
49. Dobermann D, Swift JA, Field LM (2017). Opportunities and hurdles of edible insects for food and feed. Nutr Bull; 42:293–308. doi: 10.1111/nbu.12291.
50. Duchemin E, Wegmuller F, Legault AM (2008) Urban agriculture: multi-dimensional tools for social development in poor neighbourhoods. F Actions Sci Reports 1:43–52. doi: 10.5194/facts-2-1- 2009
51. Eigenbrod C, Gruda N (2015) Urban vegetable for food security in cities. A review. Agron Sustain Dev 35:483–498. doi: 10.1007/s13593-014-0273-y
52. Eberle, U., D. Hayn, R. Rehaag, & U. Simshäuser (Eds.). 2006. Ernährungswende. Eine Herausforderung für Politik, Unternehmen und Gesellschaft. [Nutrition Change: A Challenge for Politics, Business, and Society]. Munich: Oekom (in German).
53. Erickson DL, Lovell ST, Méndez VE (2013) Identifying, quantifying and classifying agricultural opportunities for land use planning. Landsc Urban Plan 118:29–39. Doi: 10.1016/j.landurbplan.2013.05.004
54. Eriksen-Hamel N, Danso G (2010) Agronomic considerations for urban agriculture in southern cities. Int J Agric Sustain 8:86–93. doi: 10.3763/ijas.2009.0452

55. Eshel, C. A. Shepon, T. Makov and R. Milo (2014). "Land, irrigation water, greenhouse gas, and reactive nitrogen burdens of meat, eggs, and dairy production in the United States," Proceedings of the National Academy of 26 Sciences of the United States of America, vol. 111, no. 33, pp. 11996-12001.
56. Enteleca, (2001). Tourist attitudes towards regional and local foods', research report to the Countryside Agency and the Ministry of Agriculture, Fisheries and Food, London
57. Erickson A, Kramer-LeBlanc C (1996). Ecolabels: the link between environmental preferences and green practices?, in Strategy and Policy in the Food System: Emerging Issues Eds J Caswell, R Cotterill, Proceedings of NE-165 Conference, 20-21 June 1996,Washington, DC.
58. European Commission (2011). Communication from the Commission to the European Parliament, the Council, the European Economic and Social Committee and the Committee of the Regions. Roadmap to a Resource Efficient Europe. COM/2011/0571 final. Available from: https://eur-lex.europa.eu/legal-content/EN/TXT/?uri=CELEX:52011DC0571. Accessed 15.04.2020
59. Eyles H, NiMhurchu C, Nghiem N, Blakely T (2012). Food pricing strategies, population diets, and non-communicable disease: a systematic review of simulation studies. PLoS Med. 9(12):e1001353.
60. Fernandez M, Williams J, Figueroa G, et al (2018) New opportunities, new challenges: Harnessing Cuba's advances in agroecology and sustainable agriculture in the context of changing relations with the United States. Elem Sci Anthr 6. doi: 10.1525/elementa.337
61. Foley, J.A. et al (2011). "Solutions for a cultivated planet", Nature 478, 337-342.
62. Food and Agriculture Organization (1996). Rome Declaration on World Food Security and World Food Summit Plan of Action. World Food Summit 13-17 November 1996. Rome.
63. FAO (2011). Save and Grow. A policymaker's guide to the sustainable intensification of smallholder crop production. Available from: http://www.fao.org/3/a-i2215e.pdf. Accessed 02.11.2020
64. Food and Agriculture Organization (2011a). The state of the world's land and water resources for food and agriculture (SOLAW) –

Managing systems at risk. Rome: Food and Agriculture Organization of the United Nations and London, Earthscan.

65. Food and Agriculture Organization (2011b). Energy-smart food for people and climate. Issue Paper. Rome: Food and Agriculture Organization of the United Nations.
66. FAO-WFP-IFAD (2012). The state of food insecurity in the world 2012. Economic growth is
67. necessary but not sufficient to accelerate reduction of hunger, FAO, Rome.
68. Food and Agriculture Organization of the United Nations (FAO) (2013). Healthy people depend on healthy food systems. Available from: http://www.fao.org/fileadmin/templates/getinvolved/images/WFD_issues_paper_2013_web_EN.pdf. Accessed 15.04.2020
69. Food and Agriculture Organization of the United Nations (FAO) (2014). Building a common vision for sustainable food and agriculture: principles and approaches. Rome, Italy: FAO. Available from: http://www.fao.org/3/a-i3940e.pdf. Accessed 15.04.2020
70. FAO, IFAD, UNICEF, WFP, WHO (2017) The state of food security and nutrition in the world 2017. Building resilience for peace and food security. Report of the Food and Agriculture Organization of the United Nations (FAO), Rome, Italy
71. Foley JA, DeFries R, Asner GP, Barford C, Bonan G, Carpenter SR, Chapin FS, Coe MT, Daily GC, Gibbs HK, Helkowski JH (2005). Global consequences of land use. Science 22; 309 (5734): 570-4.
72. Foley JA et al (2011). Solutions for a cultivated planet. Nature 478, 337–342 (2011).
73. Food and Agriculture Organization (2018). Sustainable Food Systems Concept and Framework. Available from : http://www.fao.org/3/ca2079en/CA2079EN.pdf. Accessed 08.04.2020
74. Food Navigator USA (2019). The Case for Traditional Foods. Available from: https://www.foodnavigator.com/Article/2019/09/03/The-case-for-traditional-foods-Production-has-to-take-place-close-to-consumption. Accessed 20.04.2020
75. Food Well Alliance (2018) Case Study: Fresh MARTA Market.
76. http://www.foodwellalliance.org/casestudy-freshmarta. Accessed 30 Jul 2019

77. Food Well Alliance (2017) Atlanta's Local Food Baseline Report
78. Foresight (2011). The Future of Food and Farming: Challenges and Choices for Global Sustainability. Final Project Report. London: Government Office for Science. Available from : https://assets.publishing.service.gov.uk/government/uploads/system/uploads/attachment_data/file/288329/11-546-future-of-food-and-farming-report.pdf. Accessed 15.04.2020
79. Fuglie, K.O., Wang, S.L. & Ball, V.E. (2012). Productivity growth in agriculture: an international perspective, CABI, Wallingford, UK.
80. Funes F, Vázquez L (2016) Avances de la Agroecologíaen Cuba. Estación Experimental de Pastos y Forrajes Indio Hatuey, Matanzas, Cuba
81. Galluzzi G, Eyzaguirre P, Negri V (2010) Home gardens: Neglected hotspots of agro-biodiversity and cultural diversity. BiodiversConserv 19:3635–3654. doi: 10.1007/s10531-010-9919-5
82. Gao Y, Wang D, Xu ML, Shi SS, Xiong JF (2018). Toxicological characteristics of edible insects in China: A historical review.Food Chem Toxicol. 2018 Sep; 119():237-251.
83. Garnett T (2014) Changing what we eat: a call for research and action on widespread adoption of sustainable healthy eating. University of Oxford, Food Climate Research Network, Oxford
84. Gaskell, G., Stares, S., Allansdottir, A., Allum, N., Castro, P., Esmer, Y., Fischler, C., Jackson, J., Kronberger, N., Hampel, J., Mejlgaard, N., Quintanilha, A., Rammer, A., Revuelta, G., Stoneman, P., Torgersen, H., & Wagner, W. (2010). Europeans and Biotechnology in 2010: Winds of Change? Brussels: European Commission.
85. GBD (2013). Risk Factors Collaborators, Global, regional, and national comparative risk assessment of 79 behavioural, environmental and occupational, and metabolic risks or clusters of risks in 188 countries, 1990-2013: A systematic analysis for the global burden of disease study 2013. Lancet 386, 2287–2323
86. Godfray, H.C. et al (2010). " Food Security: The challenge of feeding 9 billion people". Science 327, 812-818
87. Goldenburg, S. "Why global water shortages pose threat of terror and war," The Guardian, 9 February 2014.

88. Goldstein B, Hauschild M, Fernández J, Birkved M (2016) Urban versus conventional agriculture, taxonomy of resource profiles: a review. Agron Sustain Dev 36. doi: 10.1007/s13593-015-0348-4
89. Goodman D, Dupuis E M, (2002). Knowing food and growing food: beyond the production/
90. consumption debate in the sociology of agriculture. SociologiaRuralis 42 5: 22
91. Goucher L, Bruce R, Cameron DD, et al (2017) The environmental impact of fertilizer embodied in a wheat-to-bread supply chain. Nat Plants 3. doi: 10.1038/nplants.2017.12
92. Grafton RQ, Daugbjerg C, Qureshi ME. Towards food security by 2050. Food Secur. 2015;7:179–183. doi: 10.1007/s12571-015-0445-x
93. Grewal SS, Grewal PS (2012) Can cities become self-reliant in food? Cities 29:1–11. Doi: 10.1016/j.cities.2011.06.003
94. Hamilton AJ, Burry K, Mok HF, et al (2014) Give peas a chance? Urban agriculture in developing countries. A review. Agron Sustain Dev 34:45–73. doi: 10.1007/s13593-013-0155-8
95. Hancock T (2001) People, partnerships and human progress: Building community capital. Health Promot Int 16:275–280. doi: 10.1093/heapro/16.3.275
96. Hoff, H. (2011). Understanding the Nexus. Background Paper for the Bonn2011 Conference: The Water, Energy and Food Security Nexus. Stockholm, Sweden: Stockholm Environment Institute (SEI).
97. Hufnagel, J., Reckling, M. & Ewert, F. (2020) Diverse approaches to crop diversification in agricultural research. A review. Agron. Sustain. Dev. 40, 14. https://doi.org/10.1007/s13593-020-00617-4
98. Holt-Giménez E, Altieri MA (2013) Agroecology, food sovereignty, and the new green revolution. Agroecol Sustain Food Syst 37:90–102. doi: 10.1080/10440046.2012.716388
99. Horton P (2017) We need radical change in how we produce and consume food. Food Secur 9:1323–1327. doi: 10.1007/s12571-017-0740-9
100. IAASTD (2009) International Assessment of Agricultural Knowledge, Science and Technology for Development: Executive Summary of the Synthesis Report. Available from: www.agassessment.org/index.cfm. Accessed 21.06.2020

101. IHME (2018). GBD Compare. https://vizhub.healthdata.org/gbd-compare/. Accessed 02.11.2020.
102. IPBES (2018) Thematic assessment report on land degradation and restoration. Intergovernmental Science Policy Platform on Biodiversity and Ecosystem Services (IPBES), Bonn.
103. IPCC (2014). Climate Change 2014: Synthesis Report. Contribution of Working Groups I, II and III to the Fifth Assessment Report of the Intergovernmental Panel on Climate Change (Intergovernmental Panel on Climate Change, Geneva, Switzerland, 2014).
104. IWMI (2007). Comprehensive Assessment of Water Management in Agriculture. Water for food, water for life: a comprehensive assessment of water management in agriculture. London: Earthscan and Colombo: International Water Management Institute
105. Jacobi P, Amend J, Kiango S (2000) Urban agriculture in Dar-es-Salaam: providing an indispensable part of the diet. In: Bakker N, Dubbeling M, Gundel S, et al. (eds) Growing Cities, Growing Food: Urban Agriculture on the Policy Agenda. Deutsche Stiftung fur internationaleEntwicklung (DSE), Feldafing, pp 257–283
106. Jakobsen et al. (2009). , Major types of dietary fat and risk of coronary heart disease: A pooled analysis of 11 cohort studies. Am. J. Clin. Nutr. 89, 1425–1432 (2009).
107. James, C. (2010). Global Status of Commercialized Biotech/GM Crops. ISAAA Brief No. 42. Ithaca, NY: International Service for the Acquisition of Agri-Biotech Applications.
108. Jantke, K, Lottermoser F, Reinhardt J, Rothe,DStöver J (2016) Nachhaltiger Konsum, pp. 421 - 442
109. Kajikawa Y, Tacoa F, Yamaguchi K (2014) Sustainability science: the changing landscape of sustainability research. Sustain Sci 9:431–438
110. Keepin, B. (1988). Status of Major Environmental Threats (Sanderstolen, Norway: Energy Policy Foundation of Norway, Energy Policy Seminar, February 7-10 1989). W.W. Kellogg and Z.C. Zhao, "Sensitivity of Soil Moisture to Doubling of Carbon Dioxide in Climate Model Experiments," Journal of Climate, p. 348.
111. Kennard NJ (2019) Food Waste Management. In: Leal Filho W, Azul A, Brandli L, et al. (eds) Zero Hunger. Encyclopedia of the UN Sustainable Development Goals. Springer, Cham

112. Kironde JML (1992) Received Concepts and Theories in African Urbanisation and Management Strategies: The Struggle Continues. Urban Stud 29:1277–1292. doi:

113. https://doi.org/10.1080/00420989220081271

114. Klinkenberg E, McCall PJ, Hastings IM, et al (2005) Malaria and irrigated crops, Accra, Ghana. Emerg Infect Dis 11:1290–1293. doi: 10.3201/eid1108.041095

115. Klinkenberg E, McCall PJ, Wilson MD, et al (2008) Impact of urban agriculture on malaria vectors in Accra, Ghana. Malar J 7. doi: 10.1186/1475-2875-7-151

116. Kohler R, Kariuki L, Lambert C, Biesalski HK (2019). Protein, amino acid and mineral composition of some edible insects from Thailand. J Asia Pac Entomol. ;22:372–378. doi: 10.1016/j.aspen.2019.02.002

117. Koont S (2008) A Cuban Success Story: Urban Agriculture. Rev Radic Polit Econ 40:285–291. Doi: 10.1177/0486613408320016

118. Kortright R, Wakefield S (2011) Edible backyards: A qualitative study of household food growing and its contributions to food security. Agric Human Values 28:39–53. doi: 10.1007/s10460-009-9254-1

119. Kremer P, DeLiberty TL (2011) Local food practices and growing potential: Mapping the case of Philadelphia. Appl Geogr 31:1252–1261. doi: 10.1016/j.apgeog.2011.01.007

120. Kulak M, Graves A, Chatterton J (2013) Reducing greenhouse gas emissions with urban agriculture: A Life Cycle Assessment perspective. Landsc Urban Plan 111:68–78. doi:

121. 10.1016/j.landurbplan.2012.11.007

122. Landrigan PJ, Fuller R, Acosta NJR, Adeyi O, Arnold R, Basu NN, Baldé AB, Bertollini R, Bose-O'Reilly S, Boufford JI, Breysse PN, Chiles T, Mahidol C, Coll-Seck AM, Cropper ML, Fobil J, Fuster V, Greenstone M, Haines A, Hanrahan D, Hunter D, Khare M, Krupnick A, Lanphear B, Lohani B, Martin K, Mathiasen KV, McTeer MA, Murray CJL, Ndahimananjara JD, Perera F, Potočnik J, Preker AS, Ramesh J, Rockström J, Salinas C, Samson LD, Sandilya K, Sly PD, Smith KR, Steiner A, Stewart RB, Suk WA, van Schayck OCP, Yadama GN, Yumkella K, Zhong M (2017) The Lancet commission on pollution and health. Lancet pii S0140–6736(17):32345. https://doi.org/10.1016/S0140-6736(17)32345-0

123. Lang G, Miao B (2013) Food Security for China's Cities. Int Plan Stud 18:5–20. doi:
124. 10.1080/13563475.2013.750940
125. Lang T (2010) Crisis? What crisis? The normality of the current food crisis. J Agrar Chang 10:87–97. doi: 10.1111/j.1471-0366.2009.00250.x
126. Larson NI, Story MT, Nelson MC (2009) Neighborhood Environments: Disparities in Access to Healthy Foods in the U.S. Am J Prev Med 36:74–81. doi: 10.1016/j.amepre.2008.09.025
127. Lelieveld, J. S. Evans, M. Fnais, D. Giannadaki, A. Pozzer (2015). The contribution of outdoor air pollution sources to premature mortality on a global scale. Nature 525, 367–371.
128. Lin BB, Philpott SM, Jha S (2015) The future of urban agriculture and biodiversity-ecosystem services: Challenges and next steps. Basic Appl Ecol 16:189–201. doi: 10.1016/j.baae.2015.01.005
129. Liu et al.(2000). A prospective study of whole-grain intake and risk of type 2 diabetes mellitus in US women. Am. J. Public Health 90, 1409–1415.
130. Lockie S, Collie L, (2002). Feed the man meat: gendered food and theories of consumption',
131. in Restructuring Global and Regional Agricultures Transformations in Australasian Agri-food
132. Economies and Space Eds D Burch, J Goss, G Lawrence (Ashgate, Aldershot, Hants)
133. pp 255-275
134. Lovell ST, Taylor JR (2013) Supplying urban ecosystem services through multifunctional green infrastructure in the United States. LandscEcol 28:1447–1463. doi: 10.1007/s10980-013-9912-y
135. Mack EA, Tong D, Credit K (2017) Gardening in the desert: a spatial optimization approach to
136. locating gardens in rapidly expanding urban environments. Int J Health Geogr 16. doi:
137. 10.1186/s12942-017-0110-z
138. MacRae R, Gallant E, Patel S, et al (2010) Could Toronto provide 10% of its fresh vegetable

139. requirements from within its own boundaries? Matching consumption requirements with growing spaces. J Agric Food Syst Community Dev 1:105–127. Doi:10.5304/jafscd.2010.012.008

140. Mariola MJ (2008) The local industrial complex? Questioning the link between local foods and energy use. Agric Human Values 25:193–196. doi: 10.1007/s10460-008-9115-3

141. Martellozzo F, Landry JS, Plouffe D, et al (2014) Urban agriculture: A global analysis of the space constraint to meet urban vegetable demand. Environ Res Lett 9. doi: 10.1088/1748-

142. 9326/9/6/064025

143. Martin-Nagel, E. Howard, A. Wiltse and D. Duncan (2012). "The Water, Energy and Food Security Nexus - Solutions for the Green Economy," Conference Synopsis.

144. Matthys B, Vounatsou P, Raso G, et al (2006) Urban farming and malaria risk factors in a medium-sized town in Côte d'Ivoire. Am J Trop Med Hyg 75:1223–1231

145. McClintock N (2014) Radical, reformist, and garden-variety neoliberal: coming to terms with urban agriculture's contradictions. Local Environ 19:147–171. doi:10.1080/13549839.2012.752797

146. McClintock N, Cooper J, Khandeshi S (2013) Assessing the potential contribution of vacant land to urban vegetable production and consumption in Oakland, California. Landsc Urban Plan 111:46–58. doi: 10.1016/j.landurbplan.2012.12.009

147. McDougall R, Kristiansen P, Rader R (2018) Small-scale urban agriculture results in high yields but requires judicious management of inputs to achieve sustainability. Proc Natl Acad Sci 116:129–134. doi: 10.1073/pnas.1809707115

148. Millstone, E. & Lang, T. (2008). The Atlas of Food, 2nd ed. London: Earthscan.

149. Mlcek J, Rop O, Borkovcova M, Bednarova M (2014). A comprehensive look at the possibilities of edible insects as food in Europe–a review. Pol J Food NutrSci. ;64:147–157. doi: 10.2478/v10222-012-0099-8. [

150. Mok HF, Williamson VG, Grove JR, et al (2014) Strawberry fields forever? Urban agriculture in

151. developed countries: A review. Agron Sustain Dev 34:21–43. doi: 10.1007/s13593-013-0156-7

152. Molden, D. Molden (2007)., "Comprehensive assessment of water management in agriculture" in Water for Food, Water for Life: A Comprehensive Assessment of Water Management in Agriculture, D. Molden, Ed. (Earthscan, International Water Management Institute, London, Colombo, 2007).
153. Morland K, Wing S, Diez Roux A, Poole C (2002) Neighborhood characteristics associated with the location of food stores and food service places. Am J Prev Med 22:23–29. doi: 10.1016/S0749-3797(01)00403-2
154. Mougeot LJA (2005) Agropolis: The Social, Political, and Environmental Dimensions of Urban
155. Agriculture. Earthscan, International Development Research Centre, London
156. Mueller, N.D. et al. (2012). "Closing yield gaps through nutrient and water management", Nature 490, 254-257
157. Murefu TR, Macheka L, Musundire R, Manditsera FA (2019). Safety of wild harvested and reared edible insects: A review. Food Control; 101:209–224. doi: 10.1016/j.foodcont.2019.03.003.
158. Newbold T, Hudson LN, Hill SLL, et al (2015) Global effects of land use on local terrestrial
159. biodiversity. Nature 520:45–50. doi: 10.1038/nature14324
160. NFU (2011). Sugar and British Sugar UK, "UK Beet Sugar Industry: Sustainability Report 2011,".
161. Ng M, Fleming T, Robinson M, et al (2014) Global, regional and national prevalence of overweight and obesity in children and adults 1980-2013: A systematic analysis. Lancet 384:766–781. Doi: 10.1016/S0140-6736(14)60460-8.Global
162. Nongonierma AB, FitzGerald RJ (2017). Unlocking the biological potential of proteins from edible insects through enzymatic hydrolysis: A review. Innov Food Sci EmergTechnol. ;43:239–252. doi: 10.1016/j.ifset.2017.08.014.
163. Oberndorfer E, Lundholm J, Bass B, et al (2007) Green Roofs as Urban Ecosystems: Ecological Structures, Functions, and Services. Bioscience 57:823–833. doi: 10.1641/B571005
164. Oosterveer, P. & Sonnenfeld, D. (2012). Food, Globalization, and Sustainability. New York: Routledge.
165. Opitz I, Berges R, Piorr A, Krikser T (2016) Contributing to food

security in urban areas: differences between urban agriculture and peri-urban agriculture in the Global North. Agric Human Values 33:341–358. doi: 10.1007/s10460-015-9610-2

166. Park S, Yun E (2018). Edible insect food: Current scenario and future perspectives. Food Sci AnimResour Ind; 7:12–20.
167. ParrottN,Wilson N, Murdoch J, (2002). Spatializing quality: regional protection and the alternative geography of food. European Urban and Regional Studies 9 241-261.
168. Patel S, Suleria HAR, Rauf A (2019). Edible insects as innovative foods: Nutritional and functional assessments. Trends Food Sci Technol. 86:352–359. doi: 10.1016/j.tifs.2019.02.033.
169. Pearson LJ, Pearson L, Pearson CJ (2010) Sustainable urban agriculture: stocktake and opportunities. Int J Agric Sustain 8:7–19. doi: 10.3763/ijas.2009.0468
170. Pechan, P. & G. de Vries (Eds.) (2005). Genes on the Menu: Facts for Knowledge-Based Decisions. New York: Springer.
171. Poe MR, McLain RJ, Emery M, Hurley PT (2013) Urban Forest Justice and the Rights to Wild Foods, Medicines, and Materials in the City. Hum Ecol 41:409–422. doi:10.1007/s10745-013-9572-1
172. Policy Makers Summary of the Scientific Assessment of Climate Change (1990). Geneva, Report of Intergovernmental Panel on Climate Change, World Meteorological Organization of the United Nations Environment Programme.
173. Pourias J, Duchemin E, Aubry C (2015) Products from urban collective gardens: food for thought or for consumption? J Agric Food Syst Community Dev 5:175–199. doi:
174. 10.5304/jafscd.2015.052.005
175. Proksch G (2017) Creating Urban Agricultural Systems – An Integrated Approach to Design. Taylor & Francis, New York City
176. Ray, D.K., Ramankutty, N., Mueller, N.D., West, P.C. & Foley, J.A. (2012). "Recent patterns of
177. crop yield growth and stagnation", Nat Commun 3, 1293
178. Regenerative Agriculture Initiative (2017). What is Regenerative Agriculture? Available from: http://2igmzc48tf4q88z3o24qjfl8.wpengine.netdna-cdn.com/wp-content/uploads/2017/02/Regen-Ag-Definition-2.23.17-1.pdf. Accessed 22.04.2020

179. Reisch, L. 2004. Sustainable consumption as a consumer policy issue. In L. Reisch& I. Røpke (Eds.), The Ecological Eco- nomics of Consumption. pp. 175–189. Northampton, MA: Edward Elgar.
180. Renault, C. "Value of Virtual Water in Food: Principles and Virtues," 25 UNFAO, Rome, 2002.
181. Rosenzweig, C. et al. (1993). Climate Change and World Food Supply (Oxford: Oxford University Press.
182. Sage C (2013) The interconnected challenges for food security from a food regimes perspective: Energy, climate and mal consumption. J Rural Stud 29:71–80. doi:
183. 10.1016/j.jrurstud.2012.02.005
184. Saha M, Eckelman MJ (2017) Growing fresh fruits and vegetables in an urban landscape: A geospatial assessment of ground level and rooftop urban agriculture potential in Boston, USA. Landsc Urban Plan 165:130–141. doi: 10.1016/j.landurbplan.2017.04.015
185. Sánchez-Bayo F, Wyckhuys KAG (2019) Worldwide decline of the entomofauna: A review of its drivers. Biol Conserv 232:8–27. doi: 10.1016/j.biocon.2019.01.020
186. Schlosser E, (2001). Fast Food Nation: The Dark Side of the All-American Meal. Houghton Mifflin, Boston, MA.
187. Schneider, SH (1989). "The Changing Climate," Scientific American 261, p. 29.
188. SDG (2011). Global Agenda for Sustainable Livestock (GASL). Available from: https://sustainabledevelopment.un.org/partnership/?p=32865. Accessed 02.11.2020.
189. Shi, P. W. Yu, D. Z. Zen (2015).Dose–response meta-analysis of poultry intake and colorectal cancer incidence and mortality. Eur. J. Nutr. 54, 243–250.
190. Siegner A, Sowerwine J, Acey C (2018) Does urban agriculture improve food security? Examining the nexus of food access and distribution of urban produced foods in the United States: A systematic review. Sustainability 10. doi: 10.3390/su10092988
191. Smith P, et al. (2010) Competition for land. Philos Trans R Soc Lond B Biol Sci365(1554):2941–2957.
192. Smith V, Harrington J (2014) Community Food Production as Food Security: Resource and Economic Valuation in Madison, Wisconsin

(USA). J Agric Food Syst Community Dev 4:61–80. Doi: 10.5304/jafscd.2014.042.006

193. Sofi, F., Abbate, R., Gensini, G.F. &Casini, A. (2010). Accruing Evidence on Benefits of Adherence to the Mediterranean Diet on Health: An Updated Systematic Review and Meta-analysis. The American Journal of Clinical Nutrition, 92 (5), 1189-1196.
194. Springmann, M., Clark, M., Mason-D'Croz, D., Wiebe, K., Bodirsky, B.L., Lassaletta, L., de Vries, W., et al. (2018). Options for keeping the food system within environmental limits. Nature, 562(7728): 519–525.
195. Staples D and Funge-Smith S (2009). Ecosystem approach to fisheries and aquaculture: Implementing the FAO Code of Conduct for Responsible Fisheries. Available from: http://www.fao.org/3/a-i0964e.pdf. Accessed 02.11.20
196. Statistics Canada (2016) Census Program. https://www12.statcan.gc.ca/census-recensement/index-eng.cfm. Accessed 29 May 2019
197. Stevens, W. (1989). "Governments Start Preparing for Global Warming Disasters," New York Times, November 14.
198. Strawn K, Brown E, David J, Bakker H (2015) Big Data in Food Safety and Quality. Available from: http://www.https://www.researchgate.net/publication/295559053 _Big_Data_in_Food_Safety_and_Quality. Accessed 02.11.20
199. Sun et al. (2010). White rice, brown rice, and risk of type 2 diabetes in US men and women. Arch. Intern. Med. 170, 961–969
200. Sustainable Development Commission (SDC). 2005. Sustainability Implications of the Little Red Tractor Scheme. London: SDC.
201. Sustainable Development Commission (SDC). 2009. Setting the Table: Advice to Government on Priority Elements of Sustainable Diets. London: SDC.
202. Tang KL, Caffrey NP, Nóbrega DB, Cork SC, Ronksley PE, Barkema HW, Polachek AJ, Ganshorn H, Sharma N, Kellner JD, Ghali WA (2017) Restricting the use of antibiotics in food-producing animals and its associations with antibiotic resistance in food-producing animals and human beings: a systematic review and meta-analysis. Lancet Planetary Health 1:e316–e327. https://doi.org/10.1016/S2542-5196(17)30141-9
203. Taylor JR, Lovell ST (2012) Mapping public and private spaces of urban agriculture in Chicago through the analysis of high-resolution

aerial images in Google Earth. Landsc Urban Plan 108:57–70. doi: 10.1016/j.landurbplan.2012.08.001

204. Thaman RR (1995) Urban food gardening in the Pacific Islands: A basis for food security in rapidly urbanising small-island states. Habitat Int 19:209–224. doi: 10.1016/0197-3975(94)00067-C
205. The Royal Society (2009) Reaping the benefits: Science and the sustainable intensification of global agriculture. The Royal Society, London
206. Thomson A, Metz M (1998) Implications of Economic Policy for Food Security: A Training Manual.FAO, Rome
207. Thow AM, Jan S, Leeder S, Swinburn B. The effect of fiscal policy on diet, obesity and chronic disease: a systematic review. Bull World Health Organ. 2010;88(8):609-14.
208. Tilman D, Clark M, Williams DR, Kimmel K, Polasky S, Packer C (2017). Future threats to biodiversity and pathways to their prevention. Nature 546 (7656): 73
209. Tischner, U. &Kjaernes, U. (2007). Sustainable consumption and production in the agriculture and food domain. In S. Lahlou& S. Emmert (Eds.), SCORE Proceedings: SCP Cases in the Field of Food, Mobility, and Housing. pp. 201–237.
210. Tomlinson I (2013) Doubling food production to feed the 9 billion: A critical perspective on a key discourse of food security in the UK. J Rural Stud 29:81–90. doi: 10.1016/j.jrurstud.2011.09.001
211. Trichopoulou, A., Costacou, T., Bamia, C. &Trichopoulos, D. (2003). Adherence to a Mediterranean Diet and Survival in a Greek Population. New England Journal of Medicine,348(26):2599-2608.
212. Turner B (2011) Embodied connections: Sustainability, food systems and community gardens. Local Environ 16:509–522. doi: 10.1080/13549839.2011.569537
213. Twiss J, Dickinson J, Duma S, et al (2003) Community Gardens: Lessons Learned From California Healthy Cities and Communities. Am J Public Health 93:1435–1438. doi: 10.3390/su8080775
214. Tzoulas K, Korpela K, Venn S, et al (2007) Promoting ecosystem and human health in urban areas using Green Infrastructure: A literature review. Landsc Urban Plan 81:167–178. doi:
215. 10.1016/j.landurbplan.2007.02.001

216. UK Government (2006). "Food Industry Sustainability Strategy,".
217. UK Government (2013). "Water use in the UK food and drink industry," 2013.
218. United Nations (2015). Sustainable Development Goals. Available from: https://sustainabledevelopment.un.org/?menu=1300. Accessed 14.04.2020
219. UN Water (2016) http://www.unwater.org/water-facts/water-food-and-energy/. Accessed 20 Dec 2017
220. UN (2019) Goal 2: Zero Hunger. Sustainable Development Goals. United Nations.
221. https://www.un.org/sustainabledevelopment/hunger/. Accessed 24 Sep 2019
222. UN Department of Economic and Social Affairs (2019) World Population Prospects 2019. United Nations, Rome
223. UN Department of Economic and Social Affairs (2018) Urbanization Prospects: The 2018 Revision. United Nations, New York City
224. UNDP (1996) Urban Agriculture: Food, Jobs, and Sustainable Cities. United Nations Development Programme, New York City
225. United States Census Bureau (2018) QuickFacts. https://www.census.gov/quickfacts/. Accessed 29 May 2020
226. United States Department of Agriculture (2017) Food Access Research Atlas - Documentation.
227. https://www.ers.usda.gov/data-products/food-access-research-atlas/documentation/.
228. Accessed 13 Jun 2020
229. van der Ploeg JD (2010) The Food Crisis, Industrialized Farming and the Imperial Regime. J Agrar Chang 10:98–106
230. van Huis A (2015). Edible insects contributing to food security? Agric Food Secur. ;4:20. doi: 10.1186/s40066-015-0041-5.
231. van Huis A, Oonincx DGAB (2017). The environmental sustainability of insects as food and feed A review. Agron Sustain Dev; ;37:43. doi: 10.1007/s13593-017-0452-8
232. van Huylenbroeck G, Vandermeulen V, Mettepenningen E and verspecht A (2007). Multifunctionality of Agriculture: a Revicw of Definitions, Evidence and Instruments. Living Reviews in Landscape Research, 1:1–38.

233. van Thielen L, Vermuyten S, Storms B, Rumpold B, van Campenhout L (2019). Consumer acceptance of foods containing edible insects in Belgium two years after their introduction to the market. J Insects Food Feed.; 5:35–44. doi: 10.3920/JIFF2017.0075.

234. Vermeulen SJ, Campbell BM, Ingram JSI (2012) Climate change and food systems. Annu Rev Env Resour 37:195–222

235. Vitiello D, Nairn M (2009) Community Gardening in Philadelphia: 2008 Harvest Report. University of Pennsylvania, Philadelphia

236. Vitousek et al (1997)., Human alteration of the global nitrogen cycle : Sources and consequences published by : Ecological Society of America Stable URL. Ecol. Appl. 7, 737–750.

237. Wakefield S, Yeudall F, Taron C, et al (2007) Growing urban health: Community gardening in South-East Toronto. Health Promot Int 22:92–101. doi: 10.1093/heapro/dam001

238. Wallace JS (2000), "Increasing agricultural water use efficiency to meet future food production," Agriculture, Ecosystems and Environment, vol.82, pp. 105-119.

239. Wholesome Wave (2019) Georgia Fresh for Less. https://www.wholesomewavegeorgia.org/georgia-fresh-for-less. Accessed 30 Jul 2020

240. Wilhelm JA, Smith RG (2018) Ecosystem services and land sparing potential of urban and peri-urban agriculture: A review. Renew Agric Food Syst 33:481–494. doi: 10.1017/s1742170517000205

241. Willett, W., Rockström, J., Loken, B., Springmann, M., Lang, T., Vermeulen, S., & Jonell, M. (2019). Food in the Anthropocene: the EAT–Lancet Commission on healthy diets from sustainable food systems. The Lancet, 393(10170), 447-492.

242. Witzling L, Wander M, Phillips E (2011) Testing and educating on urban soil lead: A case of Chicago community gardens. J Agric Food Syst Community Dev 1:167–185. Doi: 10.5304/jafscd.2010.012.015

243. Whitmee S, Haines A, Beyrer C, Boltz F, Capon AG, de Souza Dias BF, Ezeh A, Frumkin H, Gong P, Head P, Horton R, Mace GM, Marten R, Myers SS, Nishtar S, Osofsky SA, Pattanayak SK, Pongsiri MJ, Romanelli C, Soucat A, Vega J, Yach D (2015) Safeguarding human health in the anthropocene epoch: report of Therockefeller foundation-

lancet commission on planetary health. Lancet 386:1973–2028. https://doi.org/10.1016/S0140-6736(15)60901-1

244. Woodwell, MG. (1989). "The Warming of the Industrialized Middle Latitudes 1985-2050: Causes and Consequences," Climate Change 15, p. 31.
245. WHO (2017) WHO guidelines on use of medically important antimicrobials in food-producing animals. World Health Organization, Geneva, Switzerland. http://who.int/foodsafety/publications/cia_guidelines/en/index.html. Accessed 20 March 2020
246. Wrigley N (2002) "Food deserts" in British cities: policy, context, and research priorities. Urban Stud 39:2029–2040
247. WWF (2013), "Water Stewardship: Perspectives on 19 business and responses to water challenges,"
248. Zenk SN, Odoms-Young AM, Dallas C, et al (2011) "You have to hunt for the fruits, the vegetables": Environmental barriers and adaptive strategies to acquire food in a low-income African American neighborhood. Heal Educ Behav 38:282–292. doi: 10.1177/1090198110372877
249. Zezza A, Tasciotti L (2010) Urban agriculture, poverty, and food security: Empirical evidence from a sample of developing countries. Food Policy 35:265–273. doi: 10.1016/j.foodpol.2010.04.007
250. Zielinska E, Karas M, Baraniak B (2018). Comparison of functional properties of edible insects and protein preparations thereof. LWT-Food Sci Technol; 91:168–174. doi: 10.1016/j.lwt.2018.01.058.

Index

D

E

F

L

M

N

O

P

Q

R

S

T

U

V